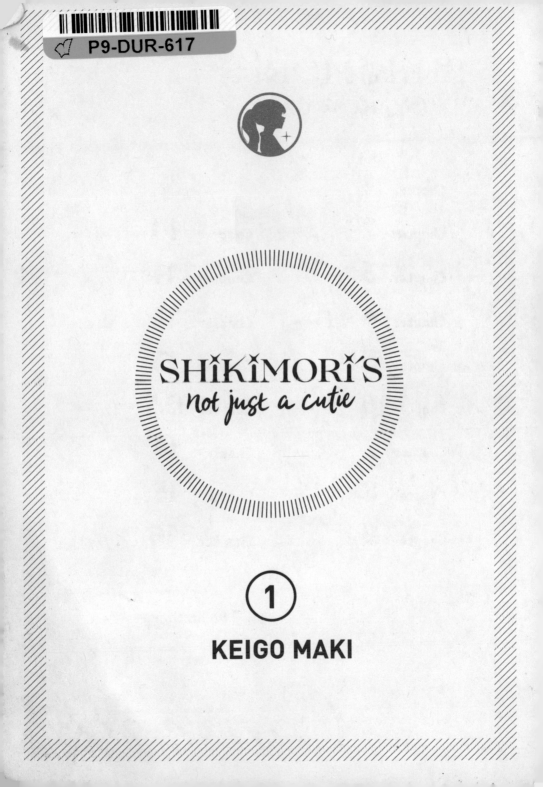

SHIKIMORI'S
not just a cutie

①

KEIGO MAKI

SHIKIMORI'S
Not just a cutie

××××××

volume.1

Contents

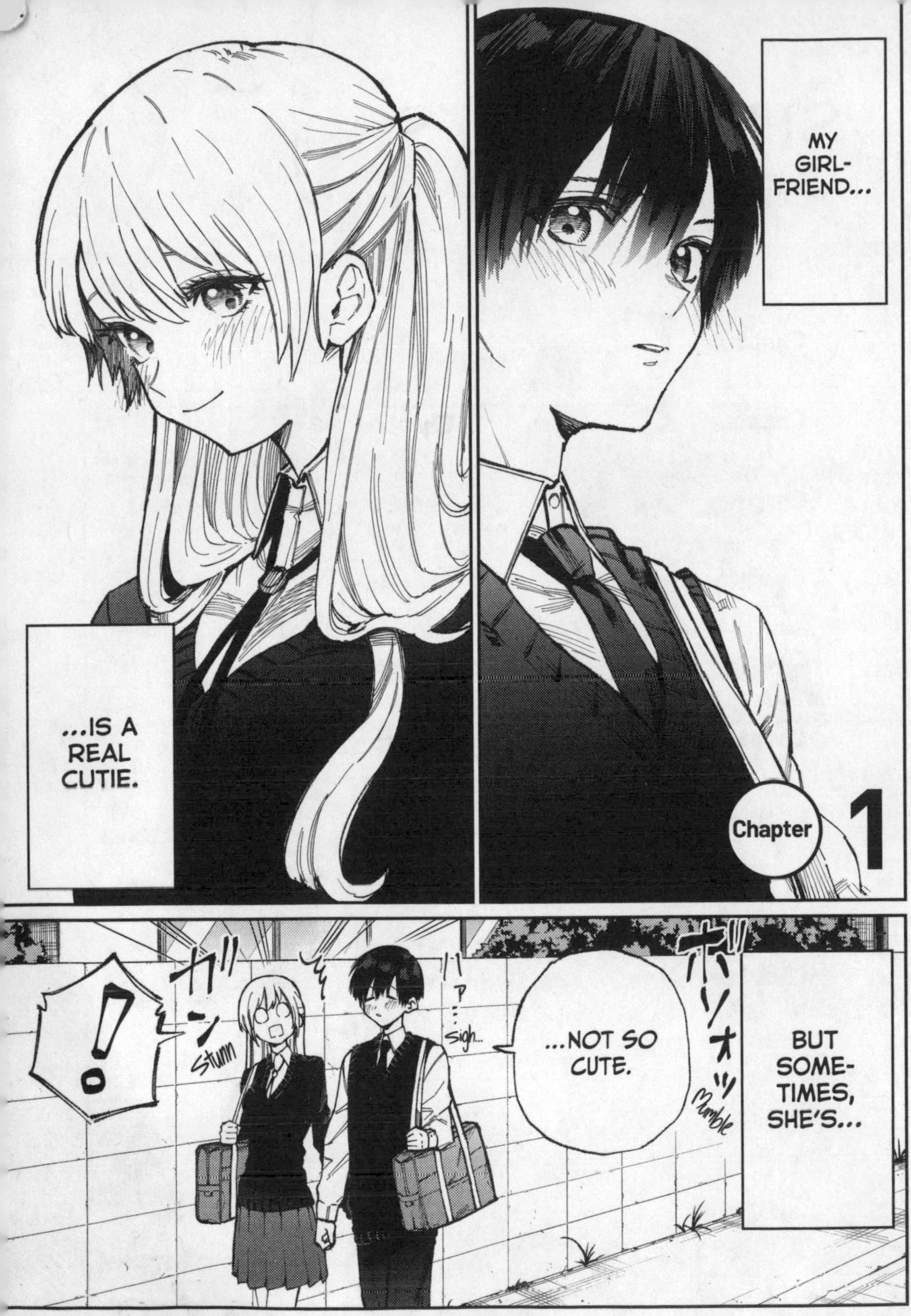
MY GIRL-FRIEND...
Chapter 1
...IS A REAL CUTIE.
BUT SOME-TIMES, SHE'S...
ボソォッ
Mumble
...NOT SO CUTE.
ハァ…
Sigh...
ガーン
Stunn
!

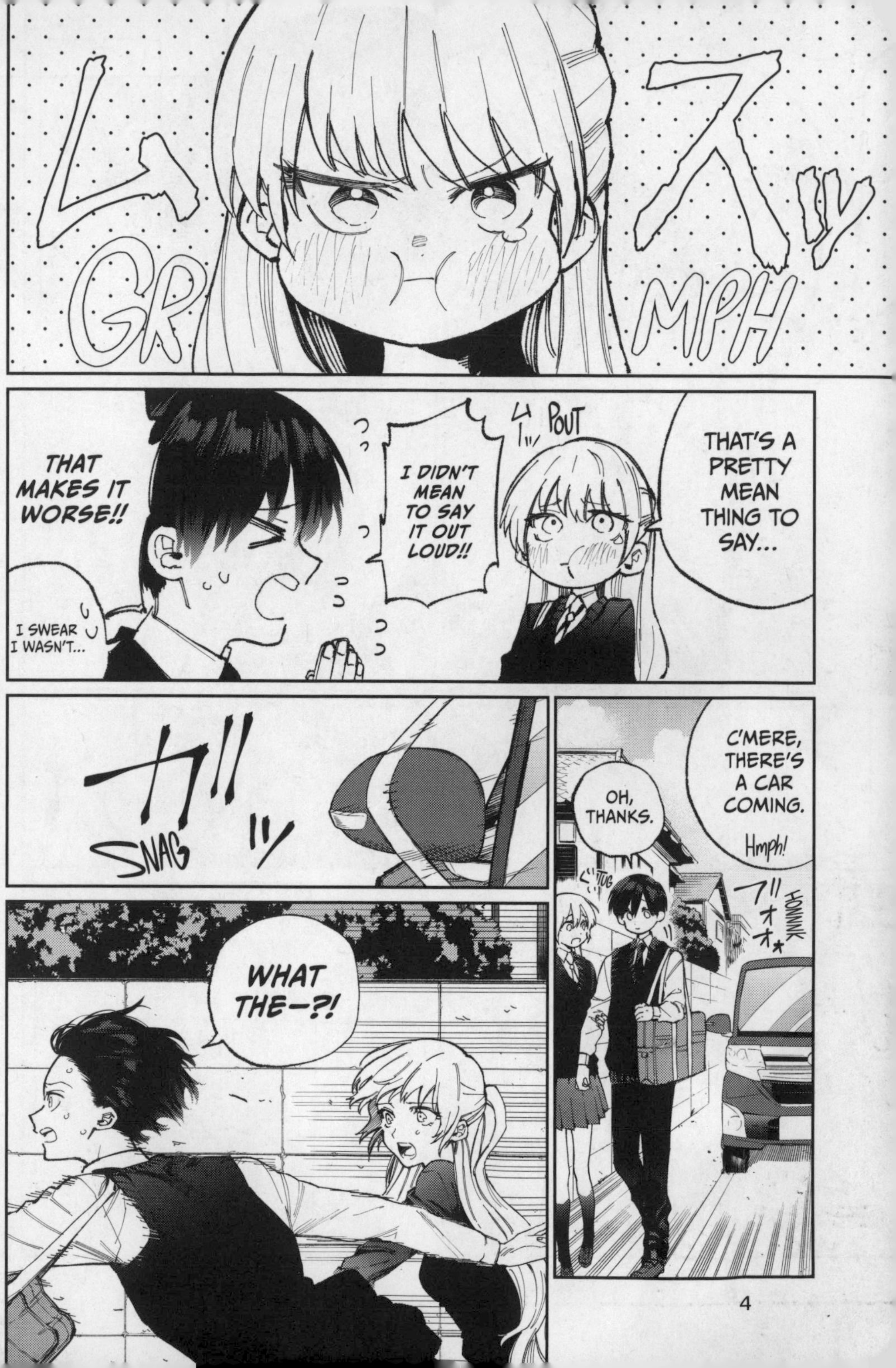
ムスッ
GRMPH
THAT'S A PRETTY MEAN THING TO SAY...
ムッ POUT
I DIDN'T MEAN TO SAY IT OUT LOUD!!
THAT MAKES IT WORSE!!
I SWEAR I WASN'T...
C'MERE, THERE'S A CAR COMING.
Hmph!
OH, THANKS.
TUG
HONNK
ガッ
SNAG
WHAT THE—?!

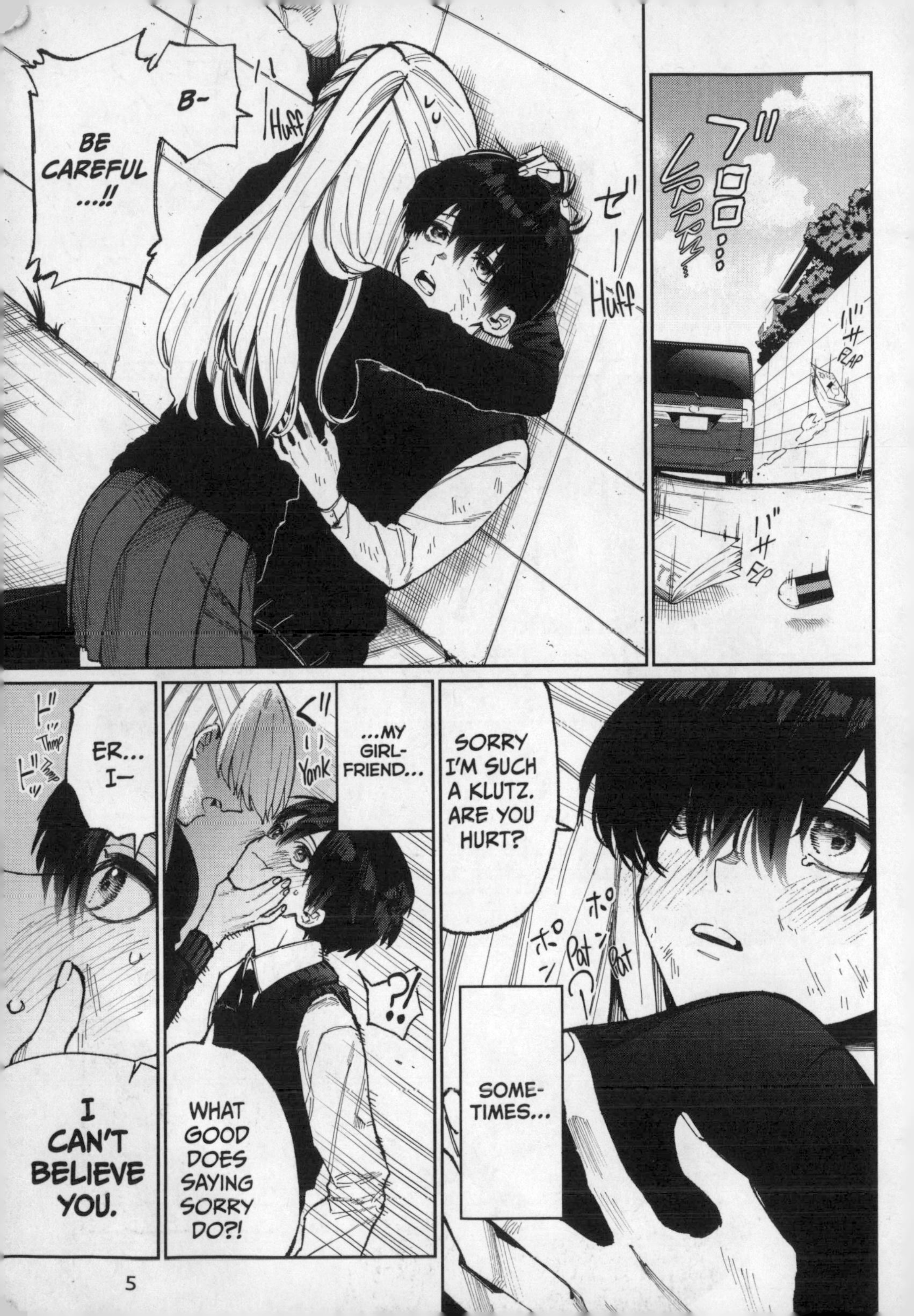

ブロロ…
VRRRM...
FLAP
FLP
ゼー
Huff
Huff
B-
BE CAREFUL ...!!
SORRY I'M SUCH A KLUTZ. ARE YOU HURT?
Pat
Pat
SOME-TIMES...
...MY GIRL-FRIEND...
Yank
?!
WHAT GOOD DOES SAYING SORRY DO?!
Thmp
Thmp
ER... I—
I CAN'T BELIEVE YOU.

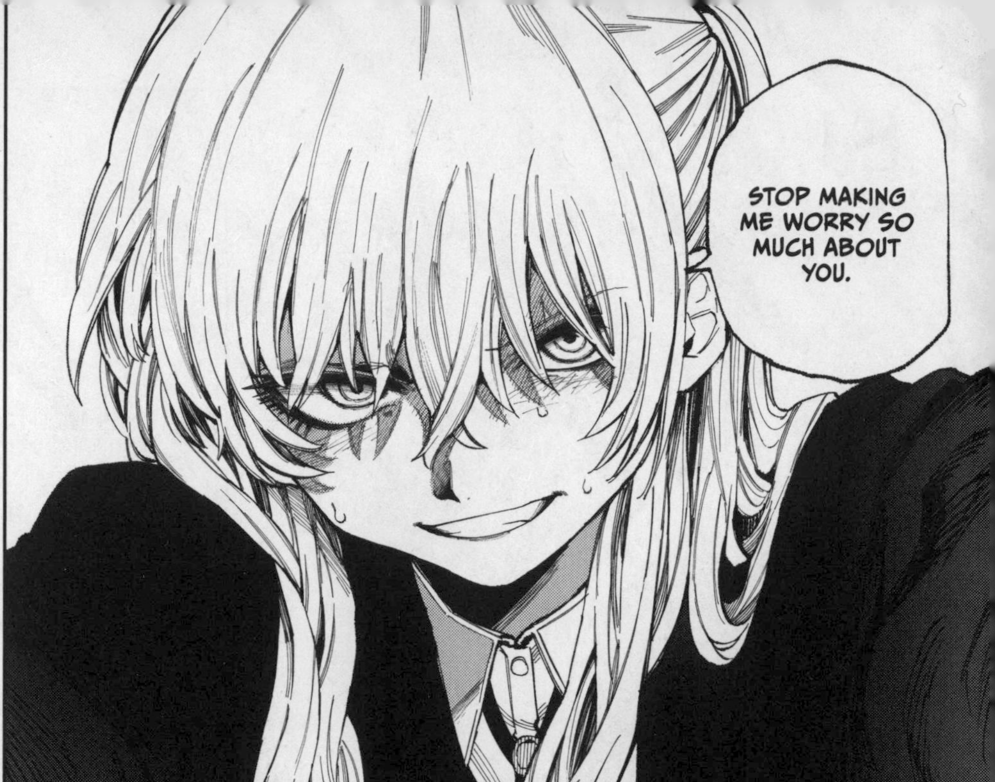
STOP MAKING ME WORRY SO MUCH ABOUT YOU.

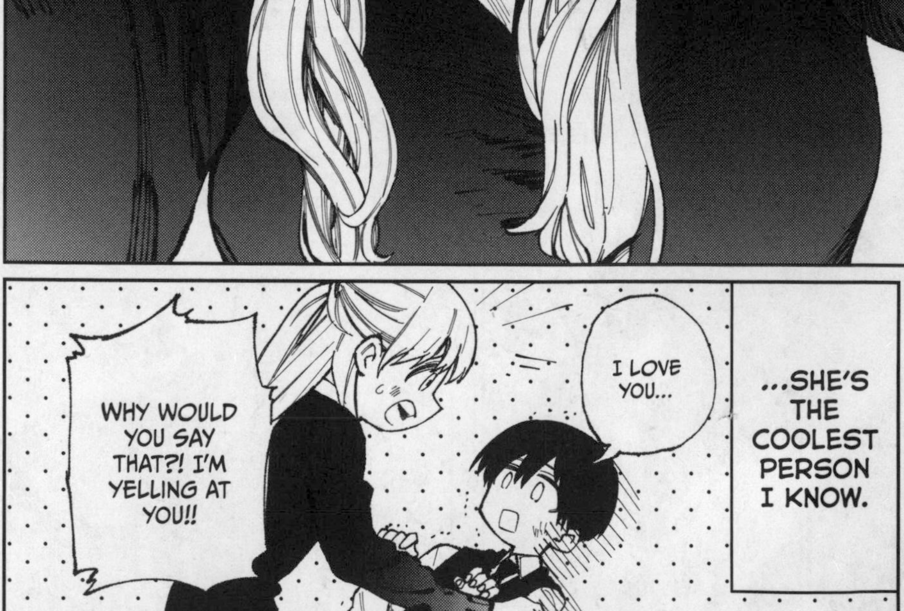
...SHE'S THE COOLEST PERSON I KNOW.
I LOVE YOU...
WHY WOULD YOU SAY THAT?! I'M YELLING AT YOU!!

Chapter 1 END

SHIKIMORI'S Not just a cutie

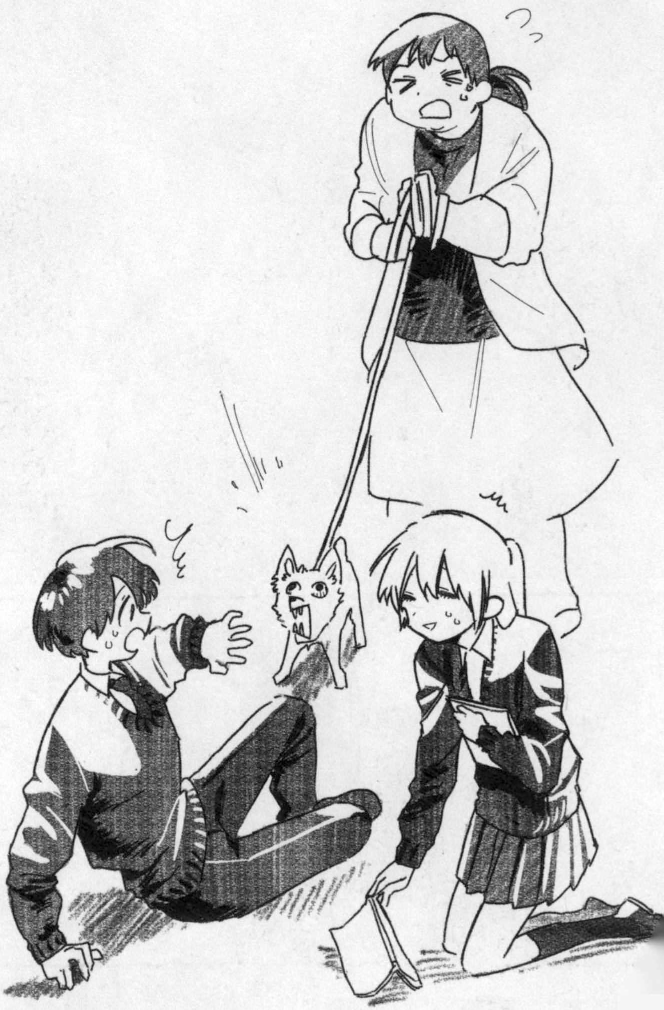

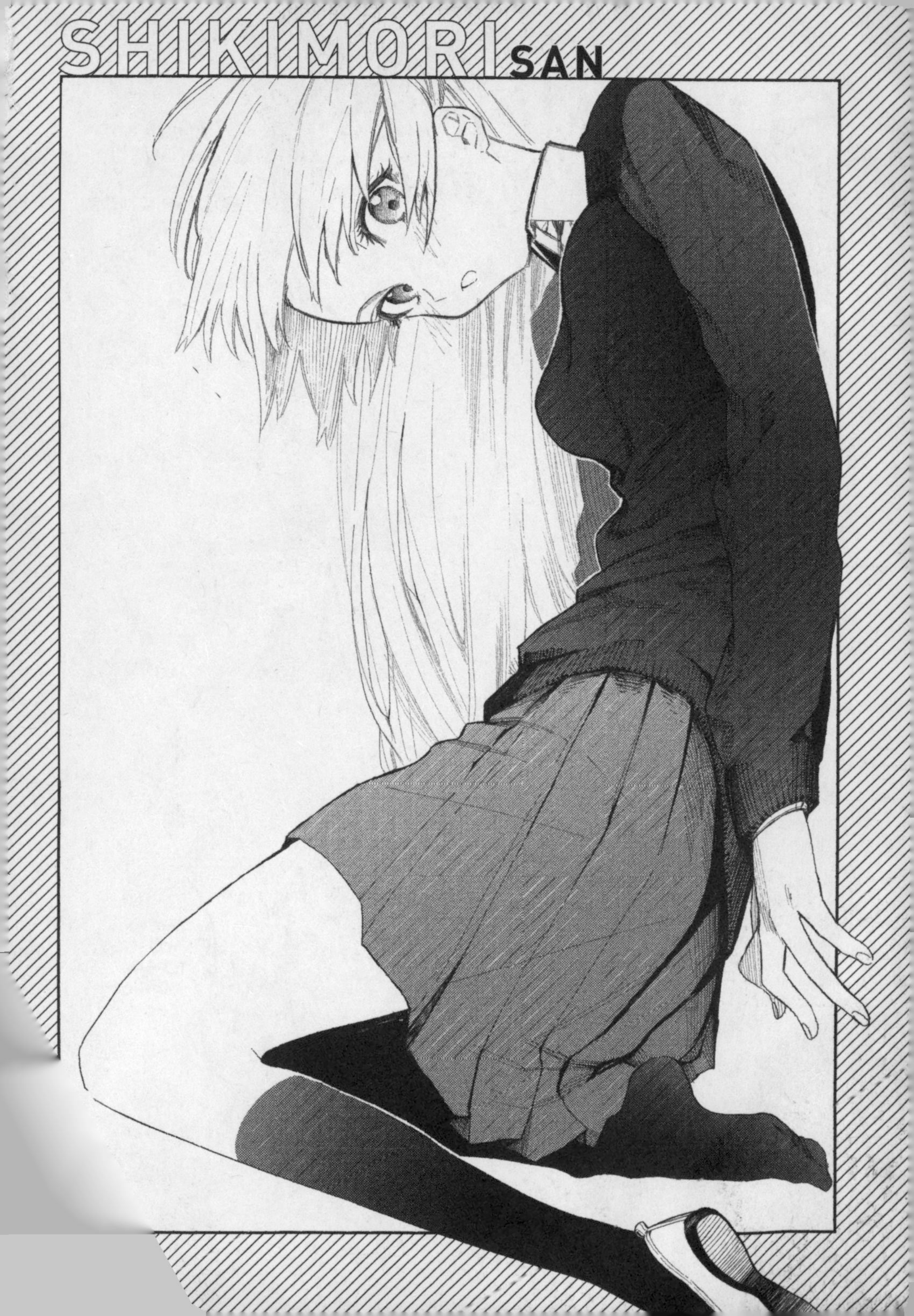
SHIKIMORI SAN

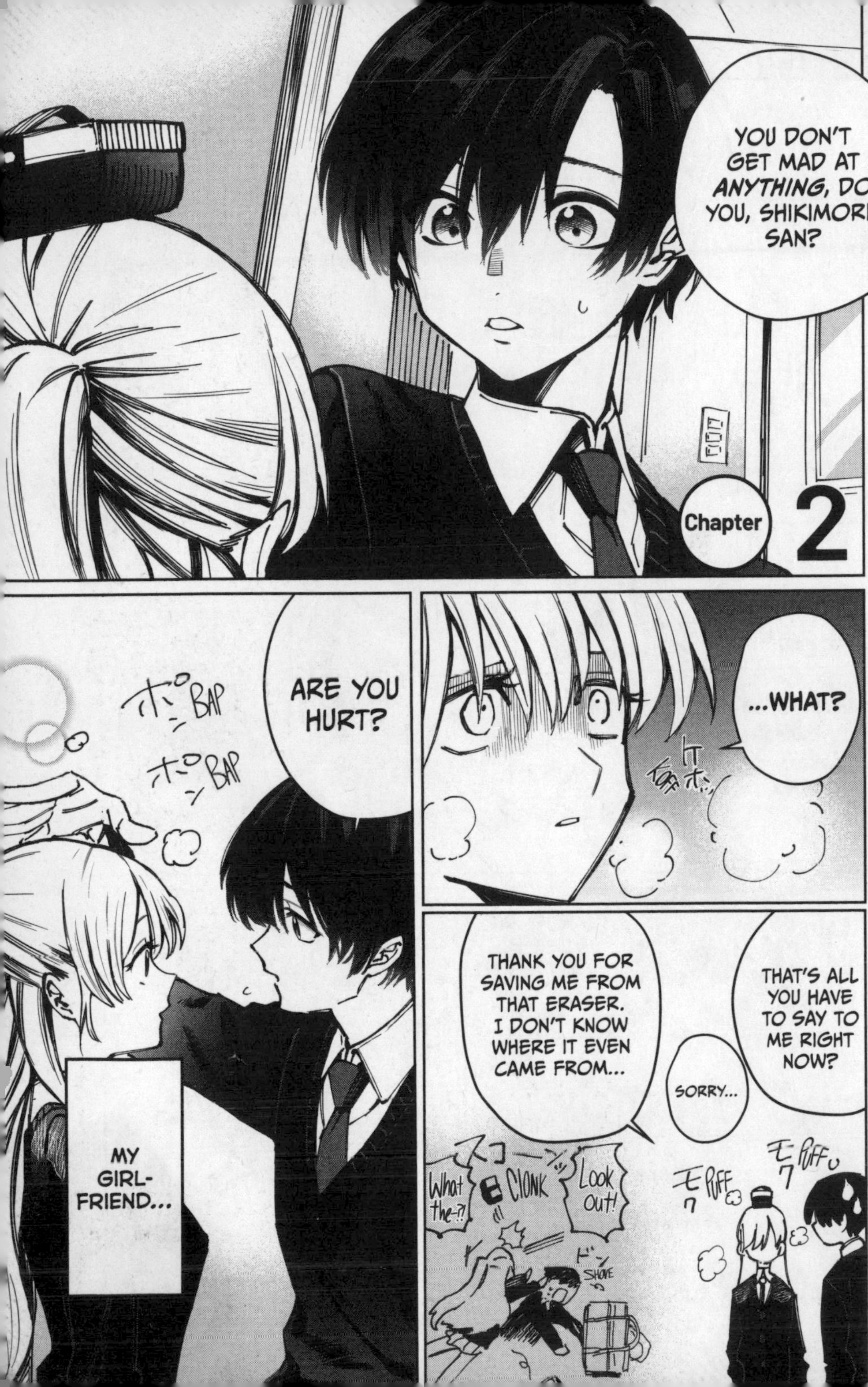
YOU DON'T GET MAD AT ANYTHING, DO YOU, SHIKIMORI-SAN?
Chapter 2
...WHAT?
KOFF
THANK YOU FOR SAVING ME FROM THAT ERASER. I DON'T KNOW WHERE IT EVEN CAME FROM...
THAT'S ALL YOU HAVE TO SAY TO ME RIGHT NOW?
SORRY...
PUFF
PUFF
Look out!
CLONK
What the-?!
SHOVE
ARE YOU HURT?
BAP
BAP
MY GIRL-FRIEND...

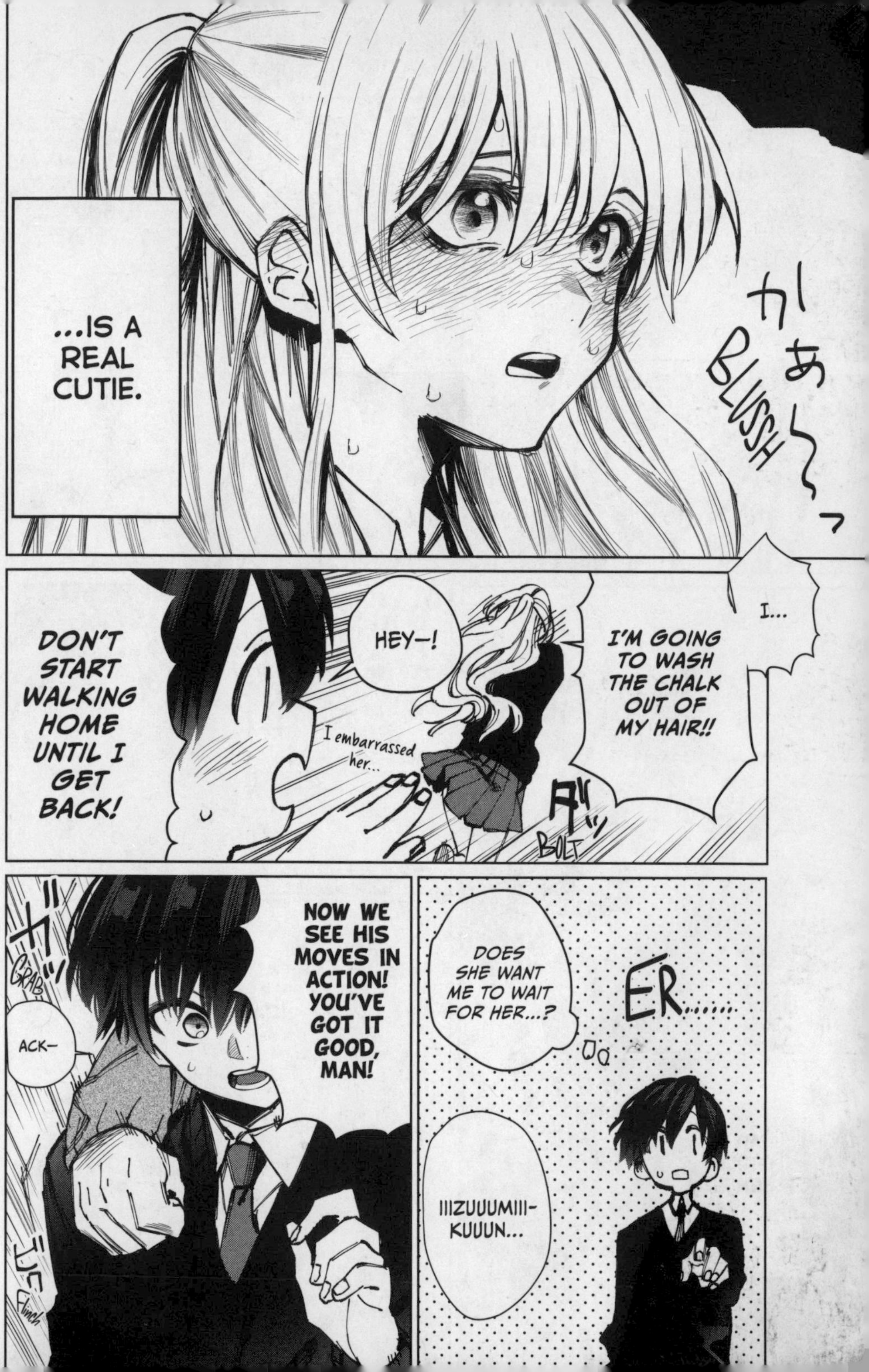
BLUSSH
...IS A REAL CUTIE.
I...
I'M GOING TO WASH THE CHALK OUT OF MY HAIR!!
BOLT
HEY—!
I embarrassed her...
DON'T START WALKING HOME UNTIL I GET BACK!
ER......
DOES SHE WANT ME TO WAIT FOR HER...?
IIIZUUUMIII-KUUUN...
NOW WE SEE HIS MOVES IN ACTION! YOU'VE GOT IT GOOD, MAN!
GRAB
ACK—
Flinch

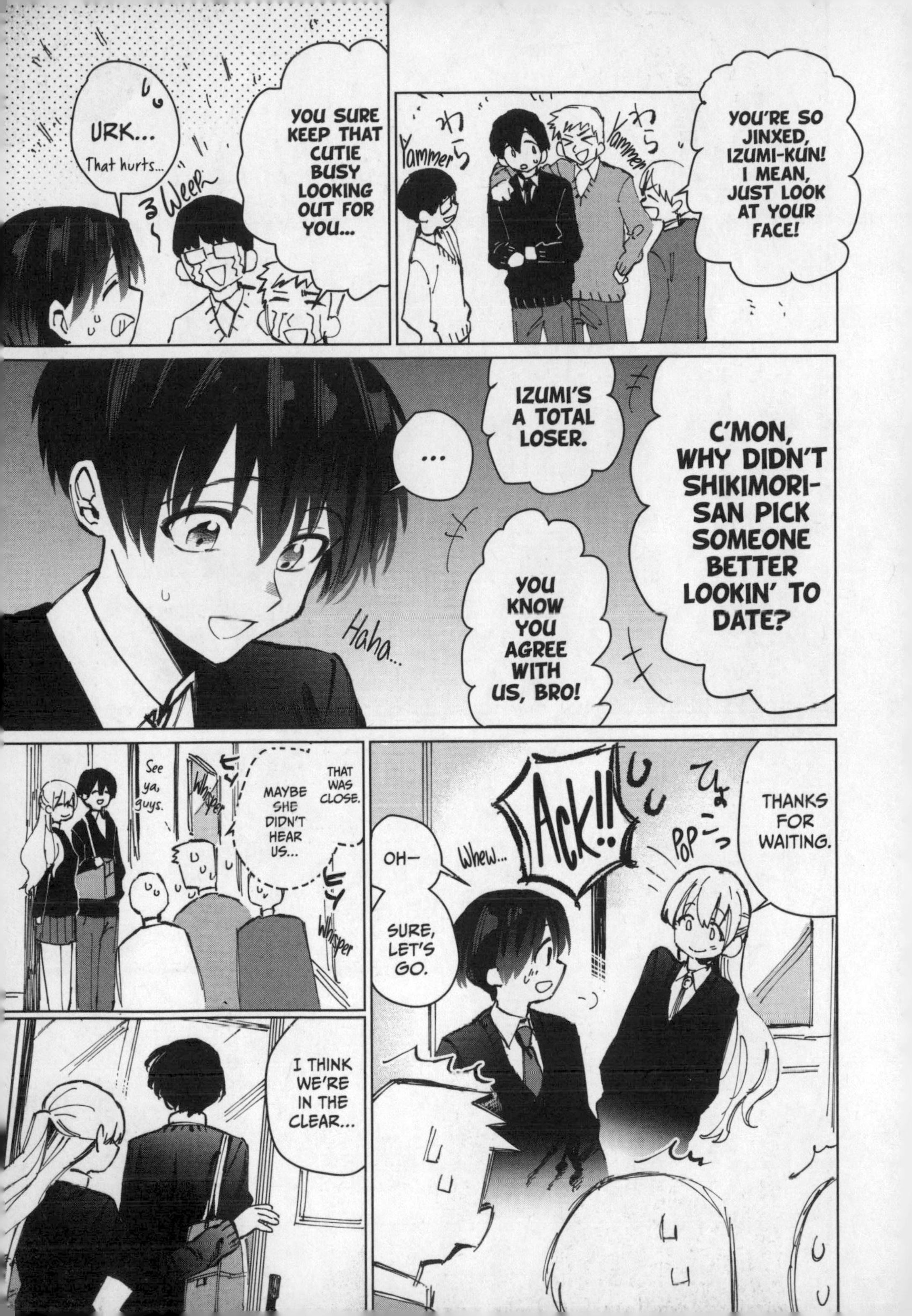
YOU'RE SO JINXED, IZUMI-KUN! I MEAN, JUST LOOK AT YOUR FACE!
Yammer
Yammer
YOU SURE KEEP THAT CUTIE BUSY LOOKING OUT FOR YOU...
URK...
That hurts...
Weep
C'MON, WHY DIDN'T SHIKIMORI-SAN PICK SOMEONE BETTER LOOKIN' TO DATE?
IZUMI'S A TOTAL LOSER.
YOU KNOW YOU AGREE WITH US, BRO!
...
Haha...
THANKS FOR WAITING.
POP
Ack!!
OH—
Whew...
SURE, LET'S GO.
THAT WAS CLOSE.
MAYBE SHE DIDN'T HEAR US...
Whisper
Whisper
See ya, guys.
I THINK WE'RE IN THE CLEAR...

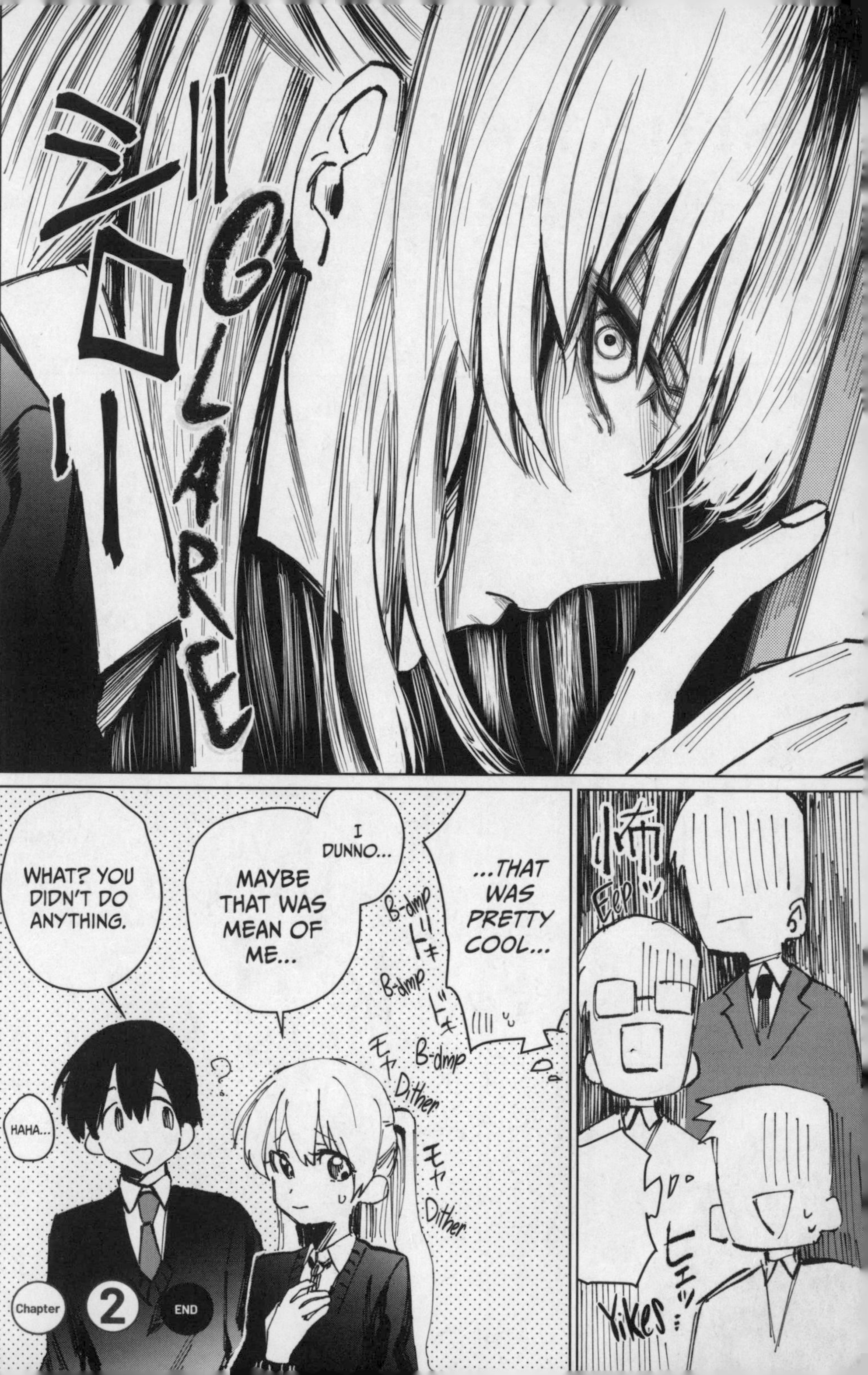
GLARE
ジロー
怖 Eep ッ
ヒエッ Yikes
...THAT WAS PRETTY COOL...
I DUNNO...
MAYBE THAT WAS MEAN OF ME...
WHAT? YOU DIDN'T DO ANYTHING.
B-dmp ドキ
B-dmp ドキ
B-dmp
モヤ Dither
モヤ Dither
HAHA...
Chapter 2 END

SHIKIMORI'S
Not just a cutie

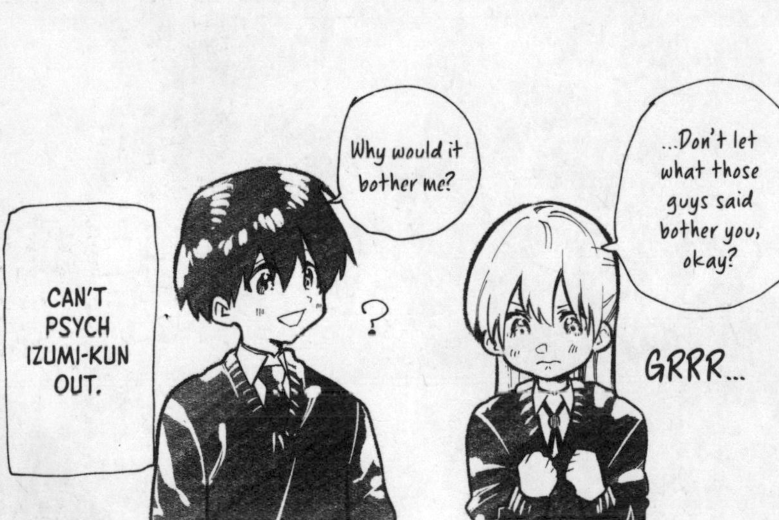
...Don't let what those guys said bother you, okay?
GRRR...
Why would it bother me?
?
CAN'T PSYCH IZUMI-KUN OUT.

IZUMI KUN

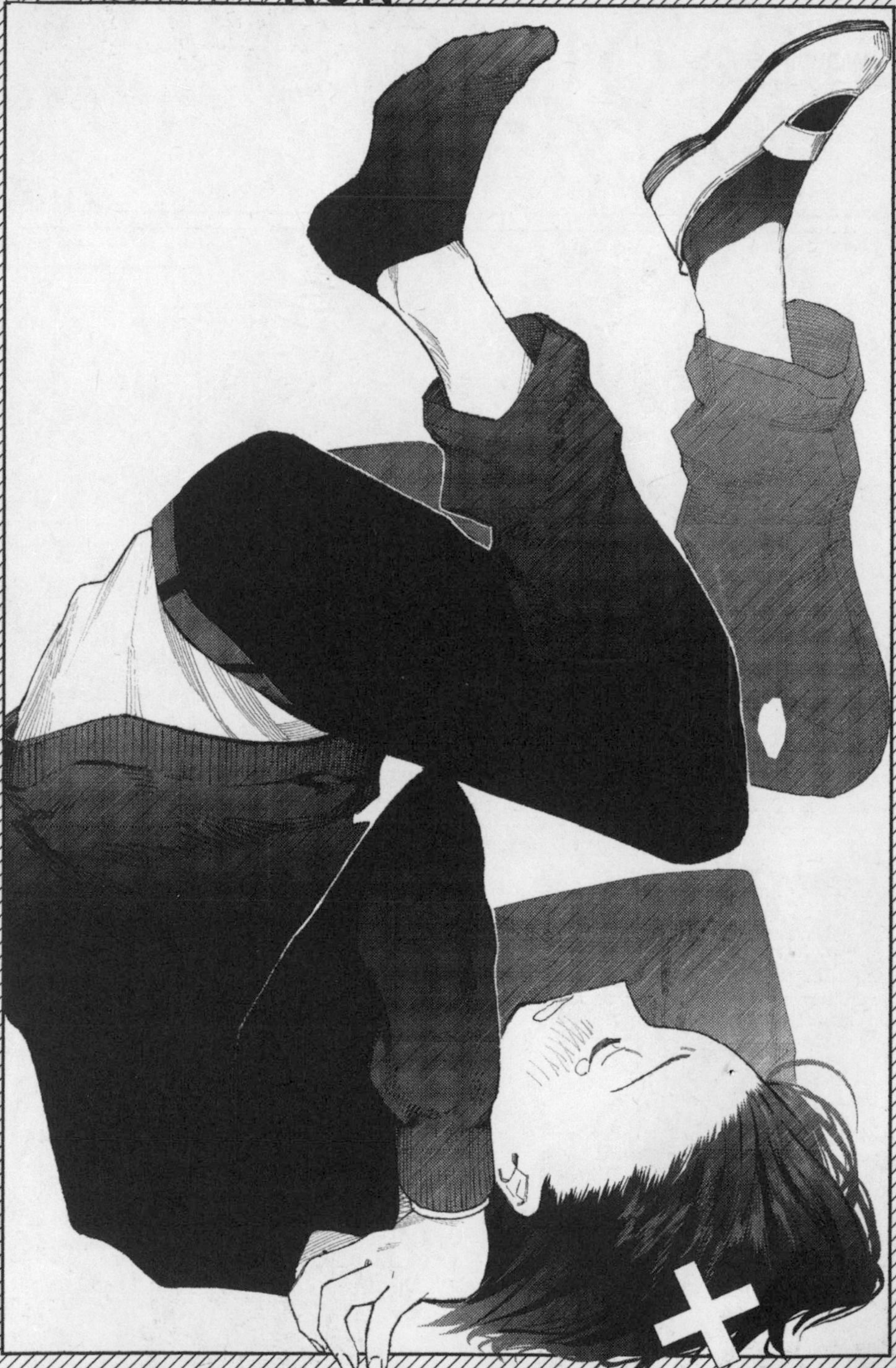

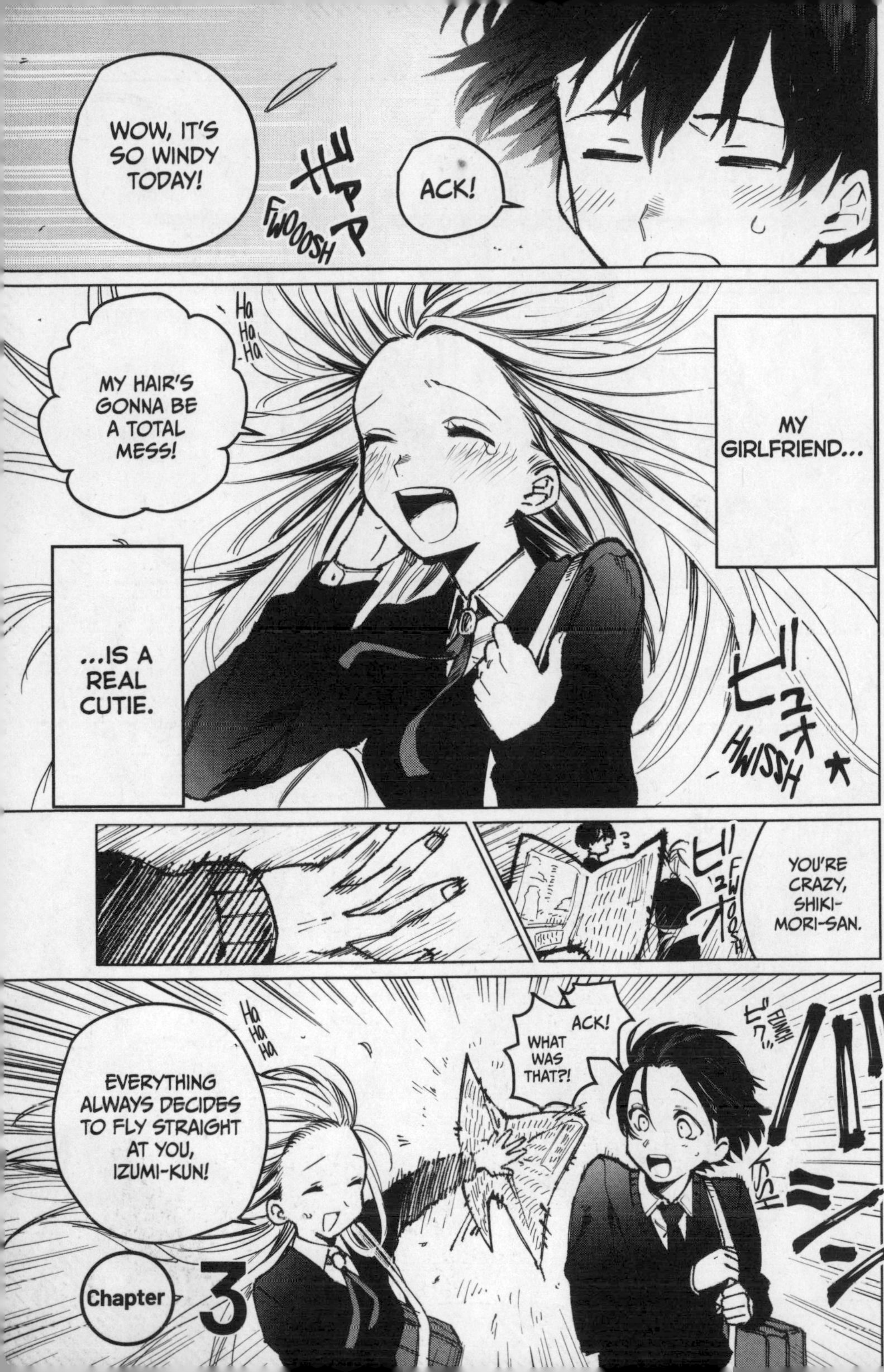

WOW, IT'S SO WINDY TODAY!
FWOOOSH
ACK!
MY GIRLFRIEND...
HWISSH
Ha Ha Ha
MY HAIR'S GONNA BE A TOTAL MESS!
...IS A REAL CUTIE.
YOU'RE CRAZY, SHIKI-MORI-SAN.
FWOOOSH
FLINCH
ACK!
WHAT WAS THAT?!
TSSH
Ha Ha Ha
EVERYTHING ALWAYS DECIDES TO FLY STRAIGHT AT YOU, IZUMI-KUN!
Chapter 3

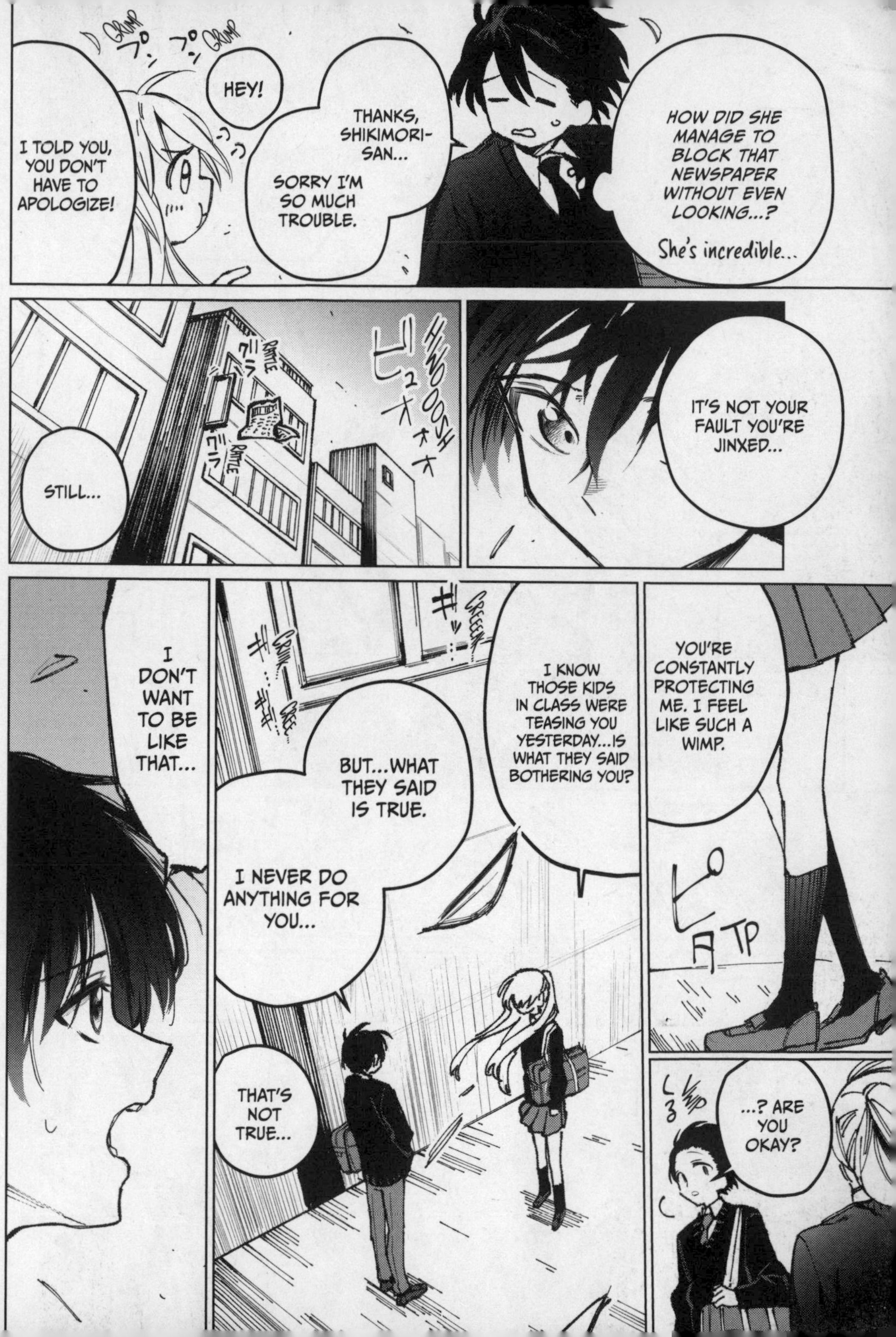
HOW DID SHE MANAGE TO BLOCK THAT NEWSPAPER WITHOUT EVEN LOOKING...?
She's incredible...
THANKS, SHIKIMORI-SAN...
SORRY I'M SO MUCH TROUBLE.
GRUMP
GRUMP
HEY!
I TOLD YOU, YOU DON'T HAVE TO APOLOGIZE!
IT'S NOT YOUR FAULT YOU'RE JINXED...
WHOOOSH
RATTLE
RATTLE
STILL...
YOU'RE CONSTANTLY PROTECTING ME. I FEEL LIKE SUCH A WIMP.
TP
VWIP
...? ARE YOU OKAY?
CREEEK
CRUNK
CREE
I KNOW THOSE KIDS IN CLASS WERE TEASING YOU YESTERDAY...IS WHAT THEY SAID BOTHERING YOU?
BUT...WHAT THEY SAID IS TRUE.
I NEVER DO ANYTHING FOR YOU...
THAT'S NOT TRUE...
I DON'T WANT TO BE LIKE THAT...

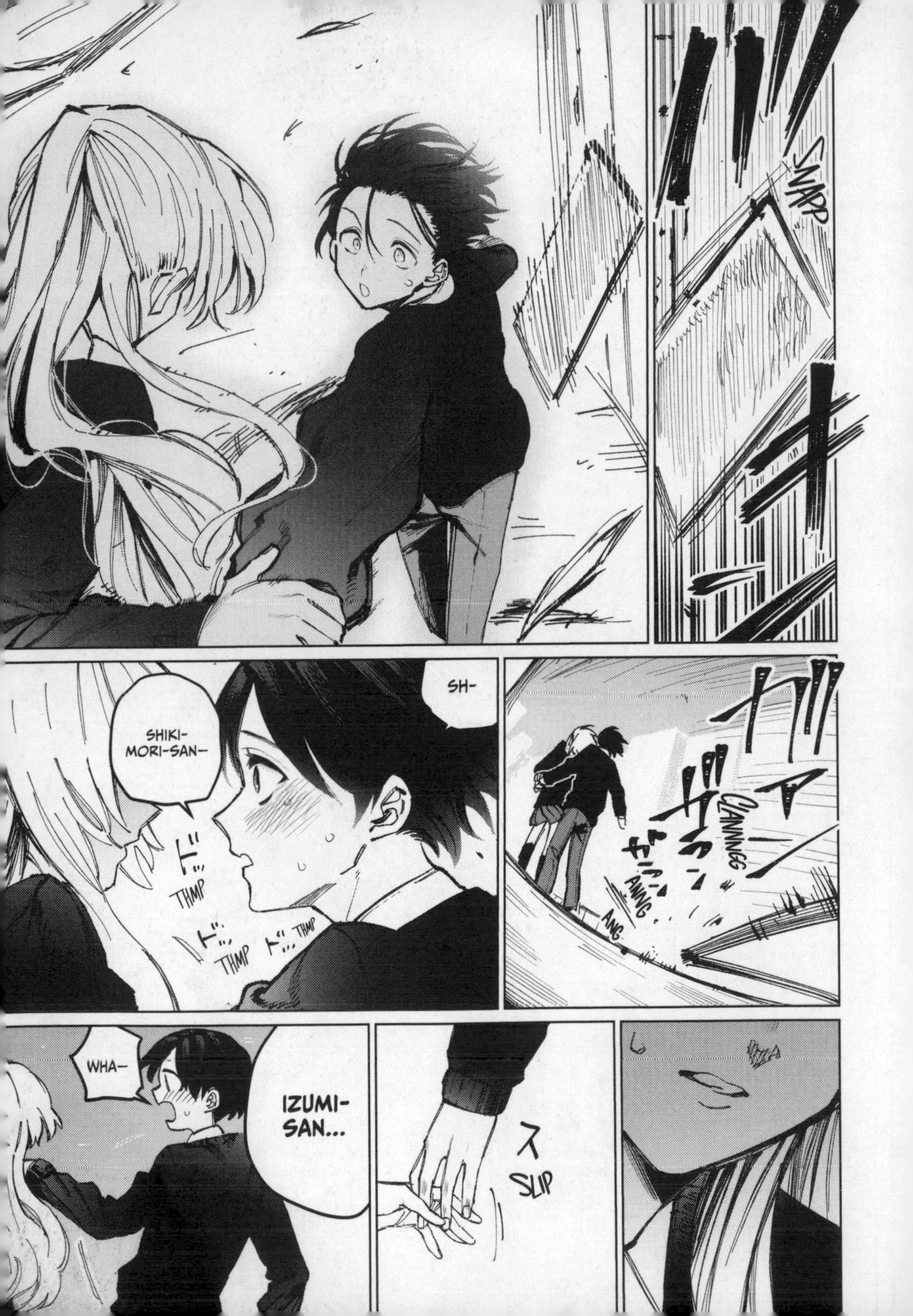
SWAPP
CLANNNGG
ANNG
ANG.
SH-
SHIKI-MORI-SAN-
THMP
THMP
THMP
IZUMI-SAN...
SLIP
WHA-

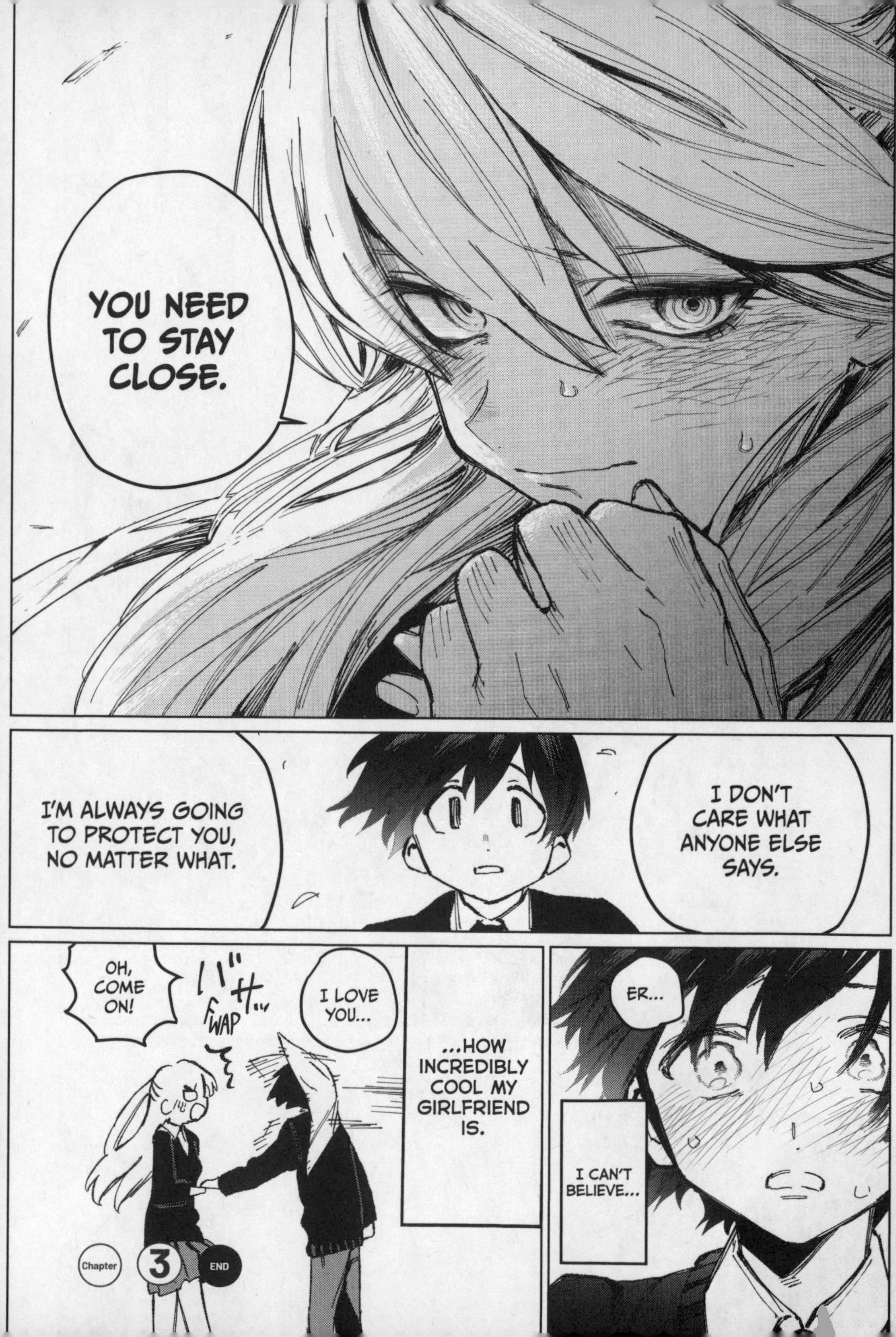
YOU NEED TO STAY CLOSE.
I DON'T CARE WHAT ANYONE ELSE SAYS.
I'M ALWAYS GOING TO PROTECT YOU, NO MATTER WHAT.
ER...
I CAN'T BELIEVE...
...HOW INCREDIBLY COOL MY GIRLFRIEND IS.
I LOVE YOU...
FWAP
OH, COME ON!
Chapter 3 END

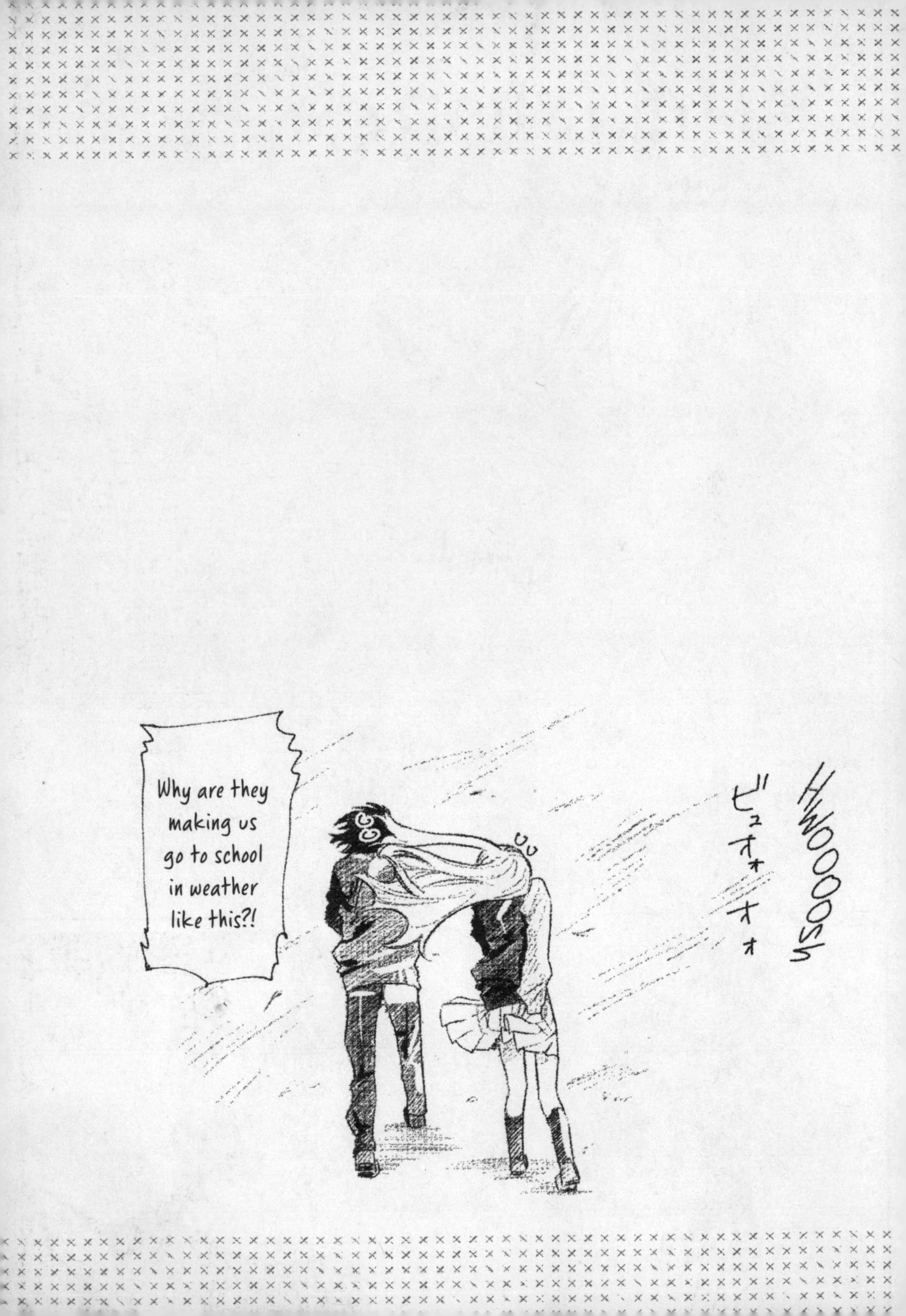
HWOOOOSH
ビュオォオォ
Why are they making us go to school in weather like this?!

SHIKIMORI'S not just a cutie

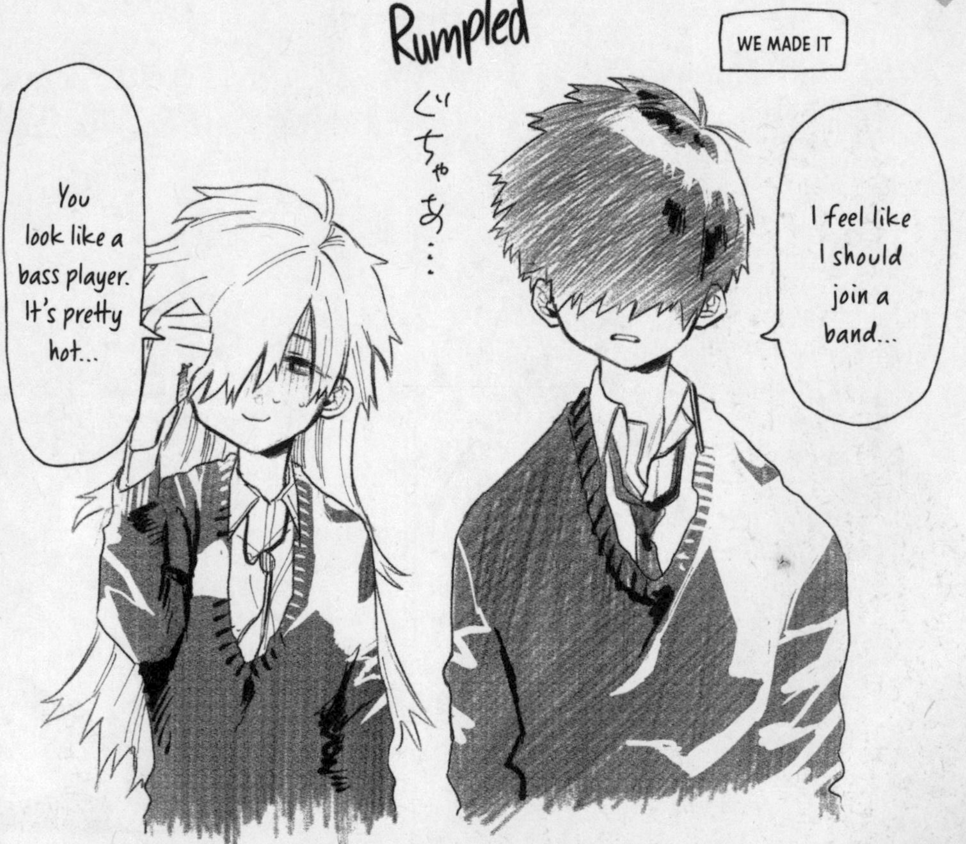
WE MADE IT
I feel like I should join a band...
Rumpled
ぐちゃあ…
You look like a bass player. It's pretty hot...

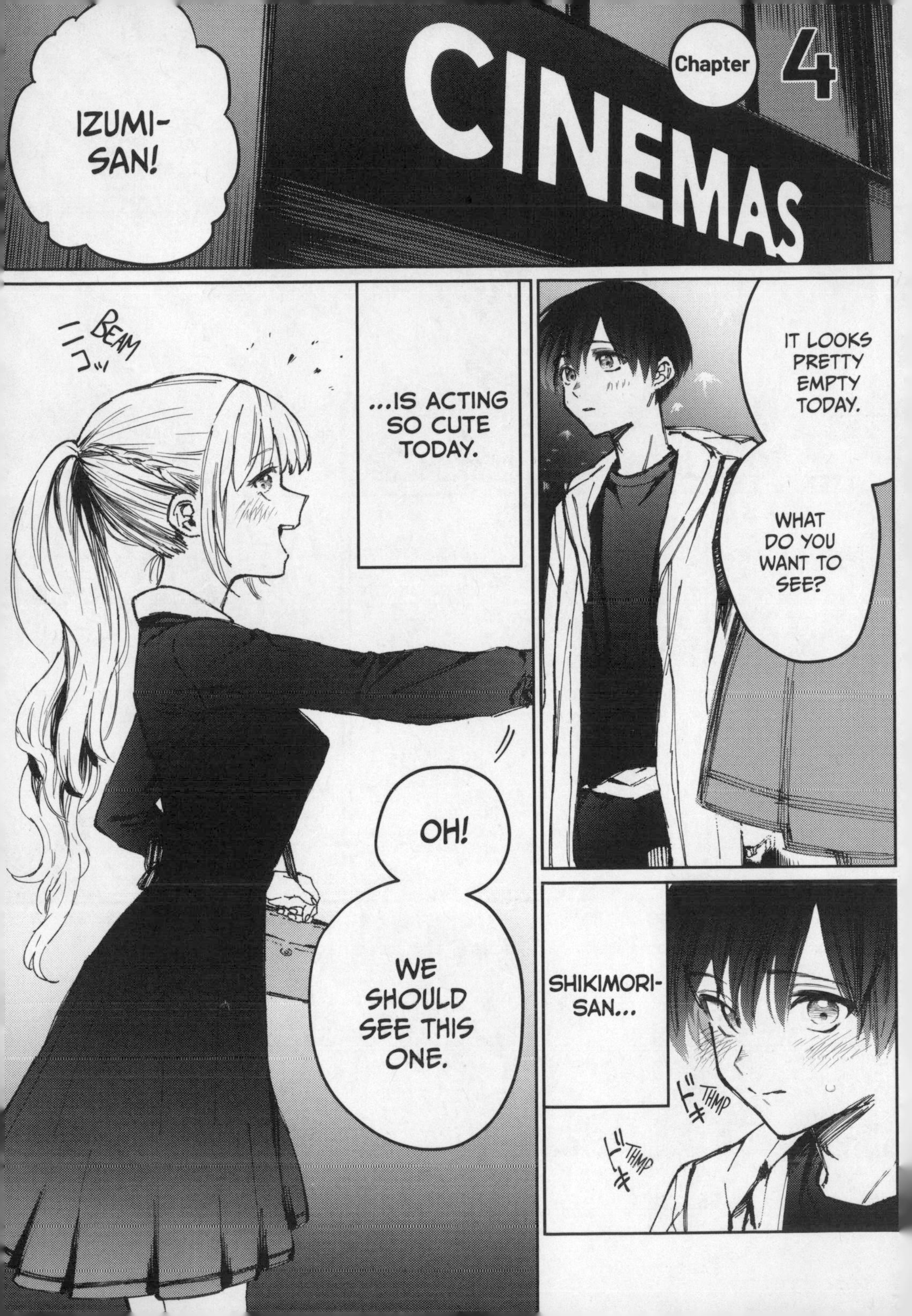
Chapter 4
CINEMAS
IZUMI-SAN!
IT LOOKS PRETTY EMPTY TODAY.
WHAT DO YOU WANT TO SEE?
SHIKIMORI-SAN...
THMP
THMP
BEAM
...IS ACTING SO CUTE TODAY.
OH!
WE SHOULD SEE THIS ONE.

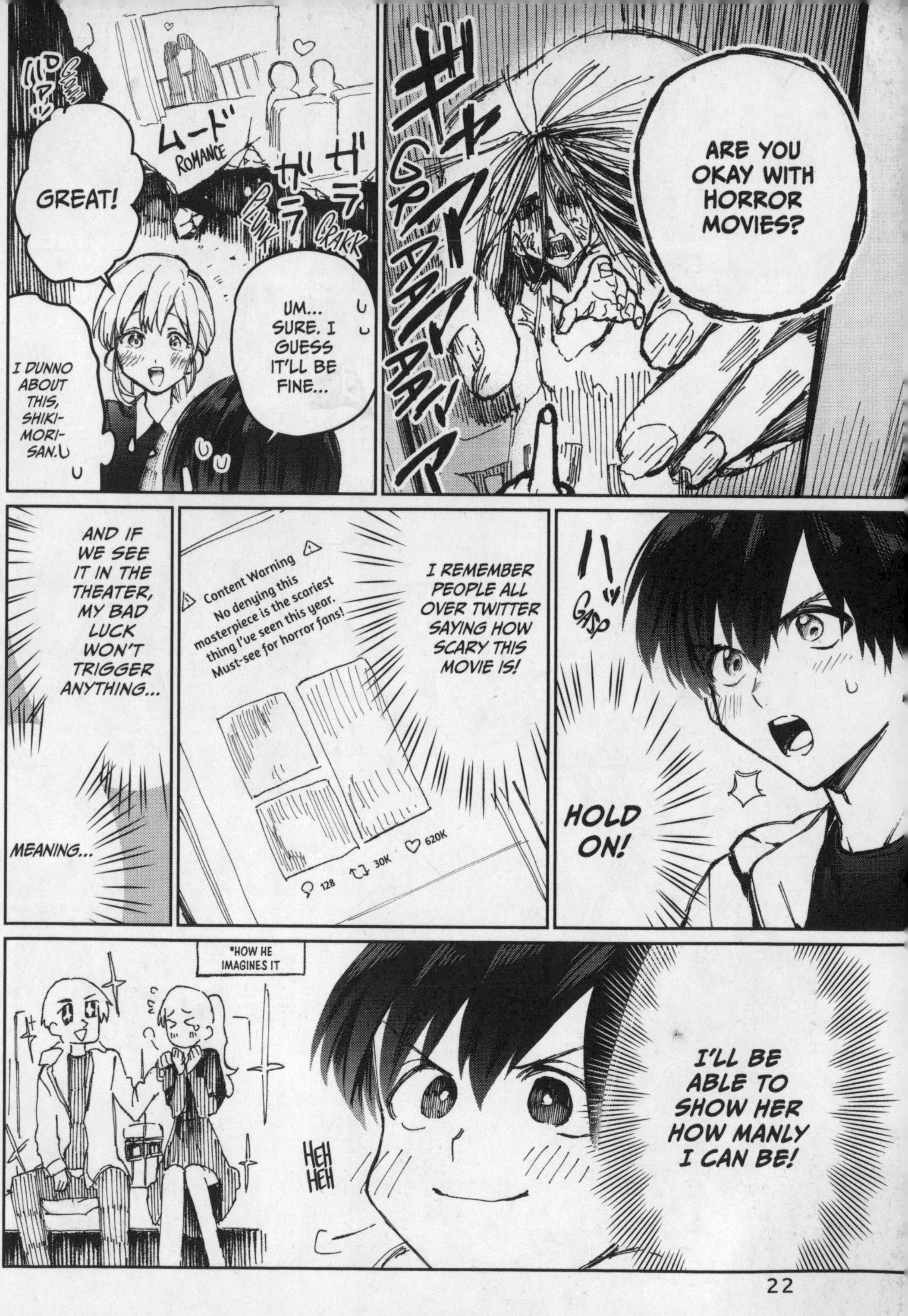
ARE YOU OKAY WITH HORROR MOVIES?
GREAT!
ムード
ROMANCE
ガラガラ
CRAKK
UM... SURE. I GUESS IT'LL BE FINE...
I DUNNO ABOUT THIS, SHIKIMORI-SAN.
ハッ
GASP
HOLD ON!
I REMEMBER PEOPLE ALL OVER TWITTER SAYING HOW SCARY THIS MOVIE IS!
Content Warning
No denying this masterpiece is the scariest thing I've seen this year. Must-see for horror fans!
128 30K 620K
AND IF WE SEE IT IN THE THEATER, MY BAD LUCK WON'T TRIGGER ANYTHING...
MEANING...
I'LL BE ABLE TO SHOW HER HOW MANLY I CAN BE!
HEH HEH
*HOW HE IMAGINES IT

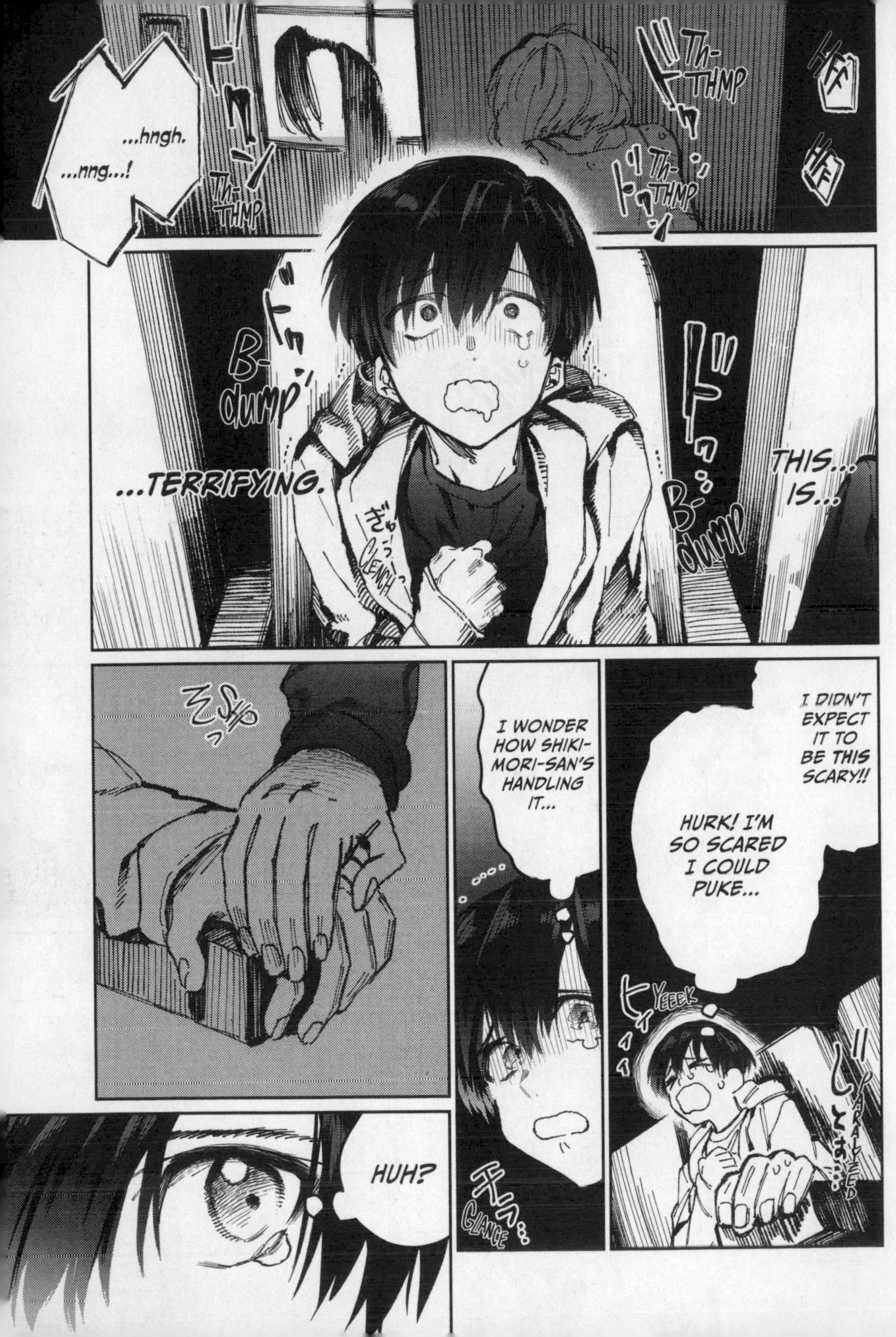
HFF
HFF
Th-THMP
Th-THMP
...hngh.
...nng...!
Th-THMP
THIS... IS...
B-dump
CLENCH
...TERRIFYING.
B-dump
I DIDN'T EXPECT IT TO BE THIS SCARY!!
HURK! I'M SO SCARED I COULD PUKE...
YEEEK
PARALYZED
I WONDER HOW SHIKIMORI-SAN'S HANDLING IT...
GLANCE
SKIP
HUH?

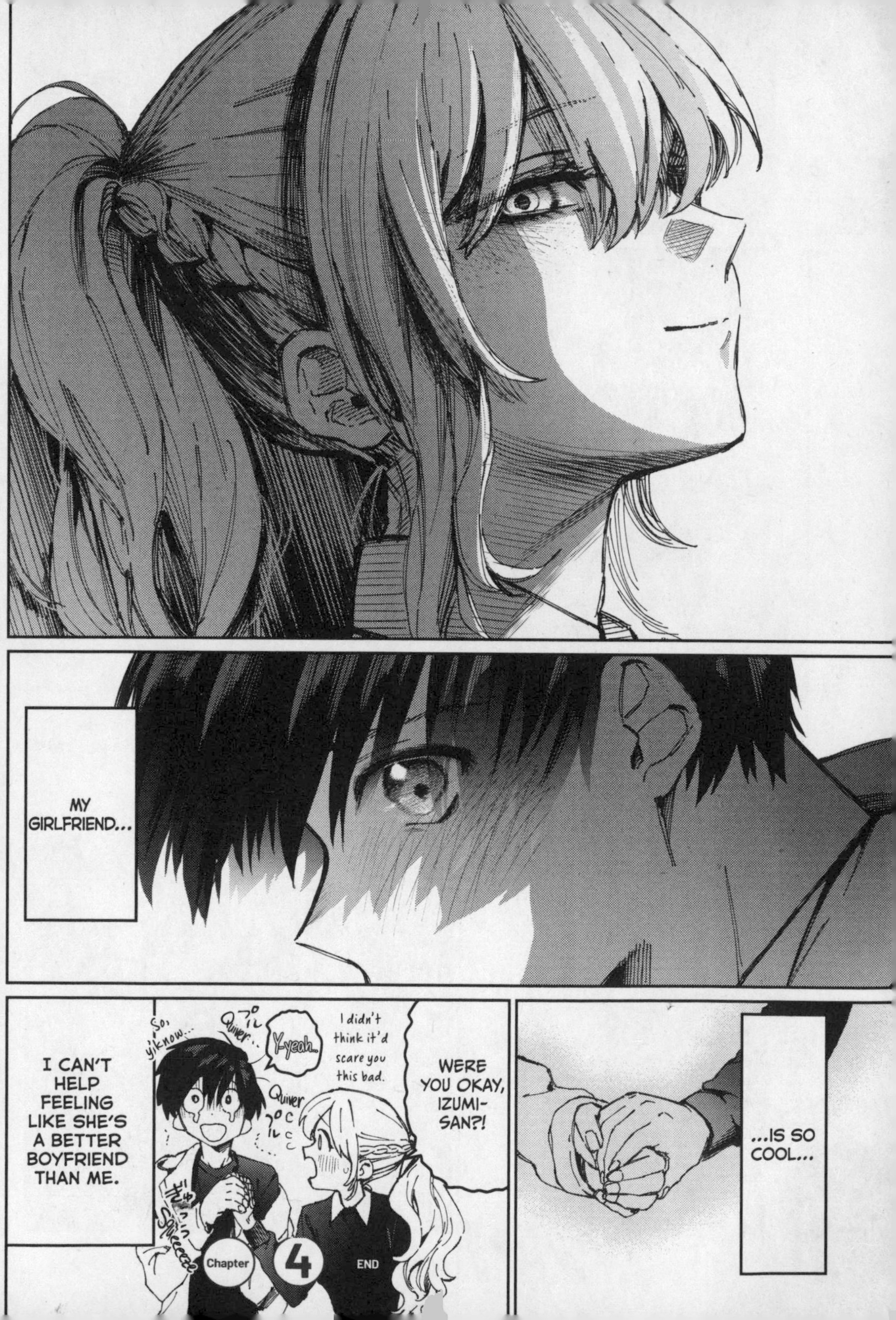
MY GIRLFRIEND...
...IS SO COOL...
WERE YOU OKAY, IZUMI-SAN?!
I didn't think it'd scare you this bad.
Y-yeah...
Quiver...
So, y'know...
Quiver
I CAN'T HELP FEELING LIKE SHE'S A BETTER BOYFRIEND THAN ME.
Squeeeeze
Chapter 4 END

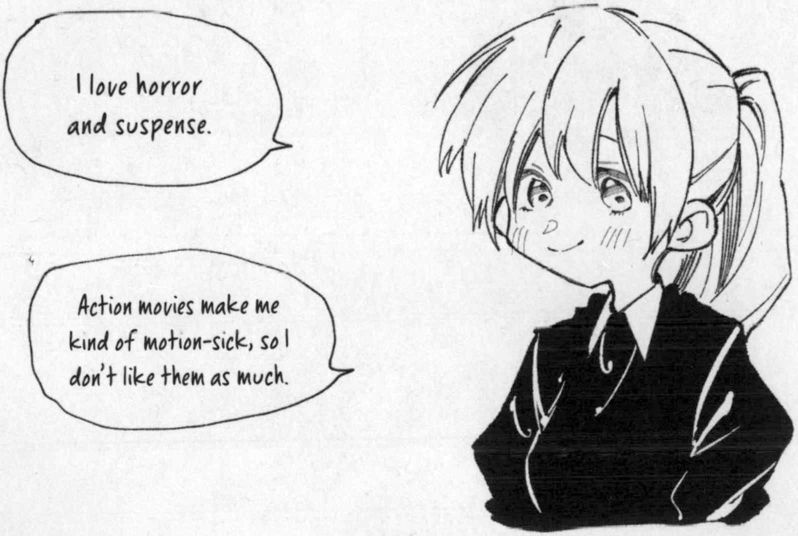
I love horror and suspense.
Action movies make me kind of motion-sick, so I don't like them as much.

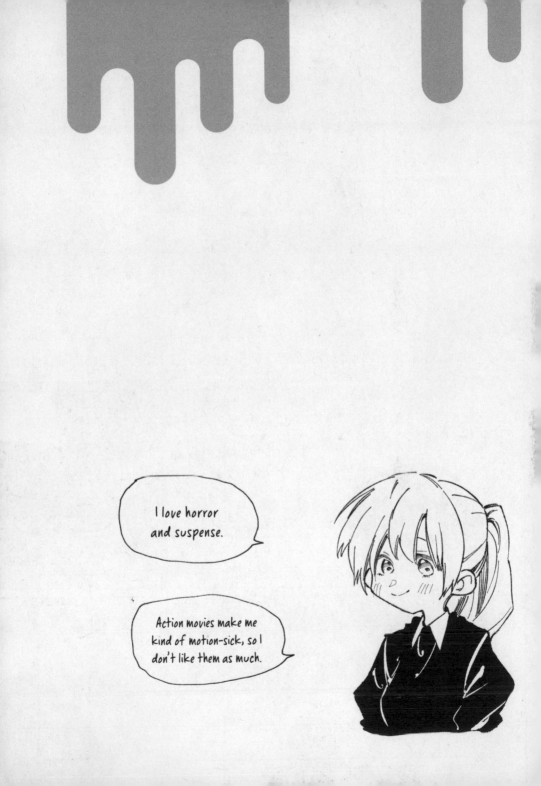

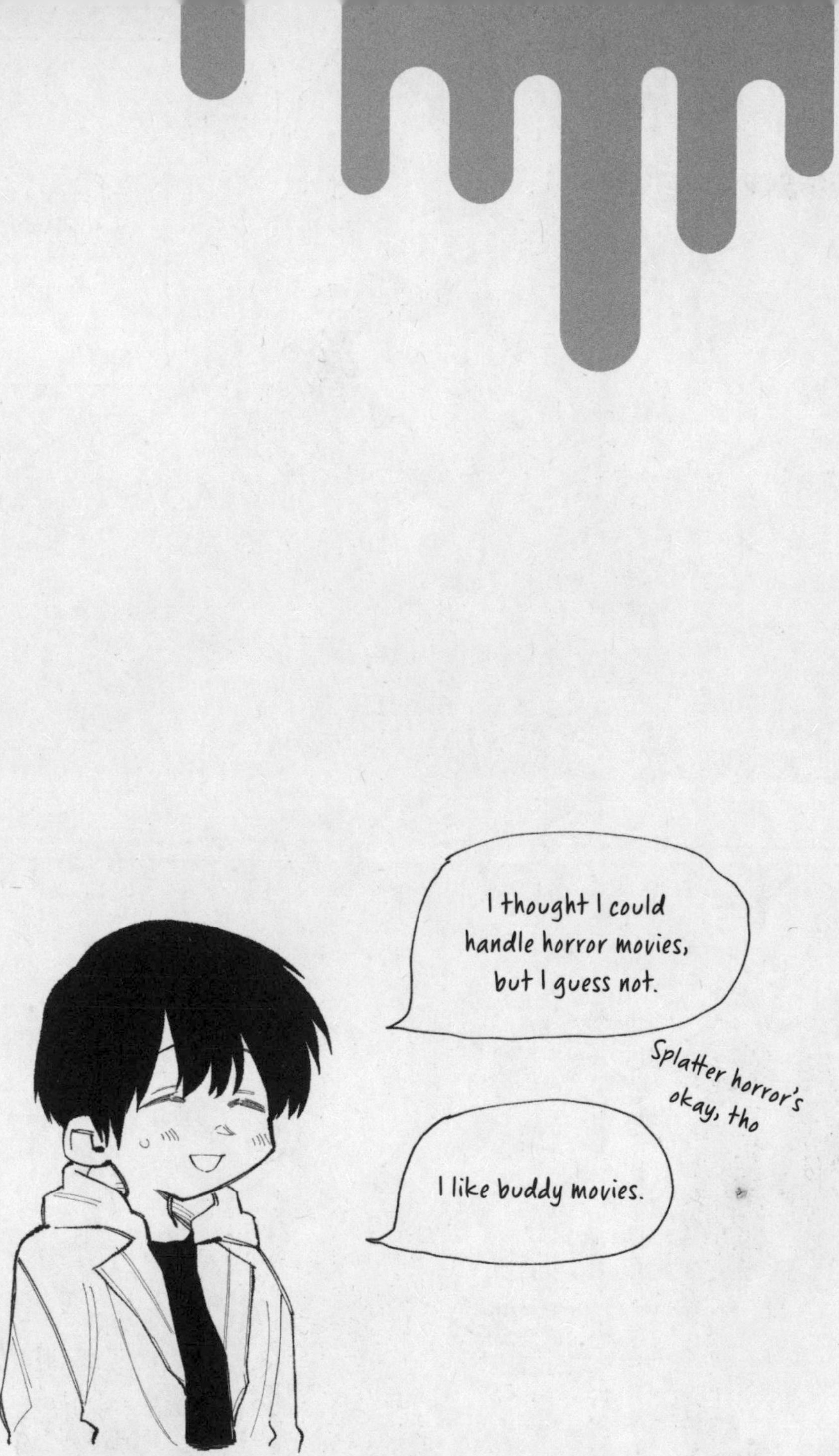
I thought I could handle horror movies, but I guess not.
Splatter horror's okay, tho
I like buddy movies.

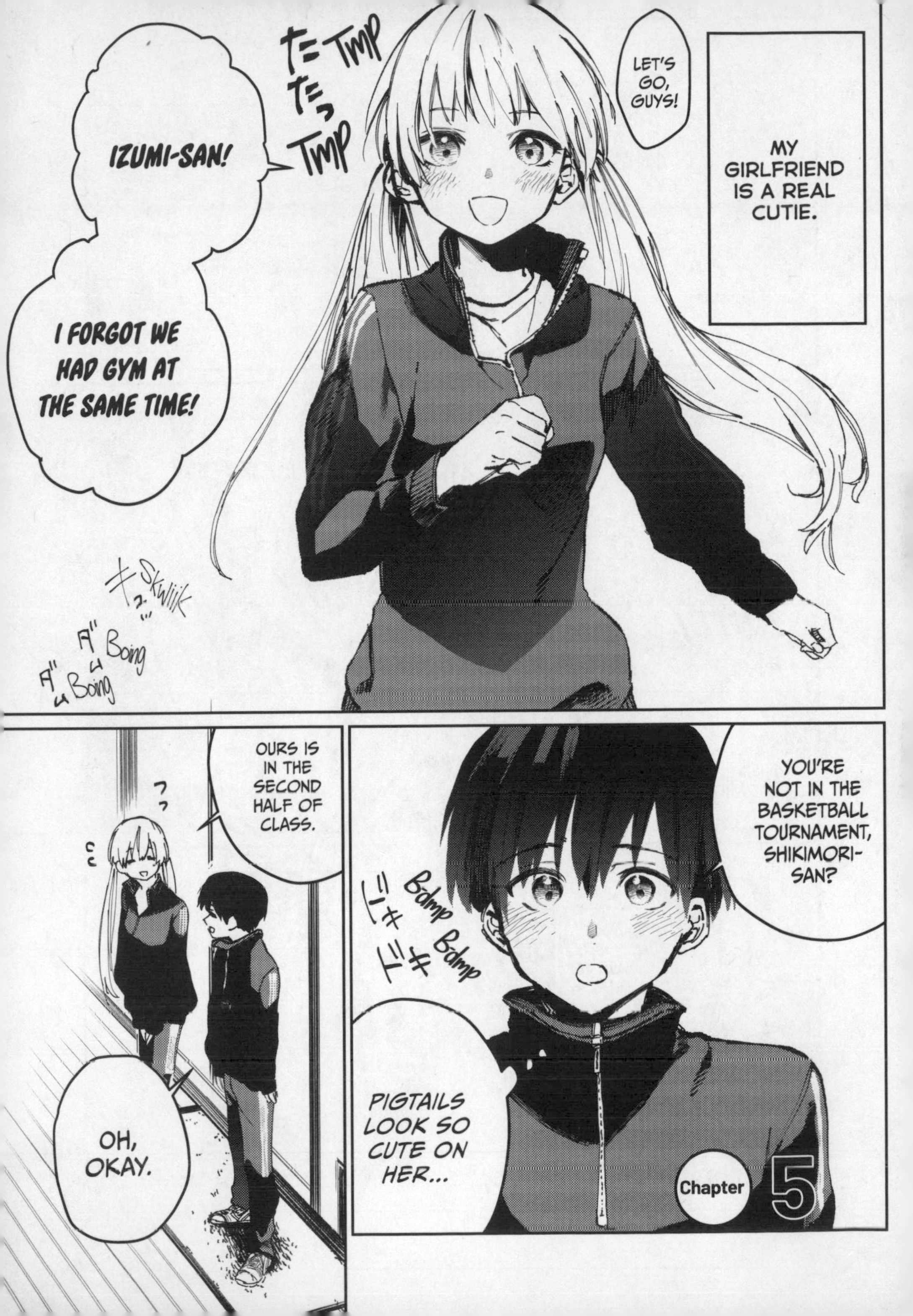
MY GIRLFRIEND IS A REAL CUTIE.
LET'S GO, GUYS!
TMP TMP
IZUMI-SAN!
I FORGOT WE HAD GYM AT THE SAME TIME!
SKWIIK
BOING BOING
YOU'RE NOT IN THE BASKETBALL TOURNAMENT, SHIKIMORI-SAN?
B-DMP B-DMP
PIGTAILS LOOK SO CUTE ON HER...
Chapter 5
OURS IS IN THE SECOND HALF OF CLASS.
OH, OKAY.

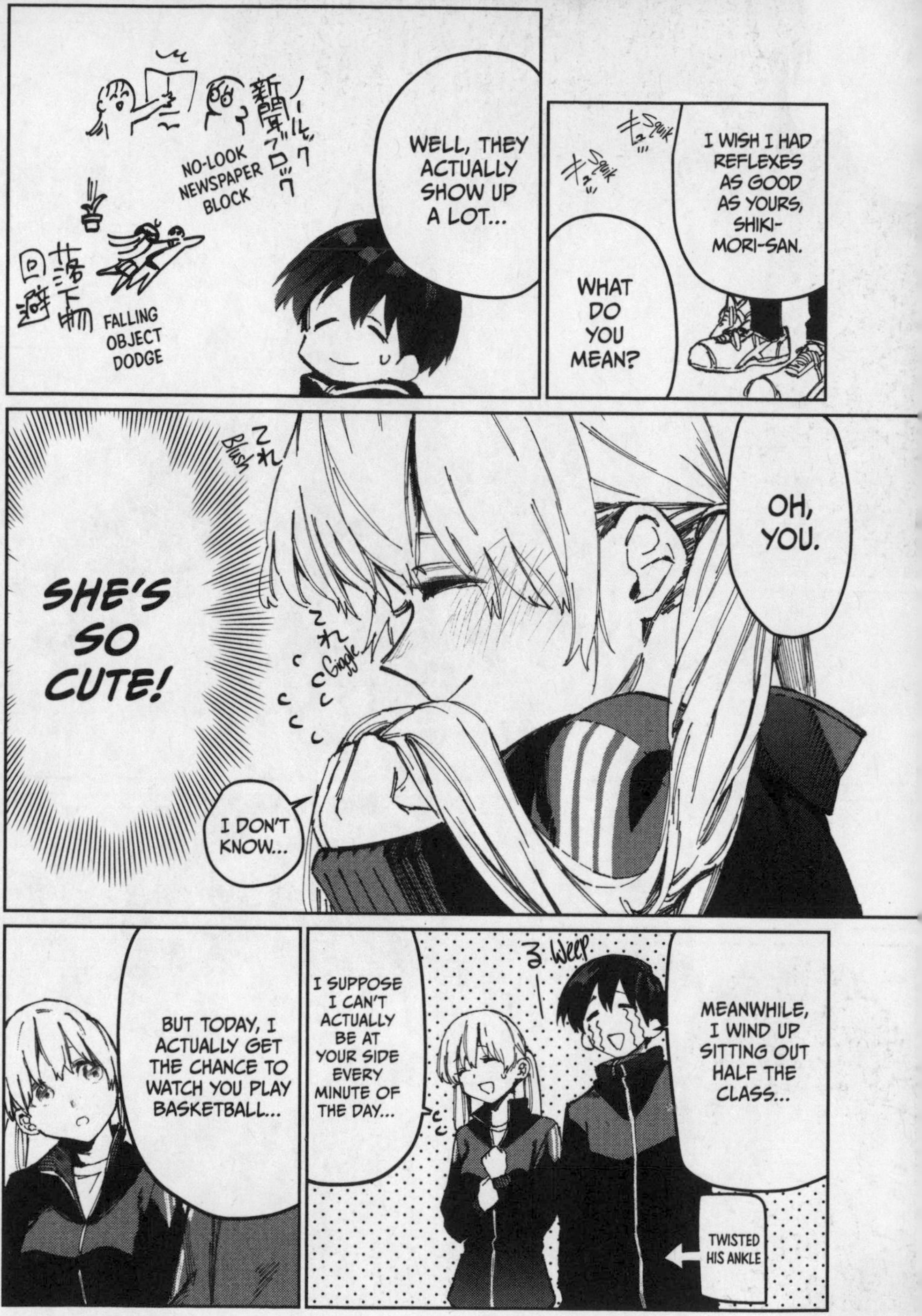
Squik
Squik
I WISH I HAD REFLEXES AS GOOD AS YOURS, SHIKI-MORI-SAN.
WHAT DO YOU MEAN?
WELL, THEY ACTUALLY SHOW UP A LOT...
NO-LOOK NEWSPAPER BLOCK
FALLING OBJECT DODGE
OH, YOU.
Blush
SHE'S SO CUTE!
Giggle
I DON'T KNOW...
Weep
MEANWHILE, I WIND UP SITTING OUT HALF THE CLASS...
I SUPPOSE I CAN'T ACTUALLY BE AT YOUR SIDE EVERY MINUTE OF THE DAY...
TWISTED HIS ANKLE
BUT TODAY, I ACTUALLY GET THE CHANCE TO WATCH YOU PLAY BASKETBALL...

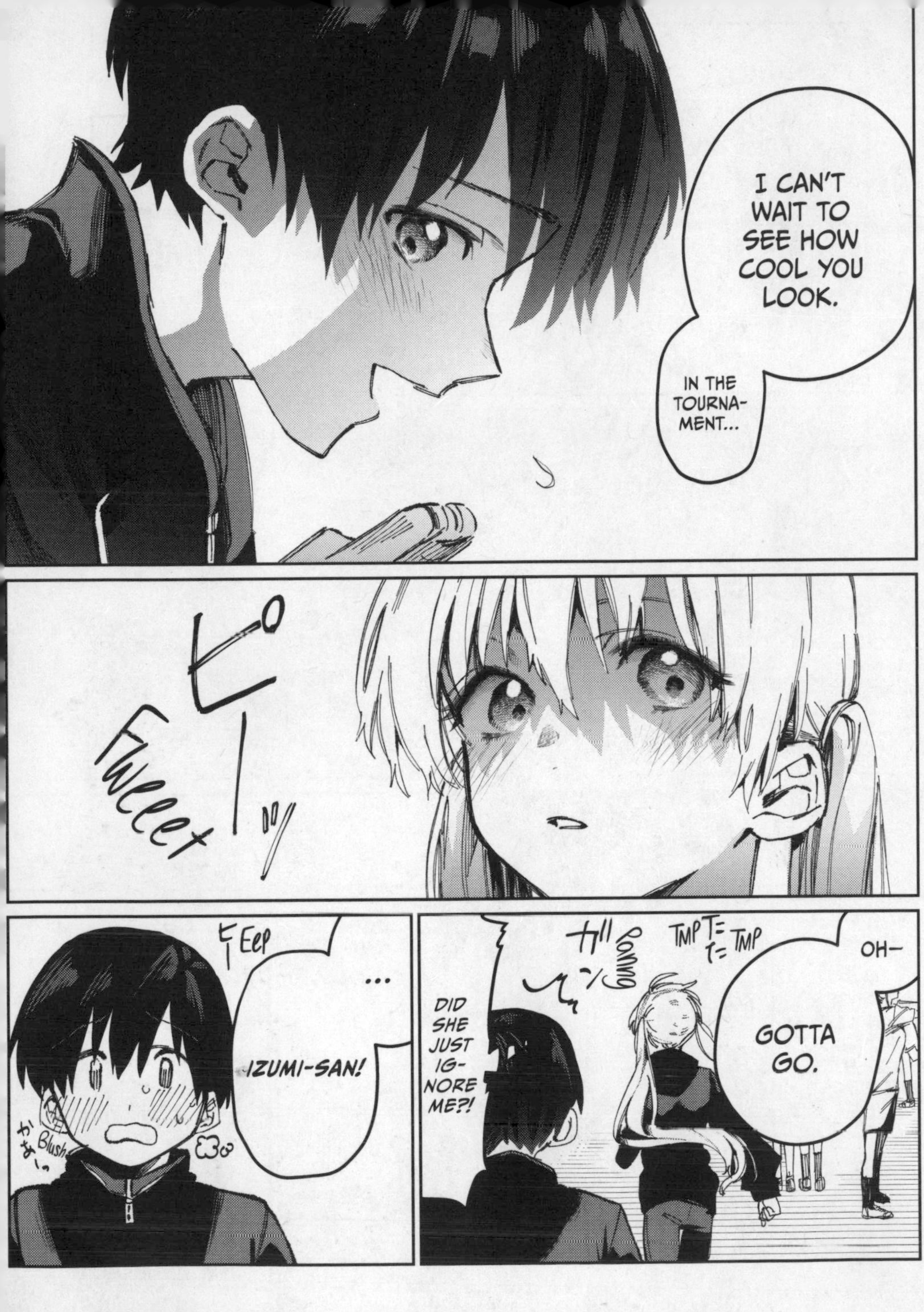
I CAN'T WAIT TO SEE HOW COOL YOU LOOK.
IN THE TOURNA-MENT...
Fweeet
OH—
GOTTA GO.
TMP TMP
DID SHE JUST IG-NORE ME?!
Eep
...
IZUMI-SAN!
Blush

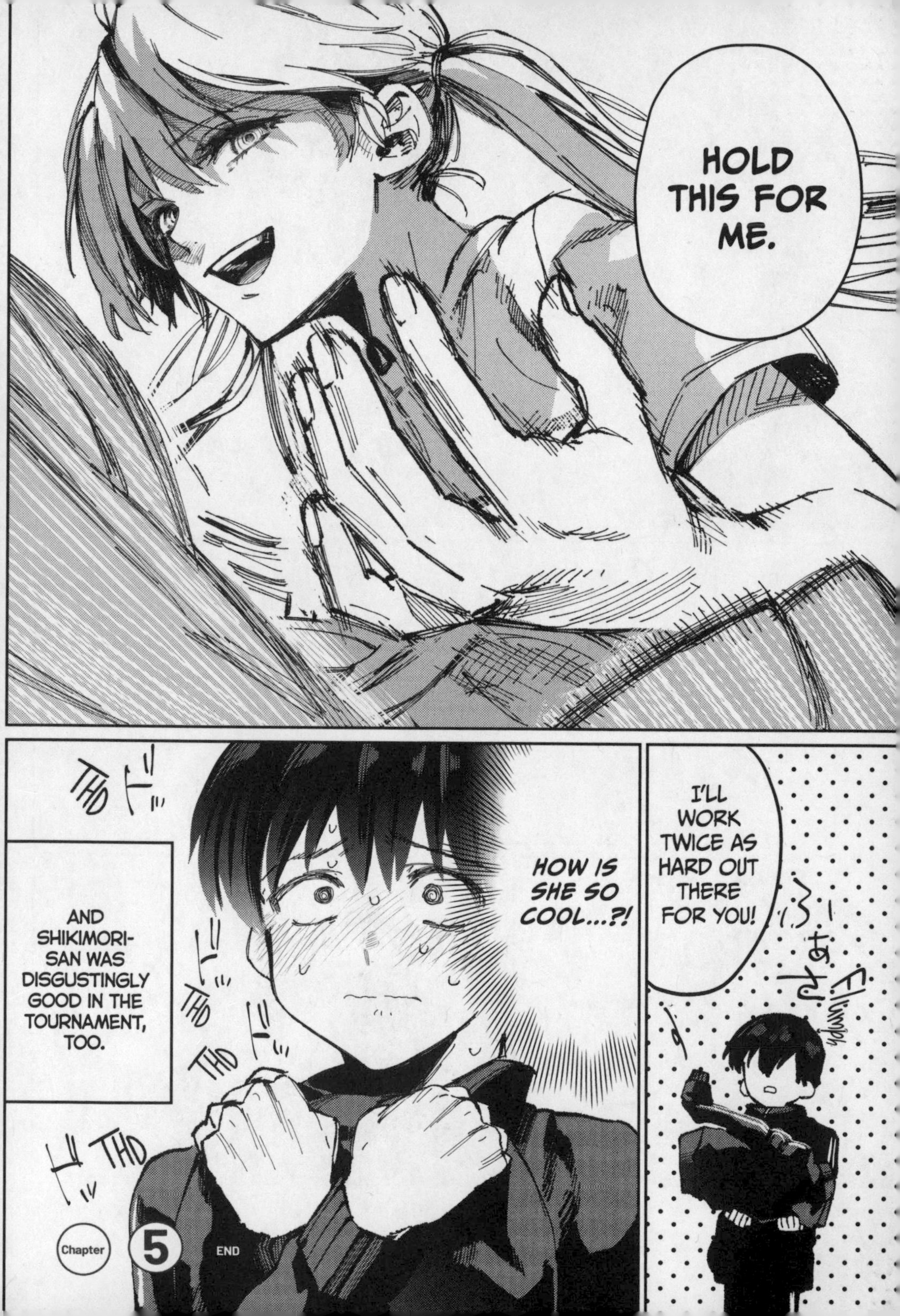
HOLD THIS FOR ME.
I'LL WORK TWICE AS HARD OUT THERE FOR YOU!
Flumph
HOW IS SHE SO COOL...?!
THD
AND SHIKIMORI-SAN WAS DISGUSTINGLY GOOD IN THE TOURNAMENT, TOO.
THD
THD
THD
Chapter 5 END

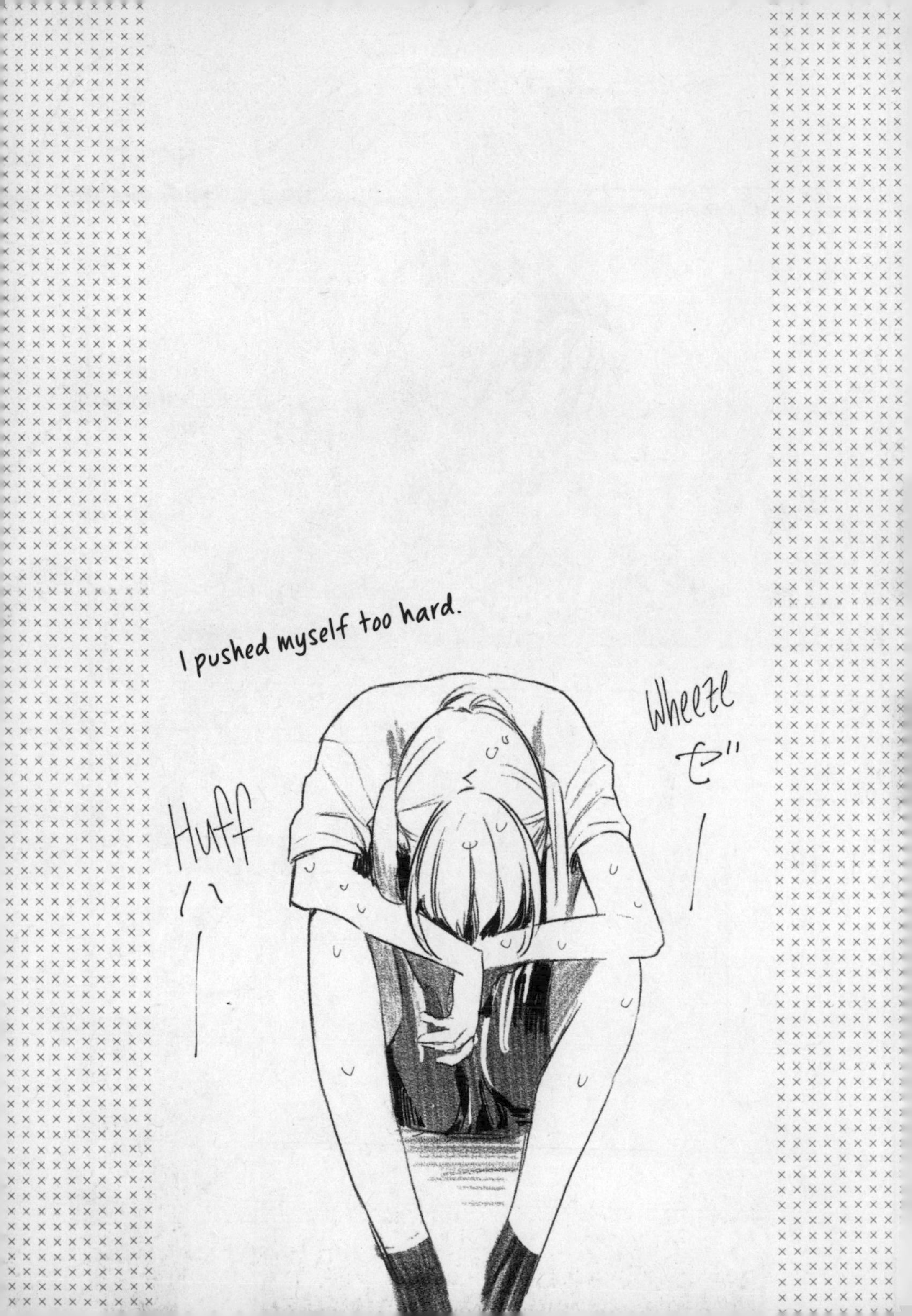
I pushed myself too hard.
Wheeze
Huff

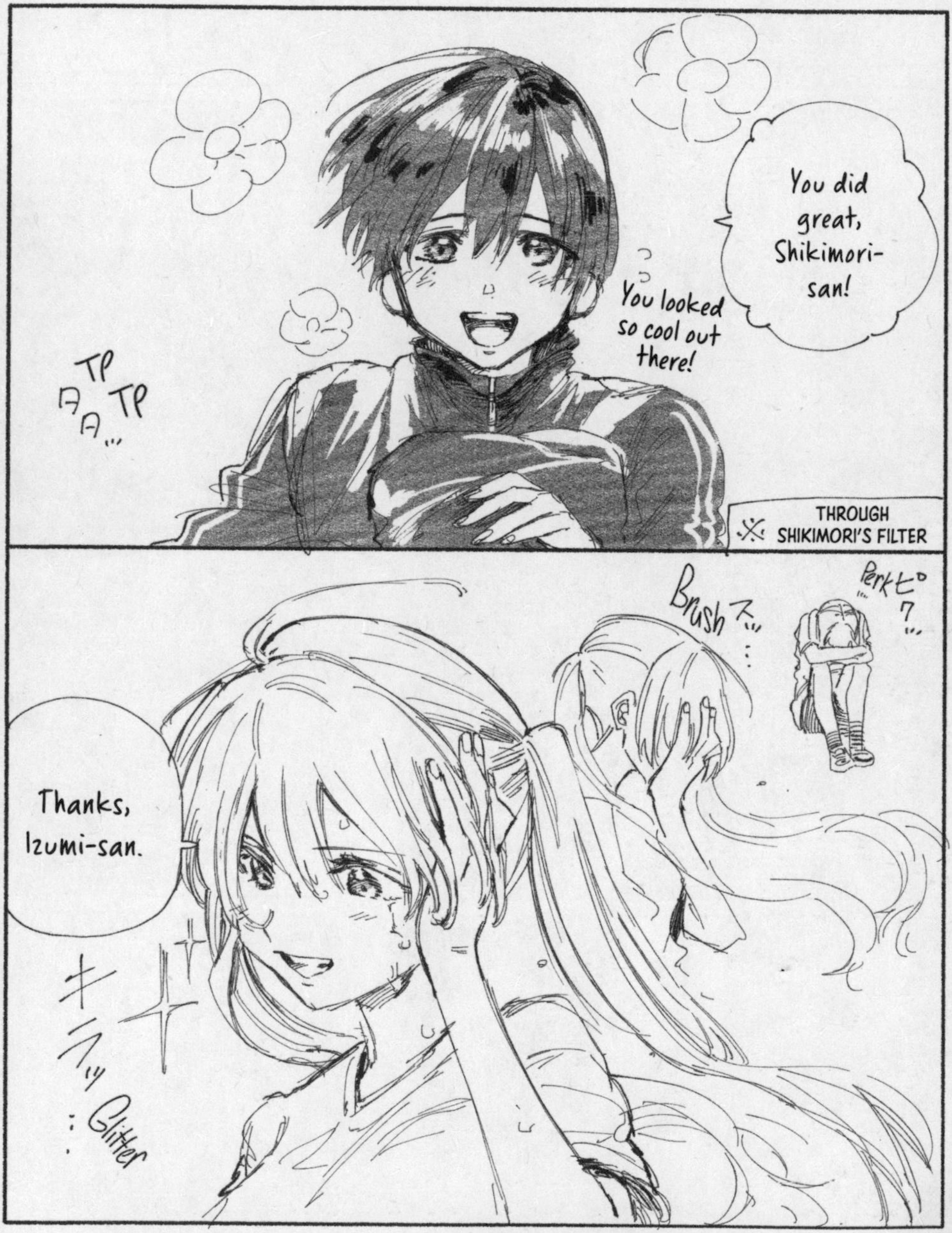
You did great, Shikimori-san!
You looked so cool out there!
TP TP
※ THROUGH SHIKIMORI'S FILTER
Perk
Brush
Thanks, Izumi-san.
Glitter

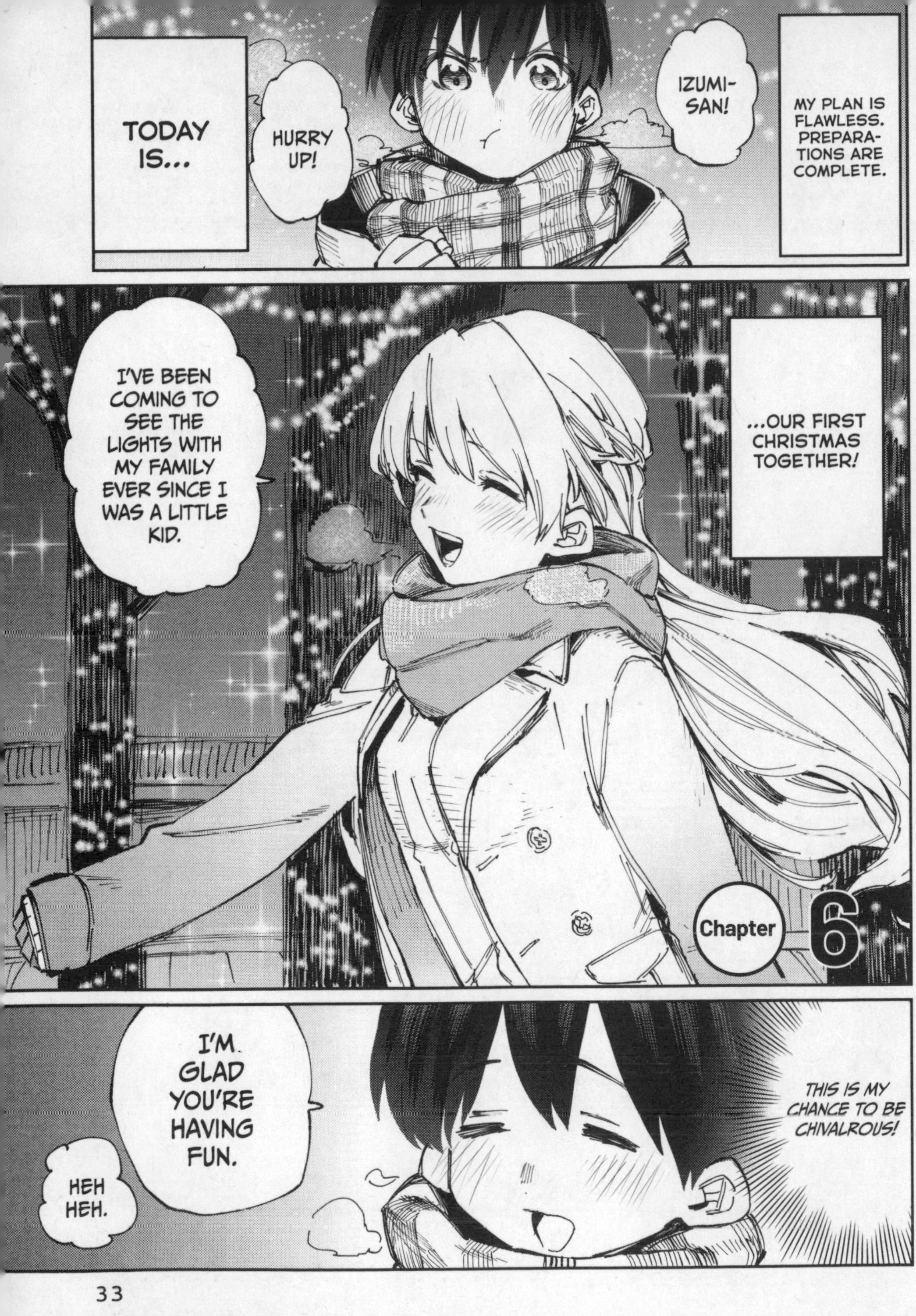
MY PLAN IS FLAWLESS. PREPARATIONS ARE COMPLETE.
IZUMI-SAN!
HURRY UP!
TODAY IS...
...OUR FIRST CHRISTMAS TOGETHER!
I'VE BEEN COMING TO SEE THE LIGHTS WITH MY FAMILY EVER SINCE I WAS A LITTLE KID.
Chapter 6
THIS IS MY CHANCE TO BE CHIVALROUS!
I'M GLAD YOU'RE HAVING FUN.
HEH HEH.

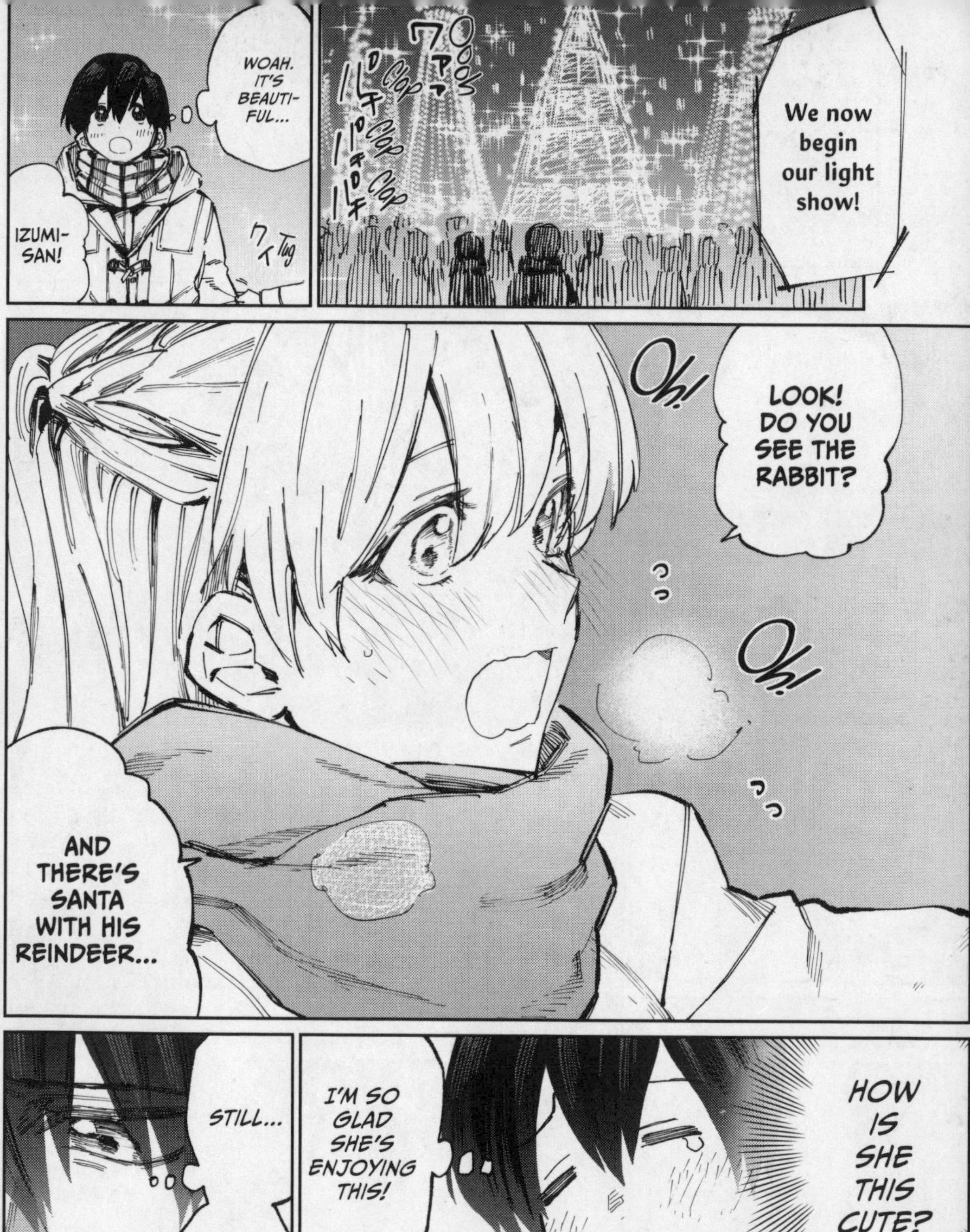
We now begin our light show!
Oooh
Clap clap clap
WOAH. IT'S BEAUTIFUL...
Tug
IZUMI-SAN!
Oh!
LOOK! DO YOU SEE THE RABBIT?
Oh!
AND THERE'S SANTA WITH HIS REINDEER...
HOW IS SHE THIS CUTE?
I'M SO GLAD SHE'S ENJOYING THIS!
Throb
STILL...
I CAN'T BELIEVE...

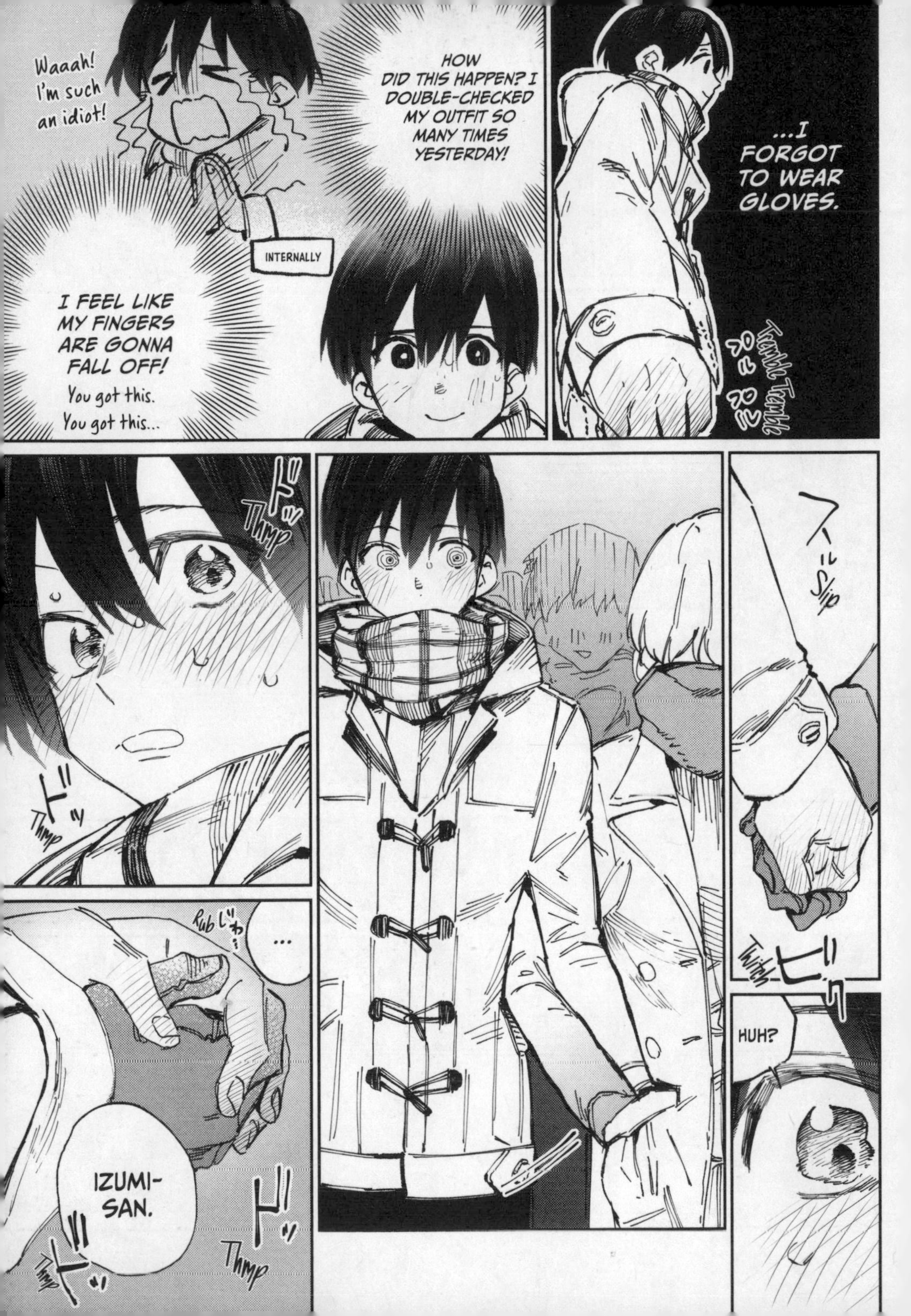
...I FORGOT TO WEAR GLOVES.
Tremble Tremble
HOW DID THIS HAPPEN? I DOUBLE-CHECKED MY OUTFIT SO MANY TIMES YESTERDAY!
Waaah! I'm such an idiot!
INTERNALLY
I FEEL LIKE MY FINGERS ARE GONNA FALL OFF!
You got this.
You got this...
Slip
Twitch
HUH?
Thmp
Thmp
Rub
...
IZUMI-SAN.
Thmp
Thmp

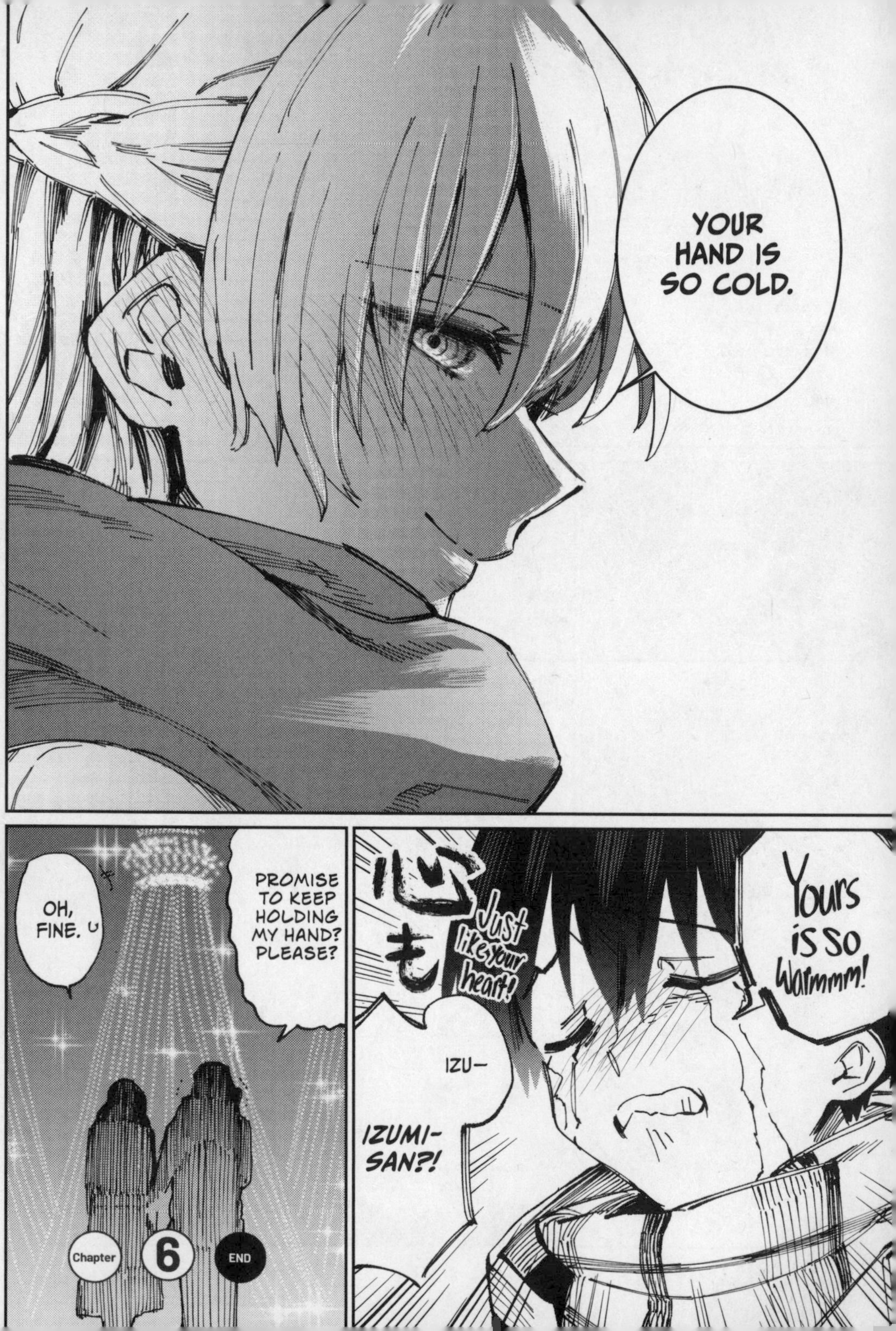
YOUR HAND IS SO COLD.
Yours is so Warmmm!
心も
Just like your heart!
IZU—
IZUMI-SAN?!
PROMISE TO KEEP HOLDING MY HAND? PLEASE?
OH, FINE.
Chapter 6 END

Annnd...

Go!

CHRISTMAS
PRESENTS

That's
crazy!

Heh.

丸かぶり
It's a twofer!

SHIKIMORI'S not just a cutie

SHiKiMORi'S
not just a cutie

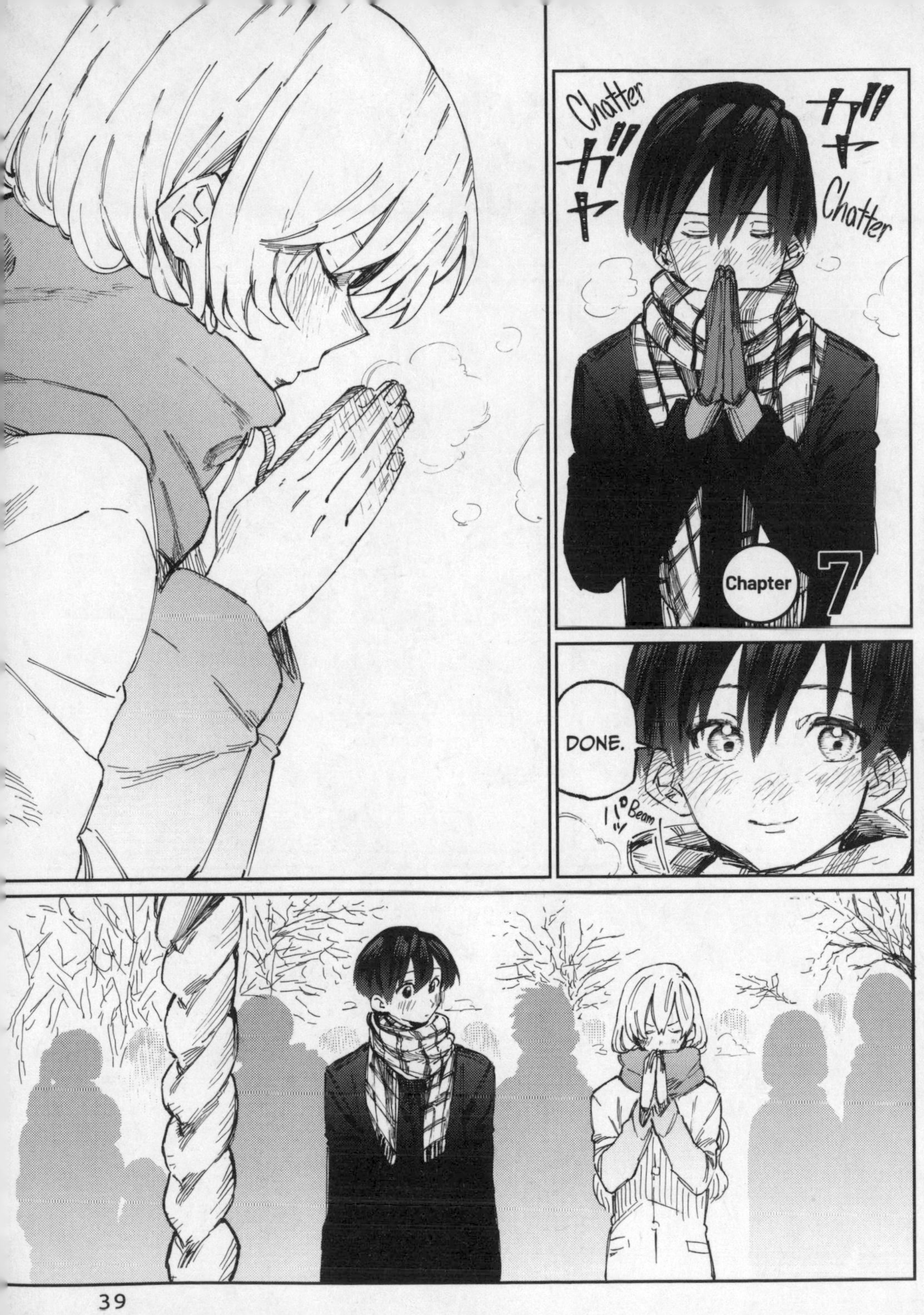
ガヤ
Chatter
ガヤ
Chatter
Chapter 7
DONE.
Beam

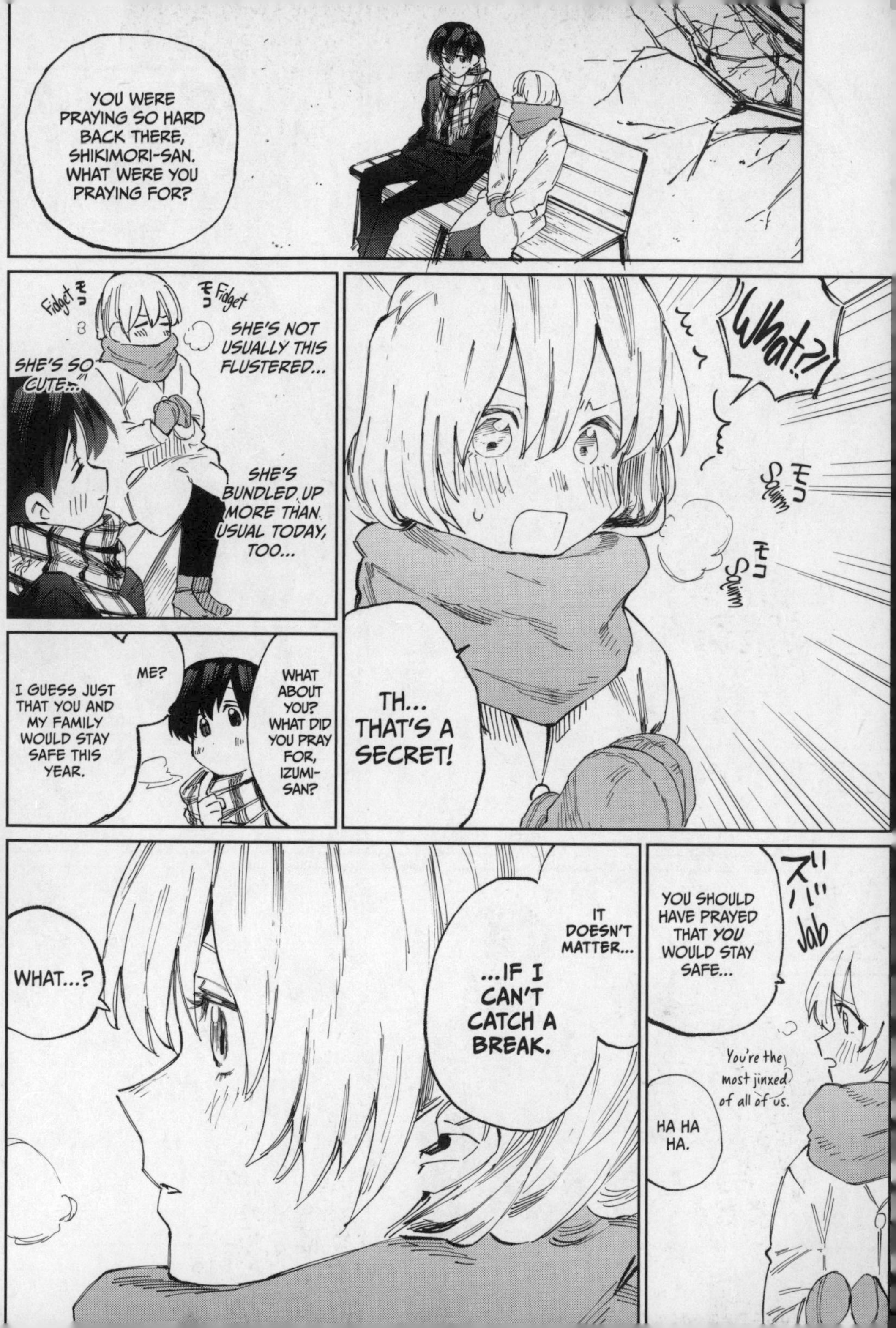
YOU WERE PRAYING SO HARD BACK THERE, SHIKIMORI-SAN. WHAT WERE YOU PRAYING FOR?
What?!
モコ Squirm
モコ Squirm
TH... THAT'S A SECRET!
モコ Fidget
モコ Fidget
SHE'S NOT USUALLY THIS FLUSTERED...
SHE'S SO CUTE...
SHE'S BUNDLED UP MORE THAN USUAL TODAY, TOO...
WHAT ABOUT YOU? WHAT DID YOU PRAY FOR, IZUMI-SAN?
ME?
I GUESS JUST THAT YOU AND MY FAMILY WOULD STAY SAFE THIS YEAR.
ズバ Jab
YOU SHOULD HAVE PRAYED THAT *YOU* WOULD STAY SAFE...
You're the most jinxed of all of us.
HA HA HA.
WHAT...?
IT DOESN'T MATTER...
...IF I CAN'T CATCH A BREAK.

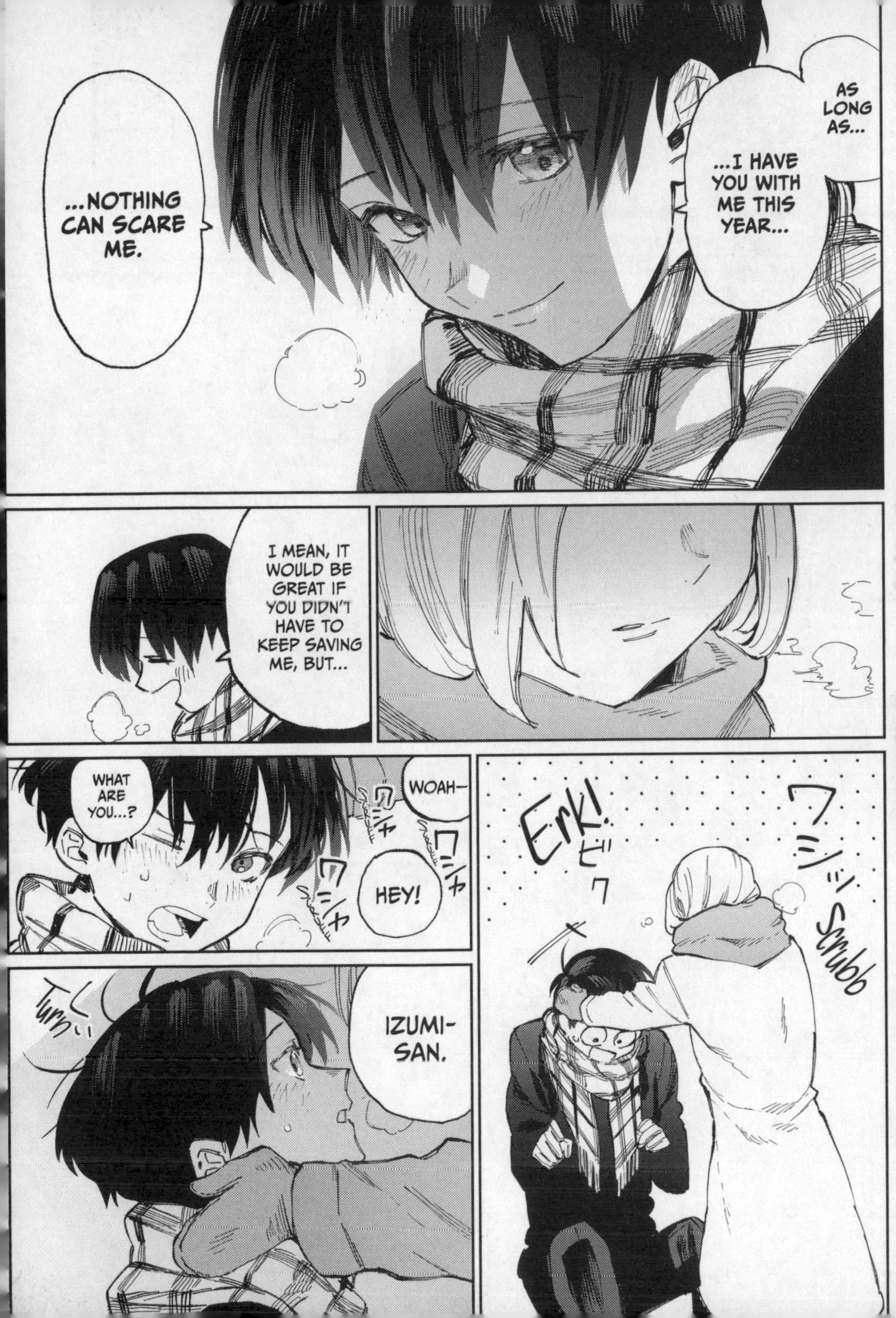
AS LONG AS...
...I HAVE YOU WITH ME THIS YEAR...
...NOTHING CAN SCARE ME.
I MEAN, IT WOULD BE GREAT IF YOU DIDN'T HAVE TO KEEP SAVING ME, BUT...
ワシッ
Scrubb
Erk!
ビクッ
WOAH—
HEY!
WHAT ARE YOU...?
IZUMI-SAN.
くるっ
Turn

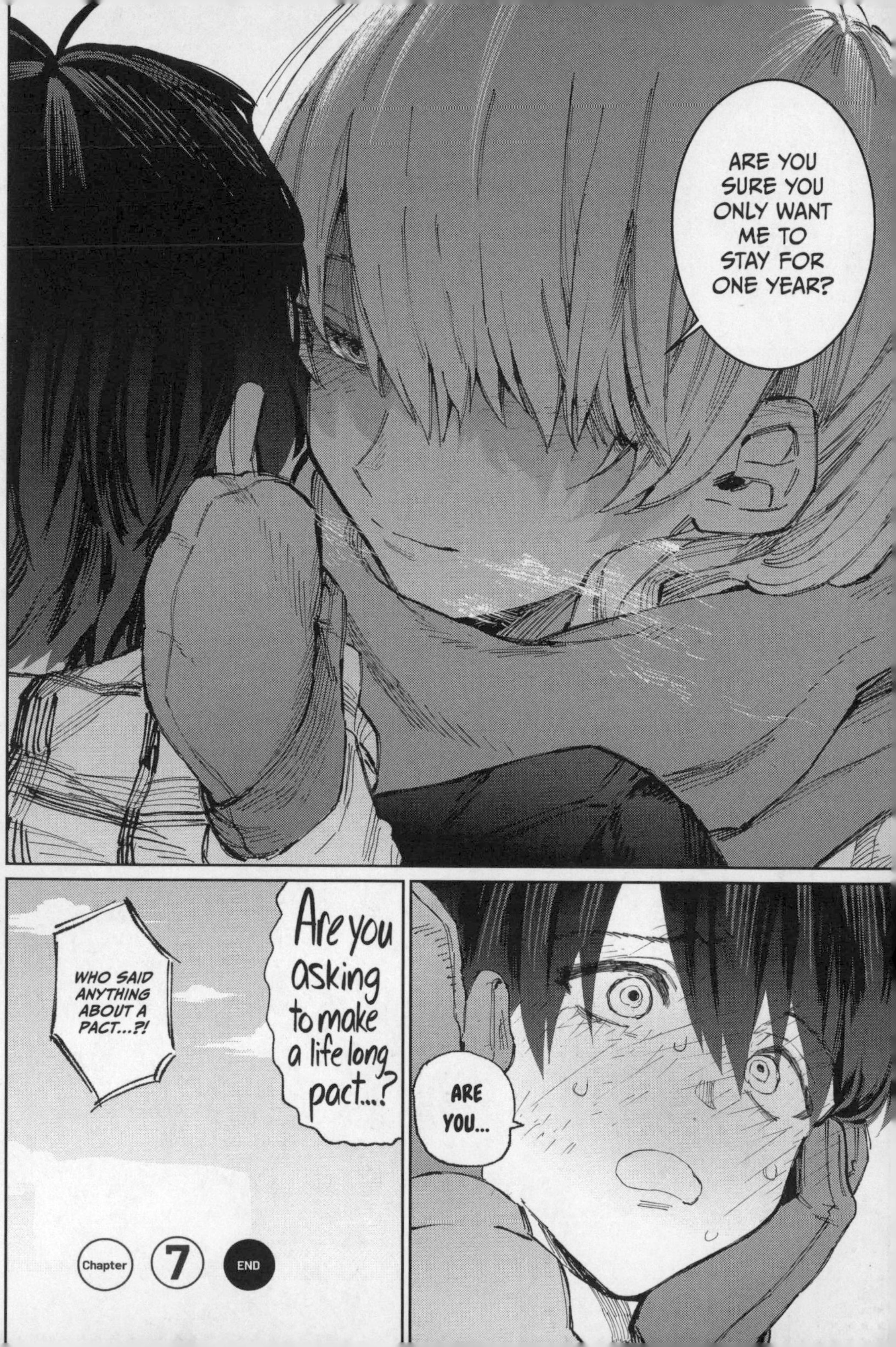
ARE YOU SURE YOU ONLY WANT ME TO STAY FOR ONE YEAR?
ARE YOU...
Are you asking to make a life long pact...?
WHO SAID ANYTHING ABOUT A PACT...?!
Chapter 7 END

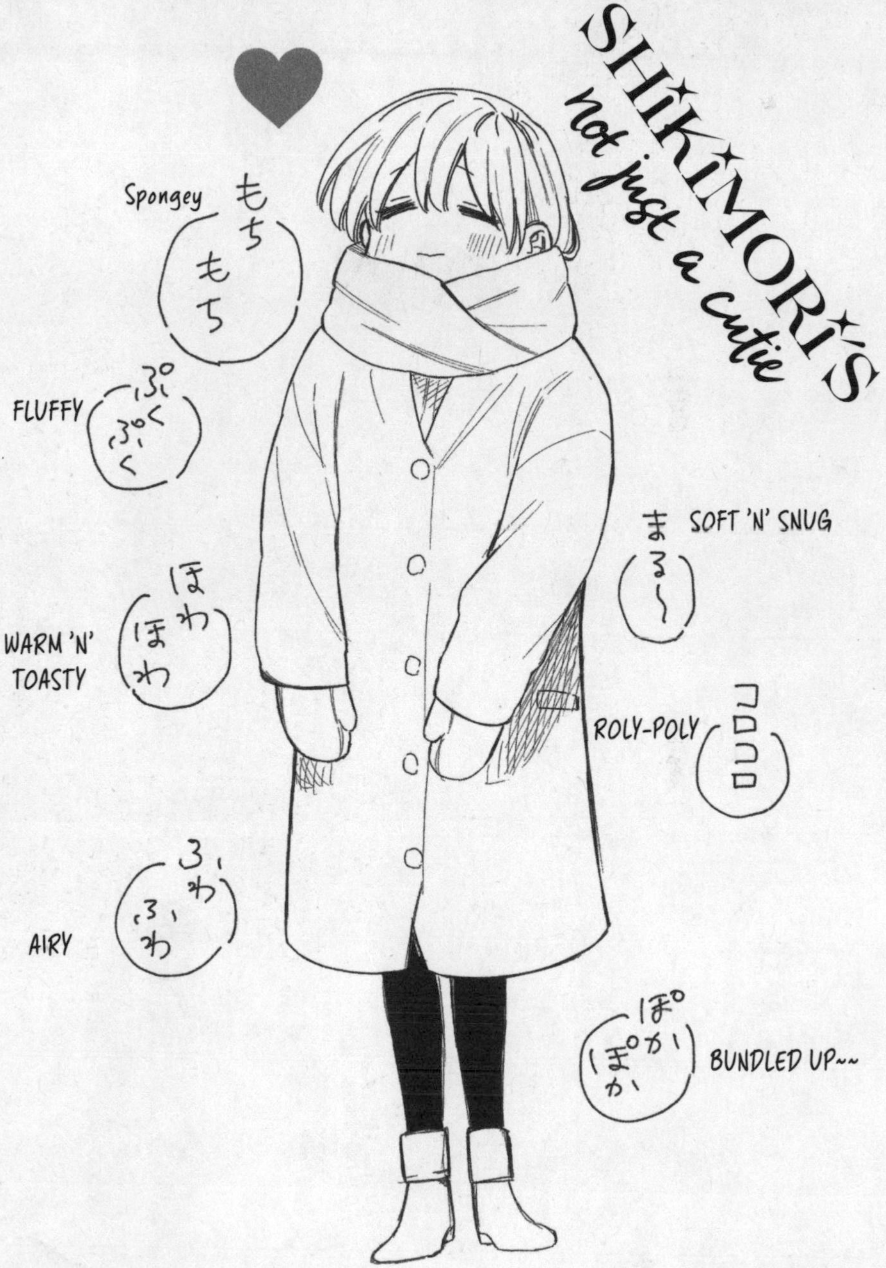
SHIKIMORI'S
not just a cutie
Spongey
もちもち
FLUFFY
ぷくぷく
WARM 'N' TOASTY
ほわほわ
AIRY
ふわふわ
SOFT 'N' SNUG
まる~
ROLY-POLY
コロコロ
BUNDLED UP~~
ぽかぽか

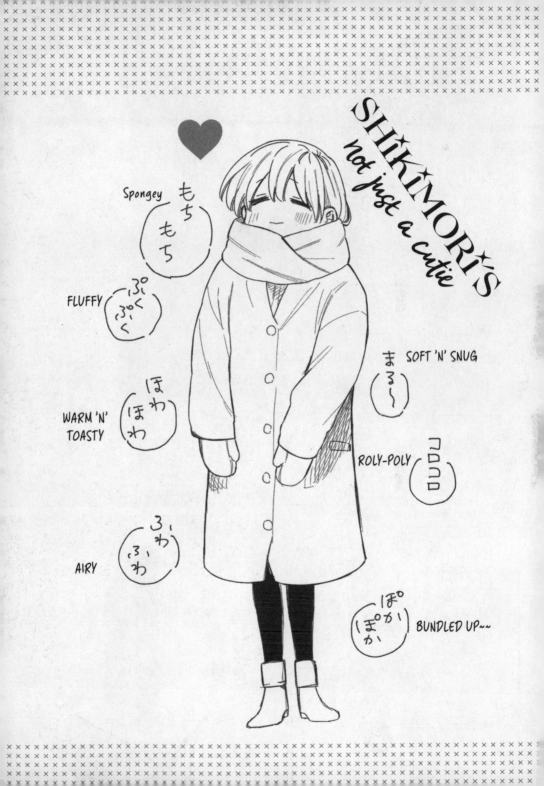

SHIKIMORI'S
not just a cutie

Hey, we match.

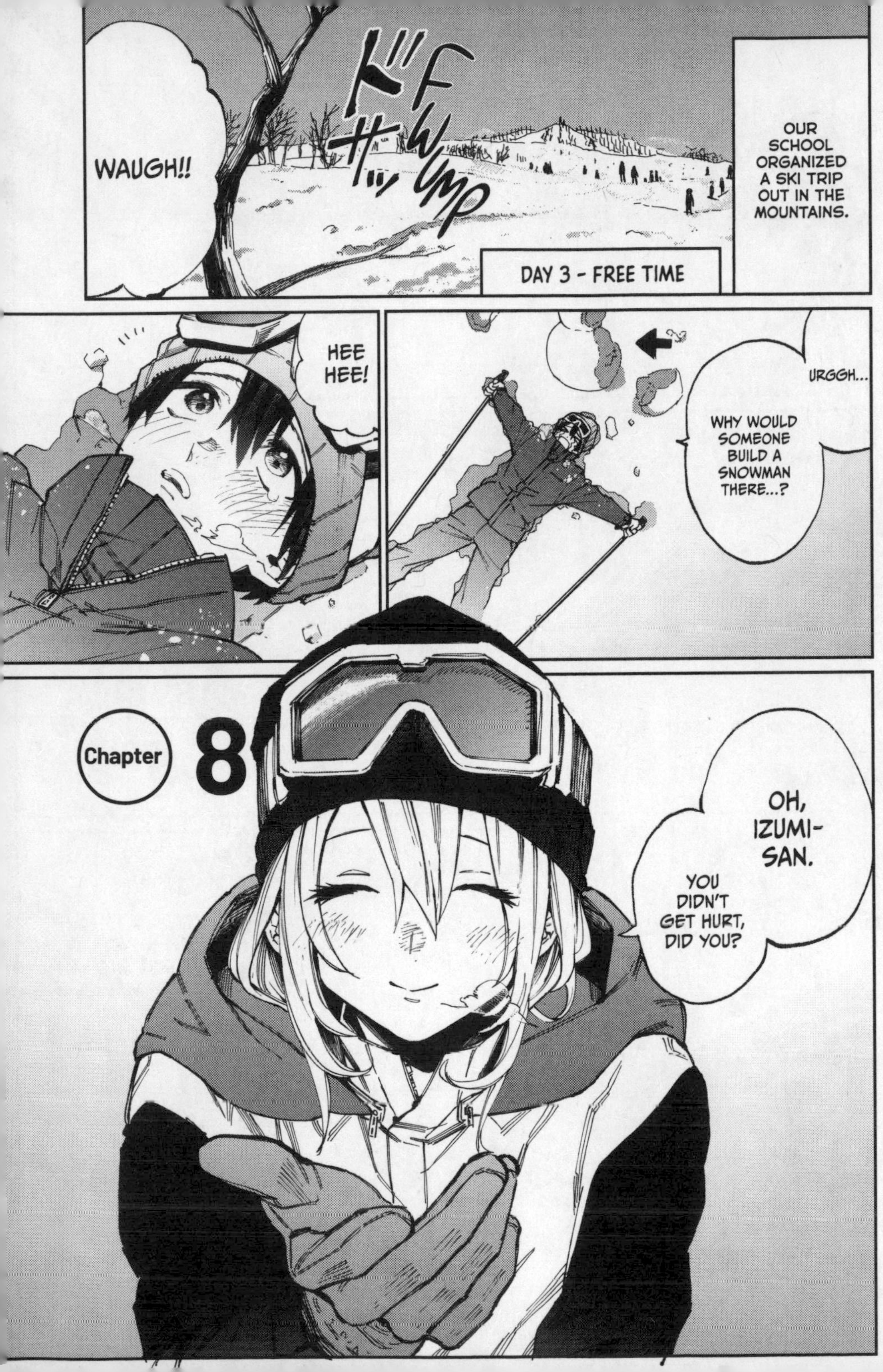
OUR SCHOOL ORGANIZED A SKI TRIP OUT IN THE MOUNTAINS.
FWUMP
DAY 3 - FREE TIME
WAUGH!!
URGGH...
WHY WOULD SOMEONE BUILD A SNOWMAN THERE...?
HEE HEE!
Chapter 8
OH, IZUMI-SAN.
YOU DIDN'T GET HURT, DID YOU?

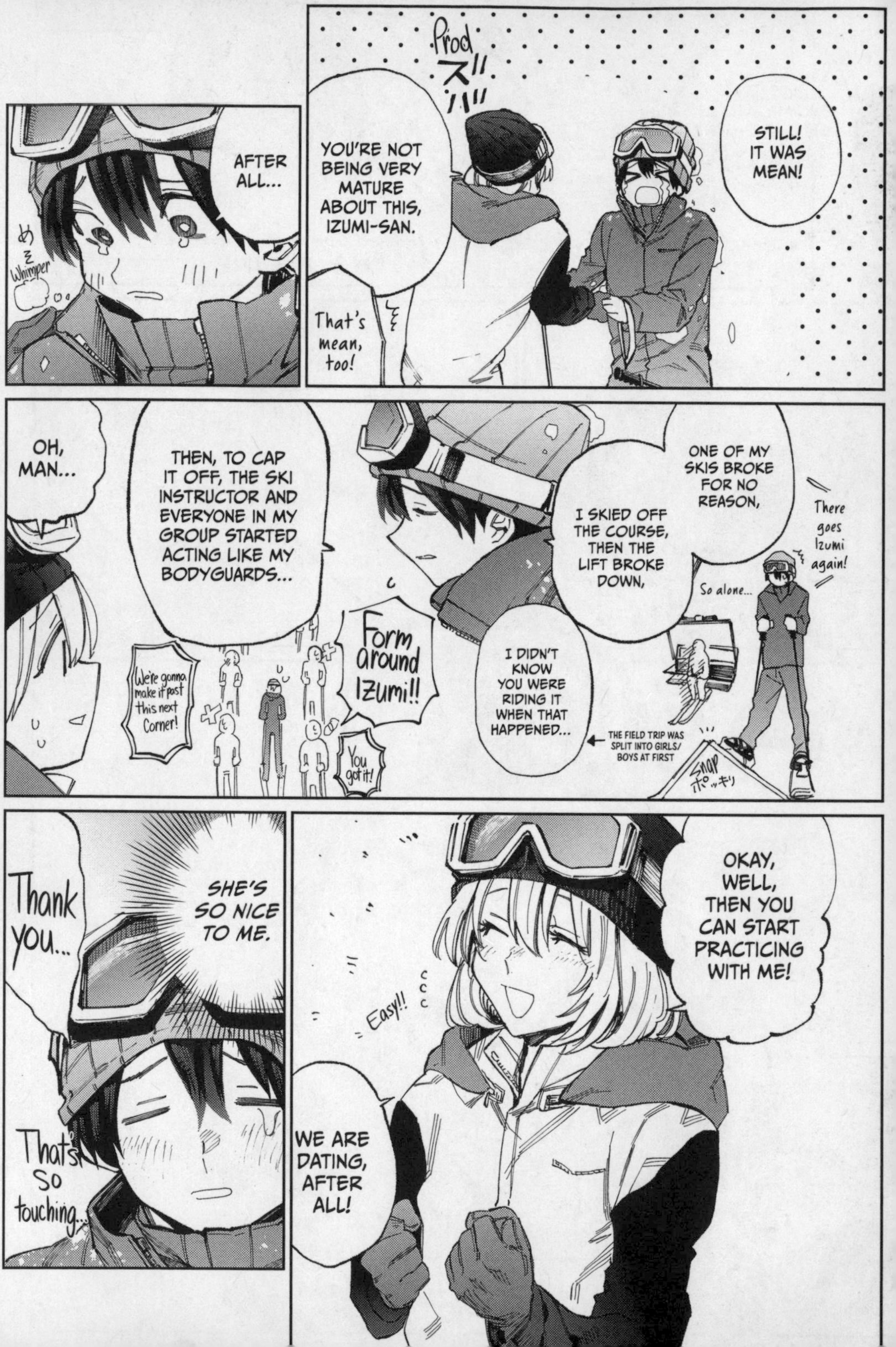
STILL! IT WAS MEAN!
Prod
ズバ
YOU'RE NOT BEING VERY MATURE ABOUT THIS, IZUMI-SAN.
That's mean, too!
AFTER ALL...
めそ
Whimper
ONE OF MY SKIS BROKE FOR NO REASON,
There goes Izumi again!
So alone...
Snap
ポッキリ
I SKIED OFF THE COURSE, THEN THE LIFT BROKE DOWN,
I DIDN'T KNOW YOU WERE RIDING IT WHEN THAT HAPPENED...
THE FIELD TRIP WAS SPLIT INTO GIRLS/BOYS AT FIRST
THEN, TO CAP IT OFF, THE SKI INSTRUCTOR AND EVERYONE IN MY GROUP STARTED ACTING LIKE MY BODYGUARDS...
Form around Izumi!!
You got it!
We're gonna make it past this next Corner!
OH, MAN...
OKAY, WELL, THEN YOU CAN START PRACTICING WITH ME!
Easy!!
WE ARE DATING, AFTER ALL!
SHE'S SO NICE TO ME.
Thank you...
That's so touching...

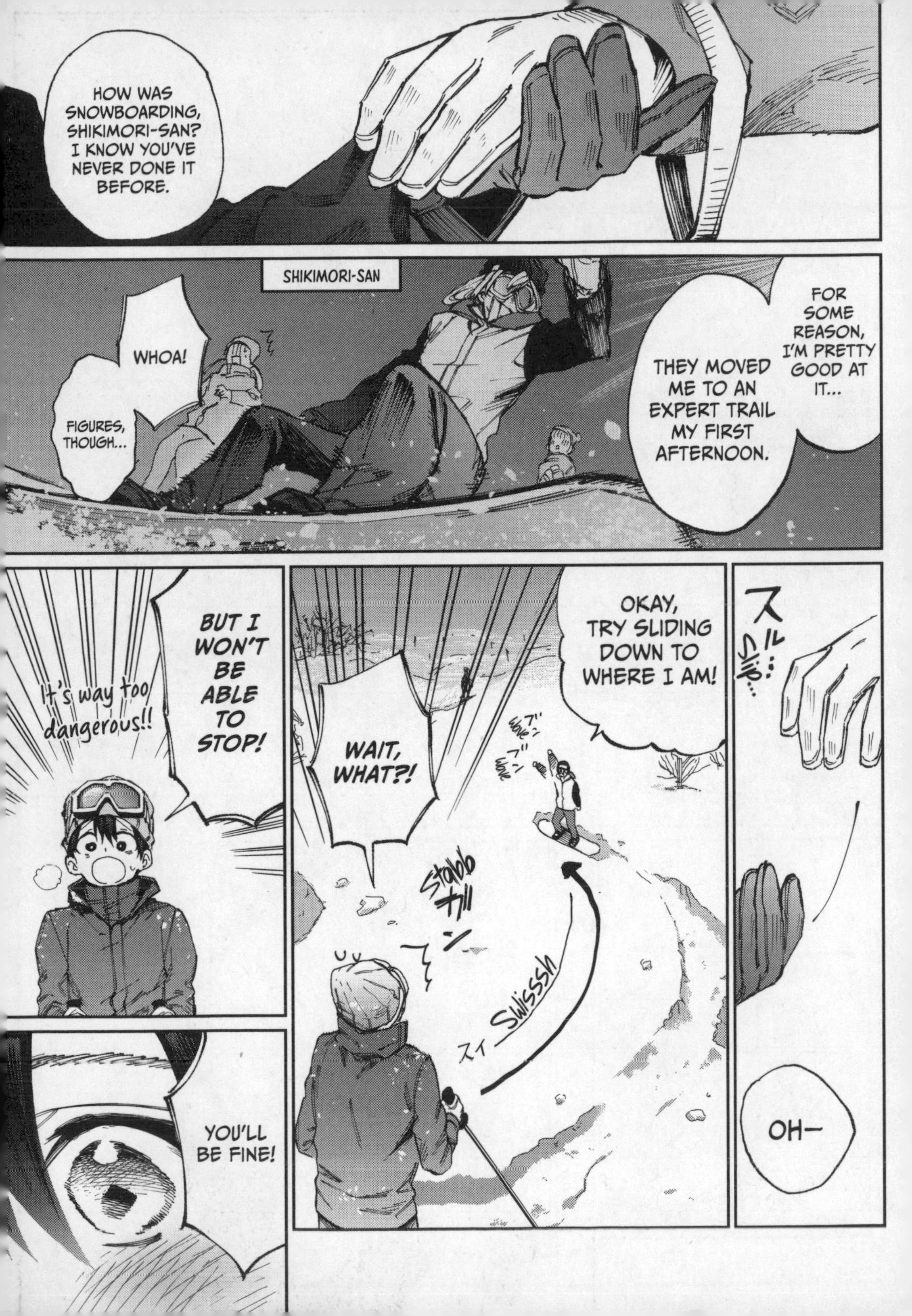
HOW WAS SNOWBOARDING, SHIKIMORI-SAN? I KNOW YOU'VE NEVER DONE IT BEFORE.
SHIKIMORI-SAN
FOR SOME REASON, I'M PRETTY GOOD AT IT...
THEY MOVED ME TO AN EXPERT TRAIL MY FIRST AFTERNOON.
WHOA!
FIGURES, THOUGH...
スル
Slip...
OH—
OKAY, TRY SLIDING DOWN TO WHERE I AM!
Wave
Wave
WAIT, WHAT?!
Stabb
Swisssh
スィー
BUT I WON'T BE ABLE TO STOP!
It's way too dangerous!!
YOU'LL BE FINE!

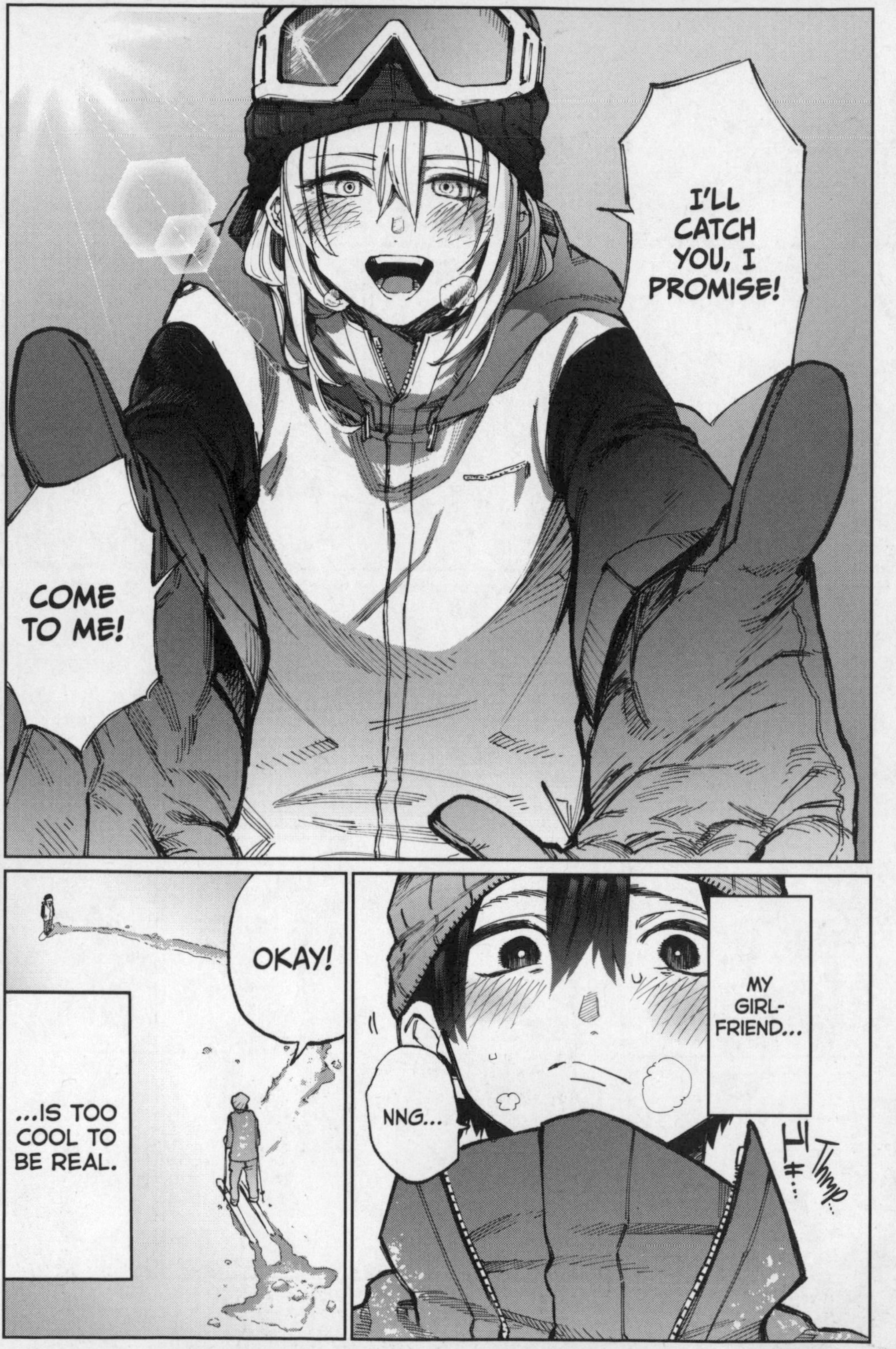
I'LL CATCH YOU, I PROMISE!
COME TO ME!
MY GIRL-FRIEND...
NNG...
Thump...
OKAY!
...IS TOO COOL TO BE REAL.

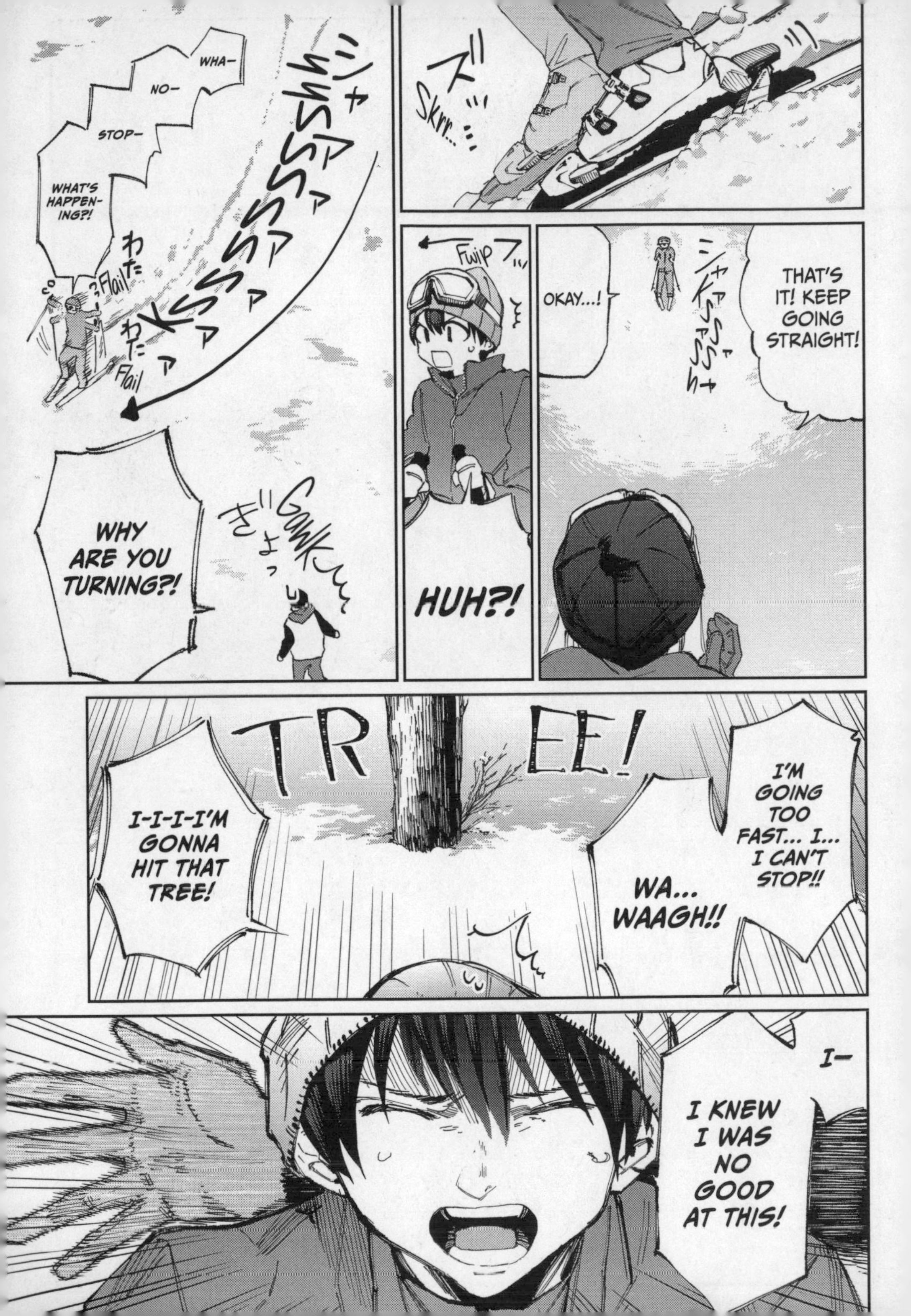
ズ
Skrr...
THAT'S IT! KEEP GOING STRAIGHT!
シャアアア
KSSSS
OKAY...!
フッ
Fwip
HUH?!
WHA—
NO—
STOP—
WHAT'S HAPPEN-ING?!
シャアアアアア
KSSSS
わた
Flail
わた
Flail
WHY ARE YOU TURNING?!
ぎょっ
Gawk
TREE!
I'M GOING TOO FAST... I... I CAN'T STOP!!
WA... WAAGH!!
I-I-I-I'M GONNA HIT THAT TREE!
I—
I KNEW I WAS NO GOOD AT THIS!

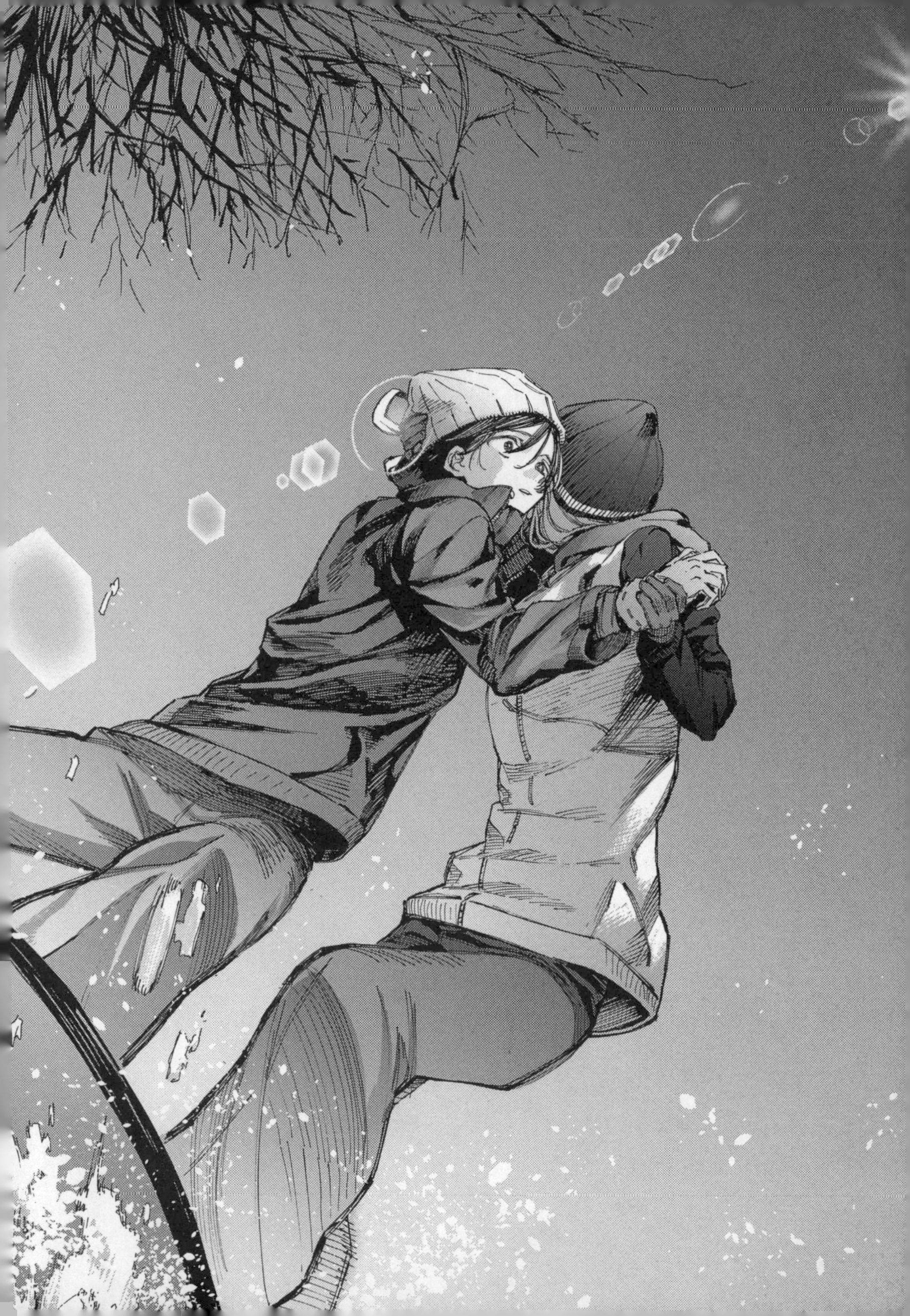

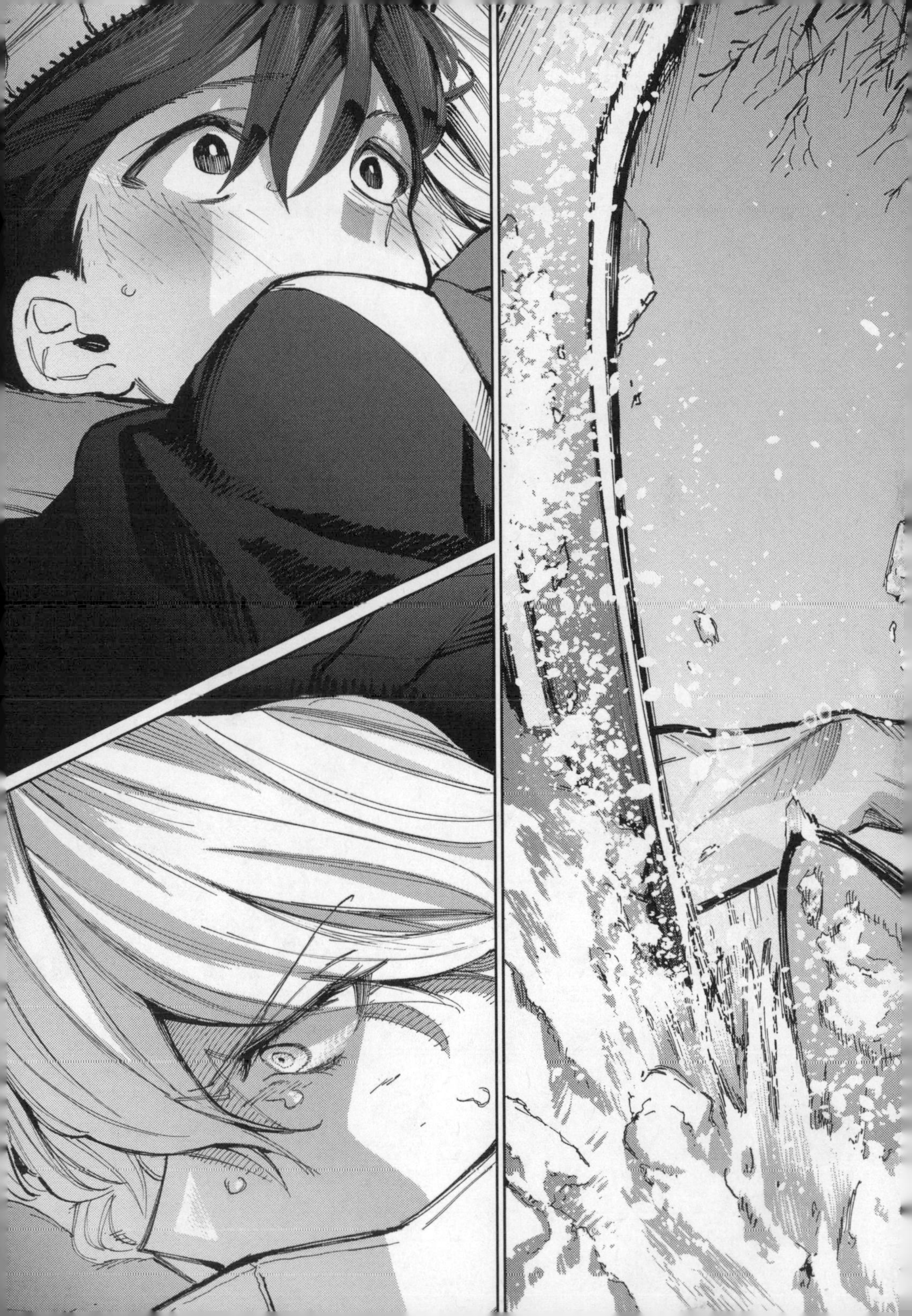

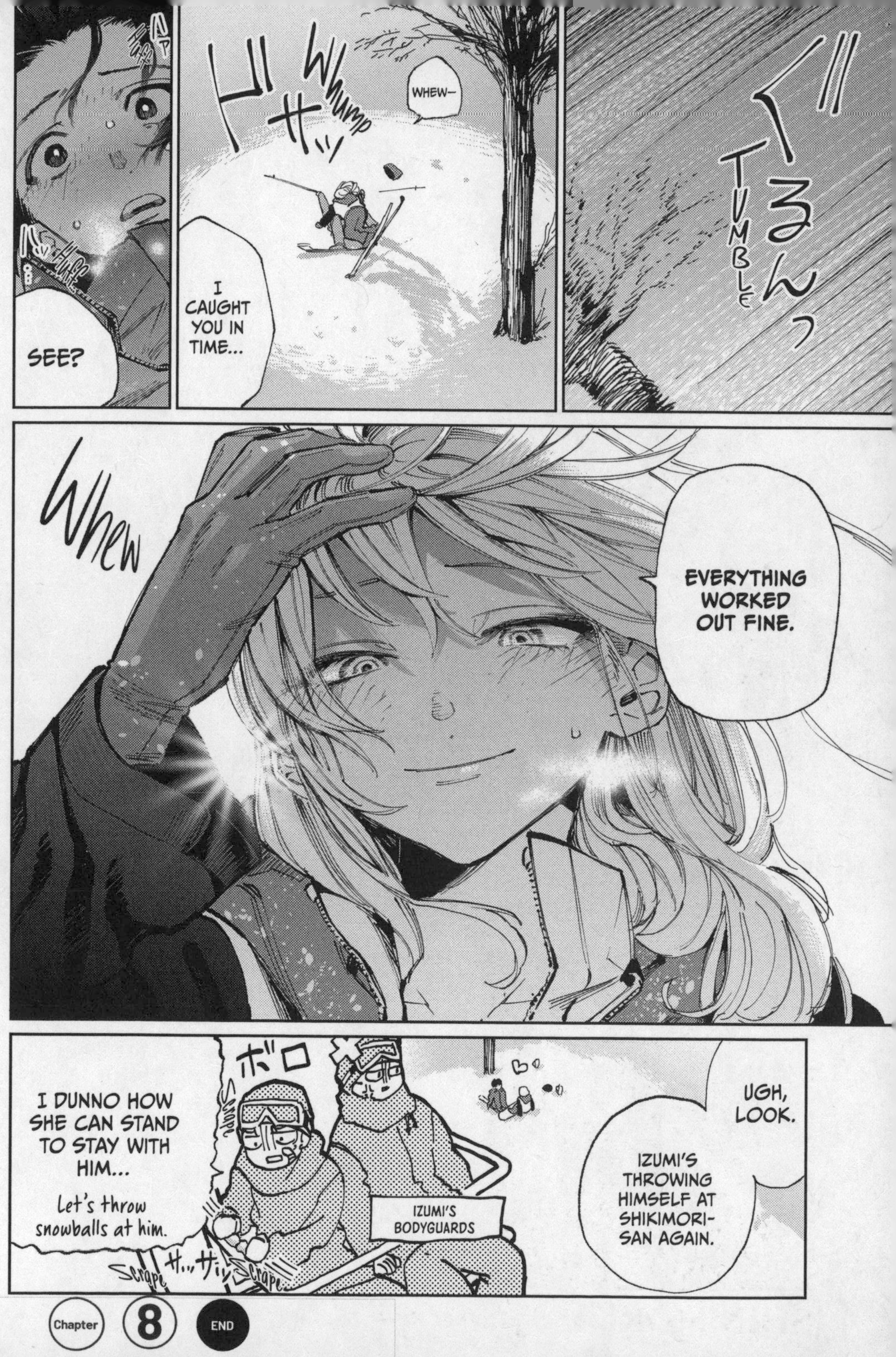
ぐるんっ
TUMBLE
ドサッ
Whump
WHEW—
I CAUGHT YOU IN TIME...
Huff
Huff
SEE?
Whew
EVERYTHING WORKED OUT FINE.
UGH, LOOK.
IZUMI'S THROWING HIMSELF AT SHIKIMORI-SAN AGAIN.
IZUMI'S BODYGUARDS
ボロ
I DUNNO HOW SHE CAN STAND TO STAY WITH HIM...
Let's throw snowballs at him.
Scrape
Scrape
Scrape

Chapter 8 END

Skiing outfit

SHIKIMORI'S not just a cutie

Thank yooou.
Izumi Bodyguard
UNNGH...

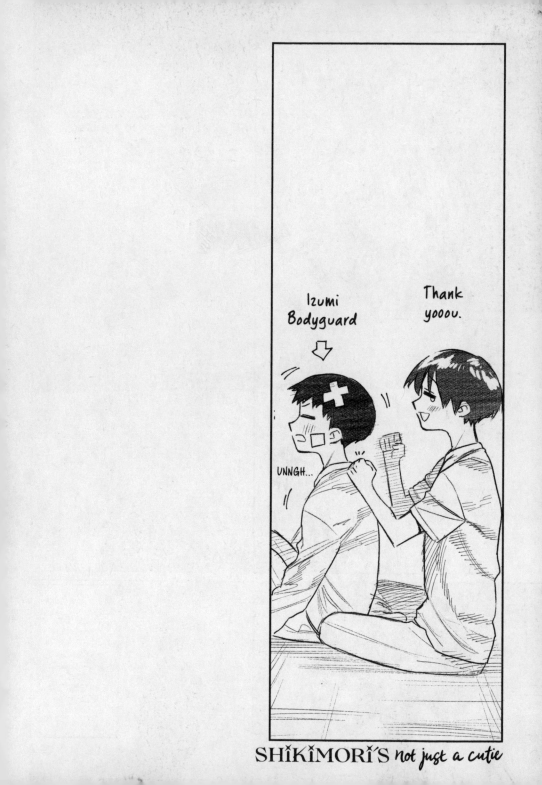

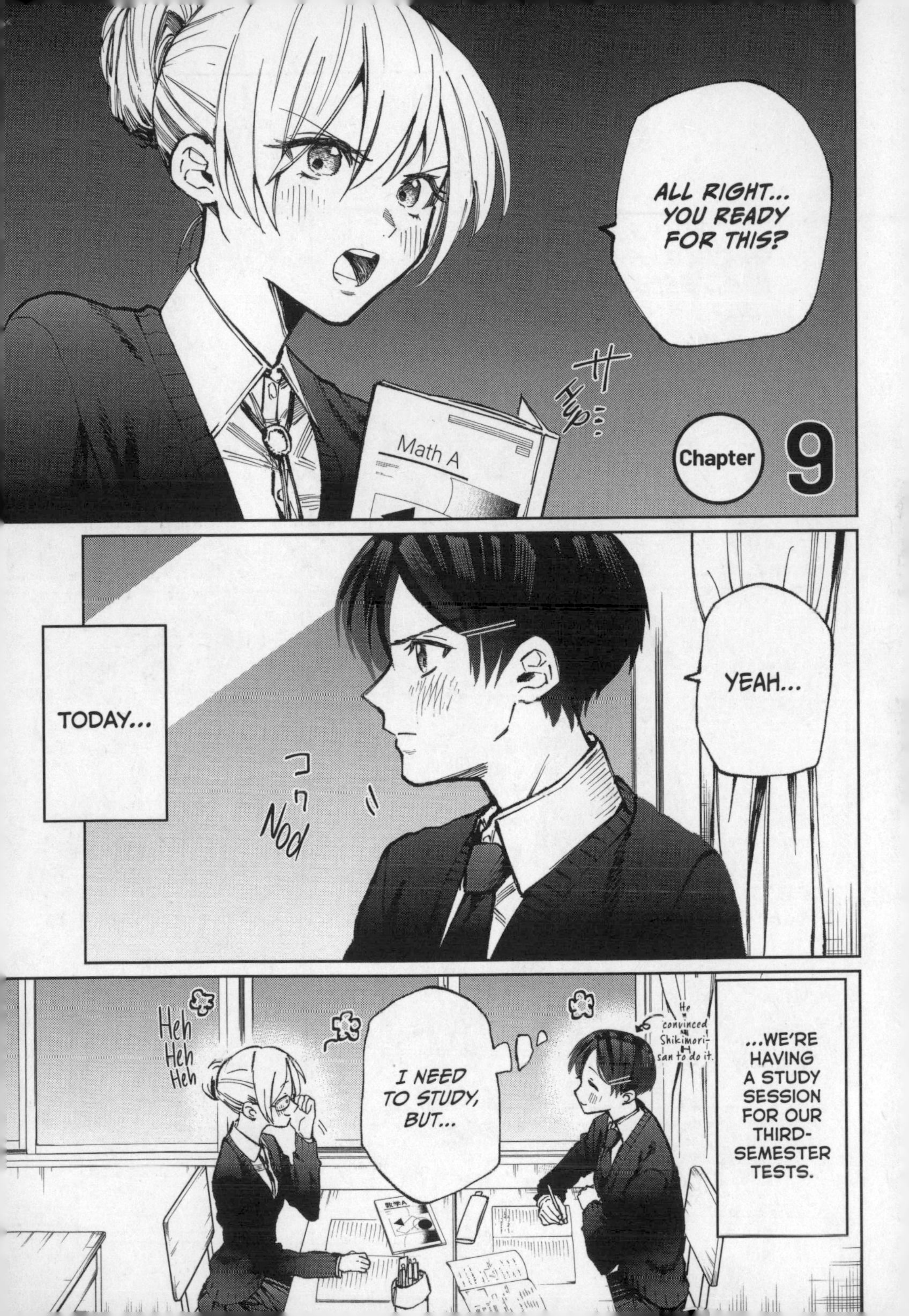
ALL RIGHT... YOU READY FOR THIS?
サ Hup
Chapter 9
YEAH...
TODAY...
コク Nod
...WE'RE HAVING A STUDY SESSION FOR OUR THIRD-SEMESTER TESTS.
He convinced Shikimori-san to do it.
I NEED TO STUDY, BUT...
Heh Heh Heh
Math A

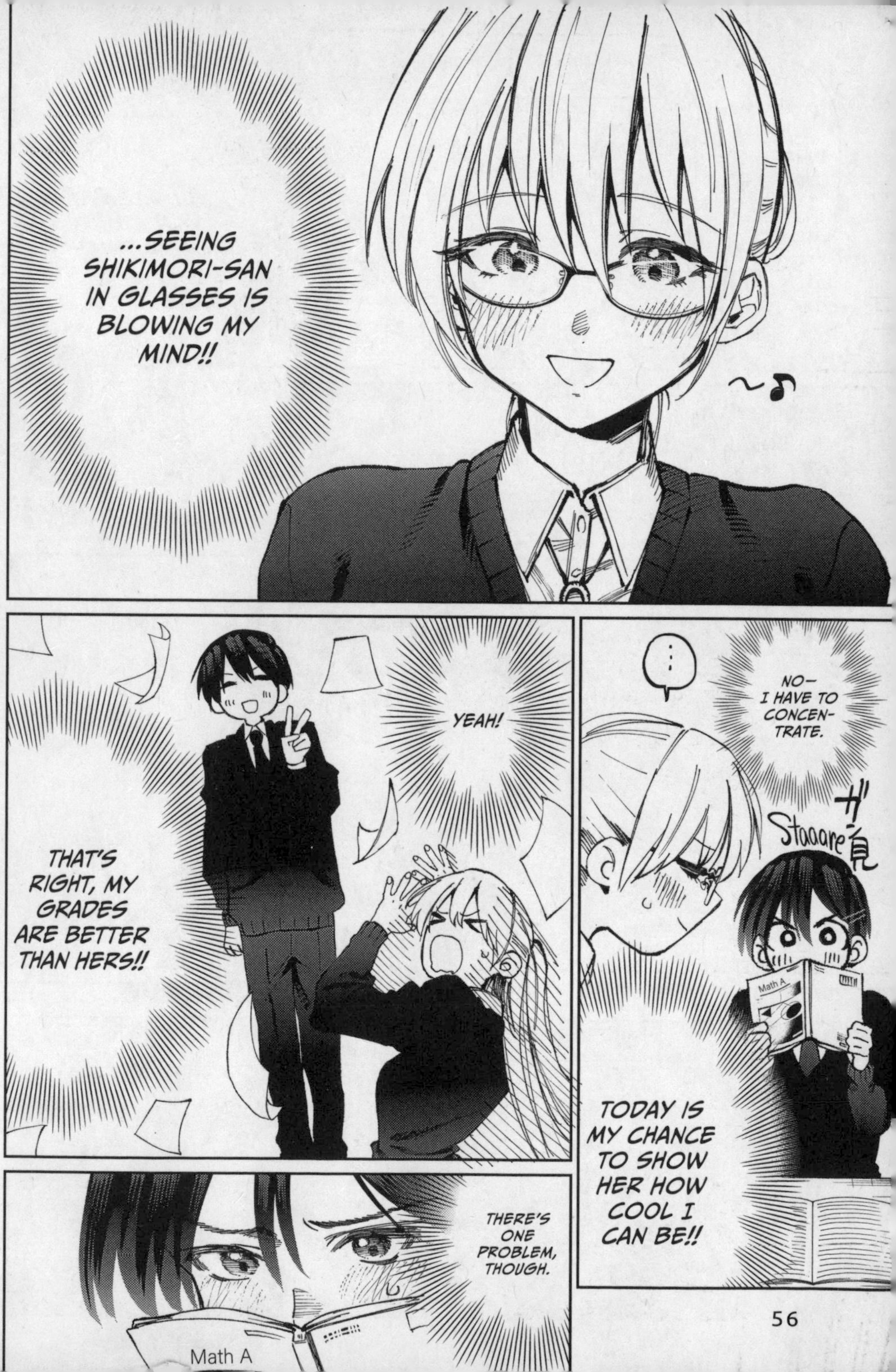
...SEEING SHIKIMORI-SAN IN GLASSES IS BLOWING MY MIND!!
~♪
…
NO— I HAVE TO CONCEN-TRATE.
Staaare
Math A
TODAY IS MY CHANCE TO SHOW HER HOW COOL I CAN BE!!
YEAH!
THAT'S RIGHT, MY GRADES ARE BETTER THAN HERS!!
THERE'S ONE PROBLEM, THOUGH.
Math A

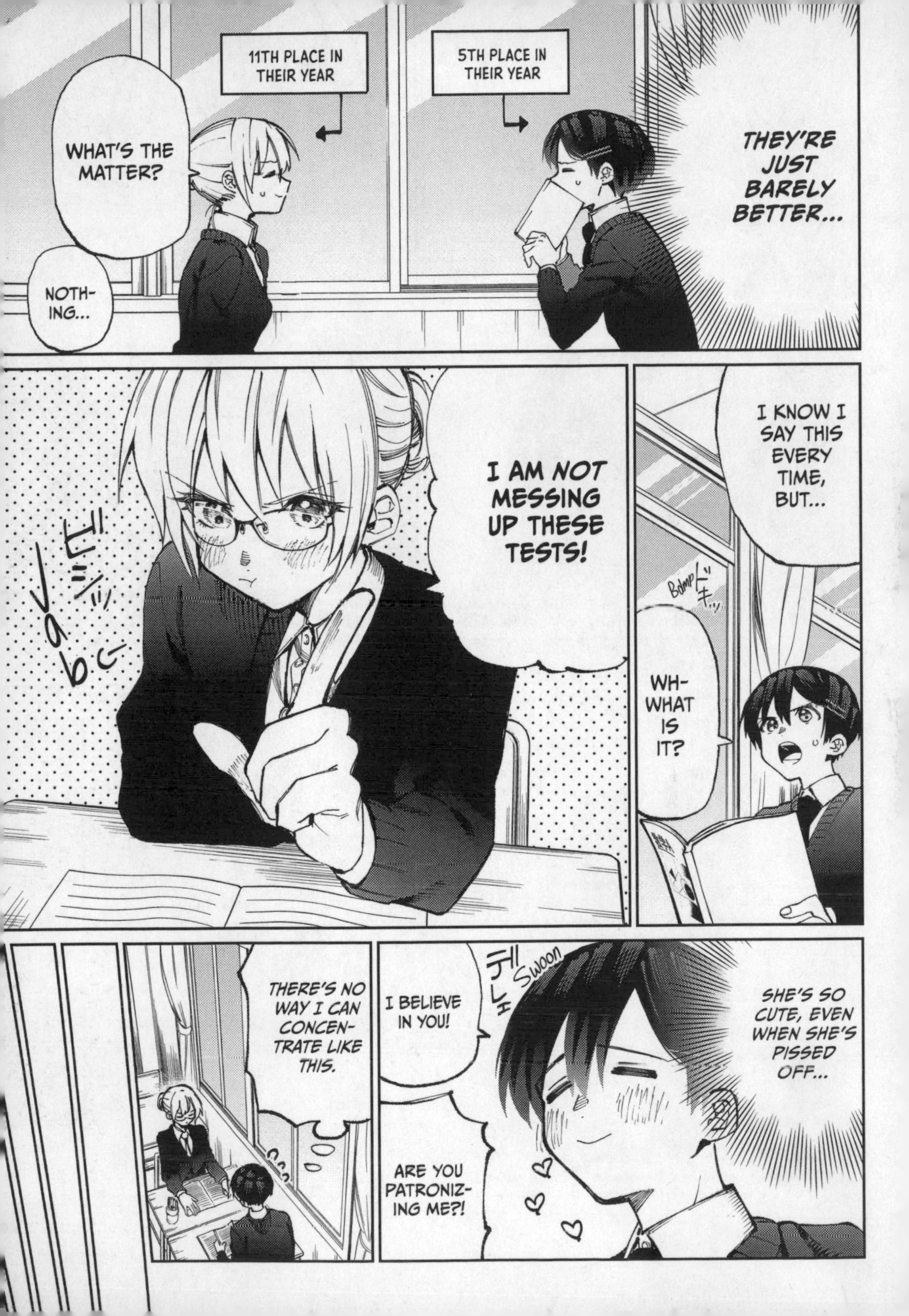
THEY'RE JUST BARELY BETTER...
5TH PLACE IN THEIR YEAR
11TH PLACE IN THEIR YEAR
WHAT'S THE MATTER?
NOTH-ING...
I KNOW I SAY THIS EVERY TIME, BUT...
Bdmp
WH-WHAT IS IT?
I AM NOT MESSING UP THESE TESTS!
SHE'S SO CUTE, EVEN WHEN SHE'S PISSED OFF...
Swoon
I BELIEVE IN YOU!
ARE YOU PATRONIZ-ING ME?!
THERE'S NO WAY I CAN CONCEN-TRATE LIKE THIS.

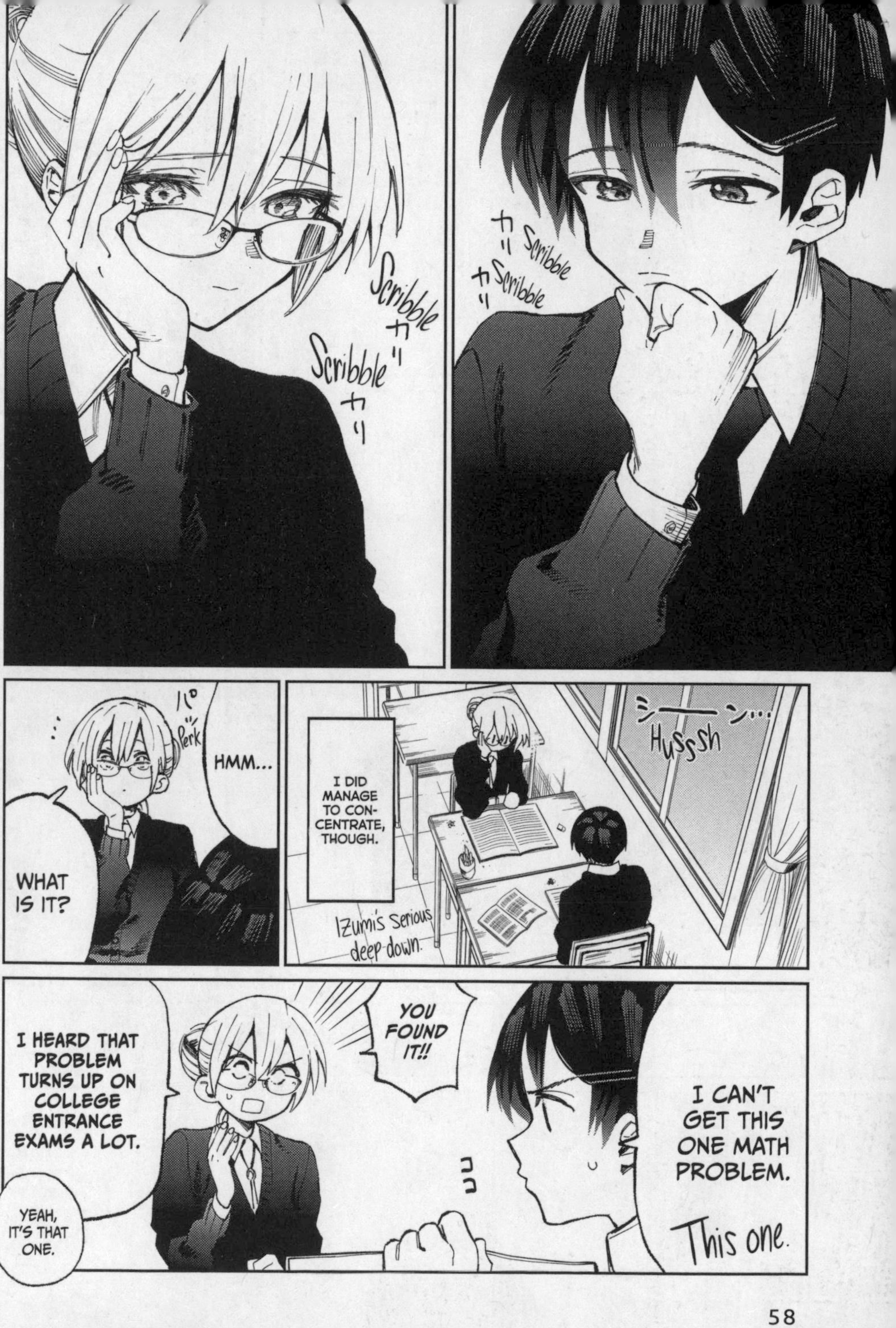
カリ Scribble
カリ Scribble
Scribble カリ
Scribble カリ
シーン… Husssh
I DID MANAGE TO CONCENTRATE, THOUGH.
Izumi's serious deep down.
HMM…
パ Perk
…
WHAT IS IT?
I CAN'T GET THIS ONE MATH PROBLEM.
This one.
コ
YOU FOUND IT!!
I HEARD THAT PROBLEM TURNS UP ON COLLEGE ENTRANCE EXAMS A LOT.
YEAH, IT'S THAT ONE.

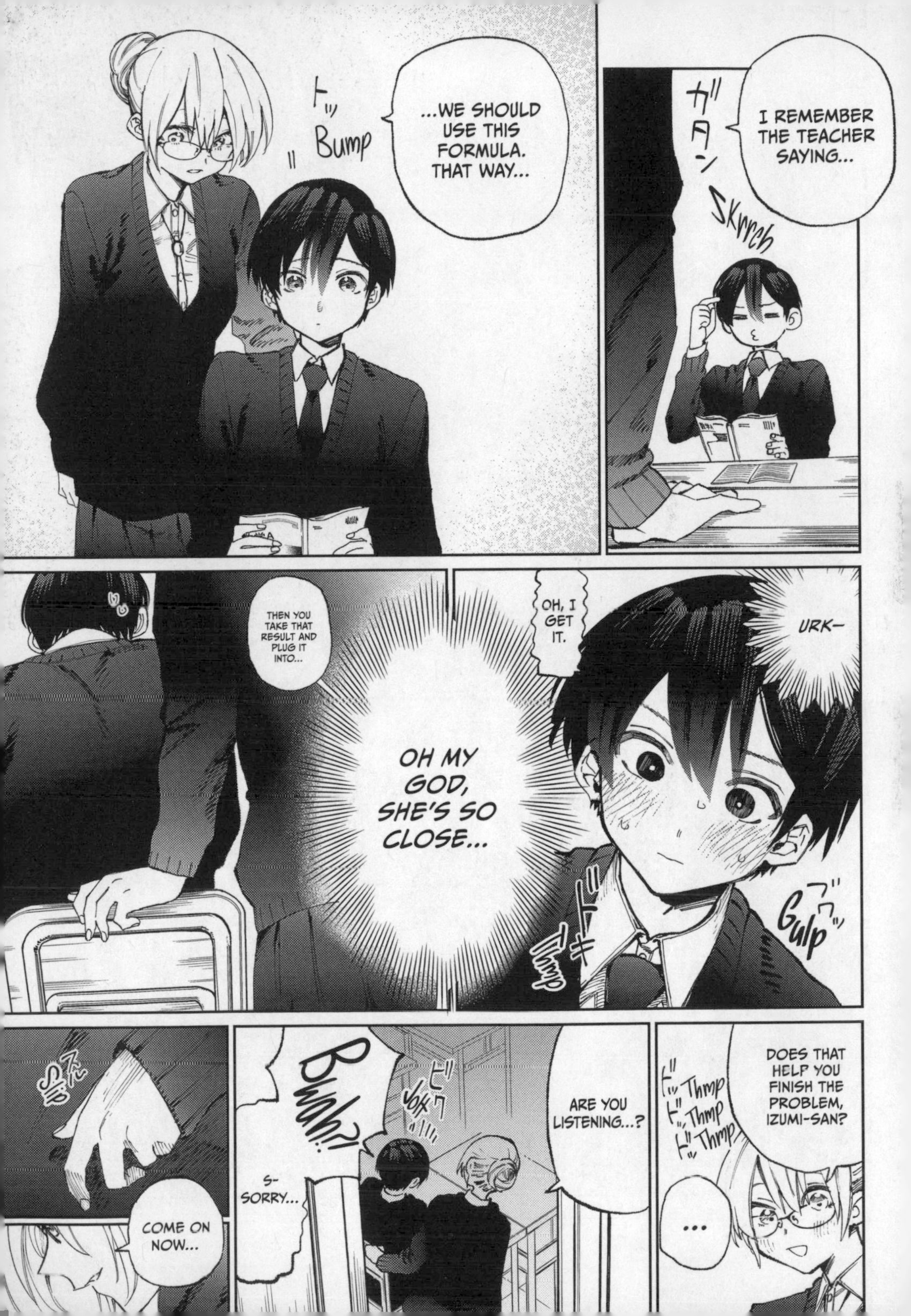
I REMEMBER THE TEACHER SAYING...
Skrrch
...WE SHOULD USE THIS FORMULA. THAT WAY...
Bump
OH, I GET IT.
URK—
Gulp
Thmp
THEN YOU TAKE THAT RESULT AND PLUG IT INTO...
OH MY GOD, SHE'S SO CLOSE...
DOES THAT HELP YOU FINISH THE PROBLEM, IZUMI-SAN?
Thmp
Thmp
Thmp
...
ARE YOU LISTENING...?
Bwah?!
Jolt
S-SORRY...
Slip
COME ON NOW...

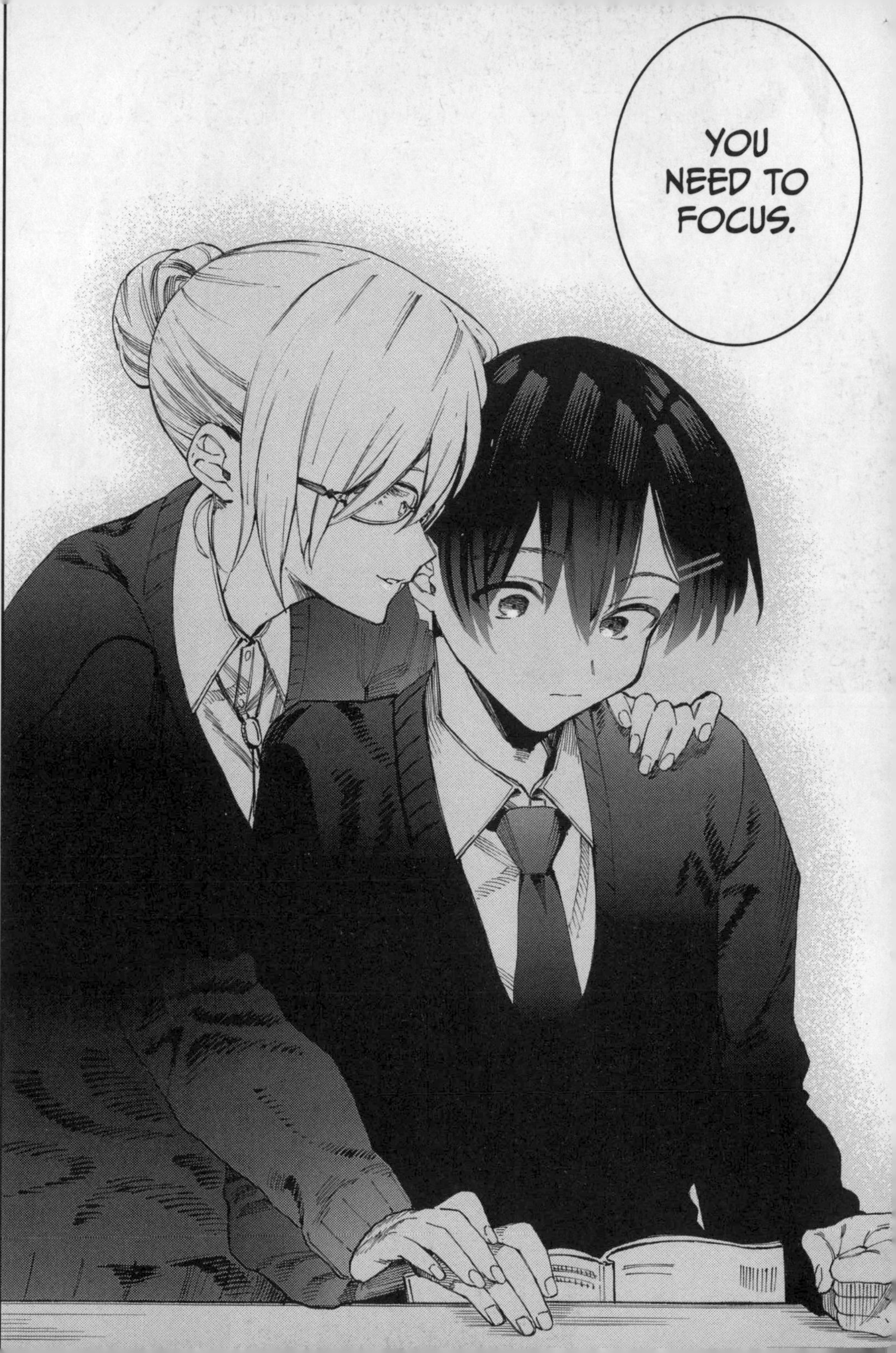
YOU NEED TO FOCUS.

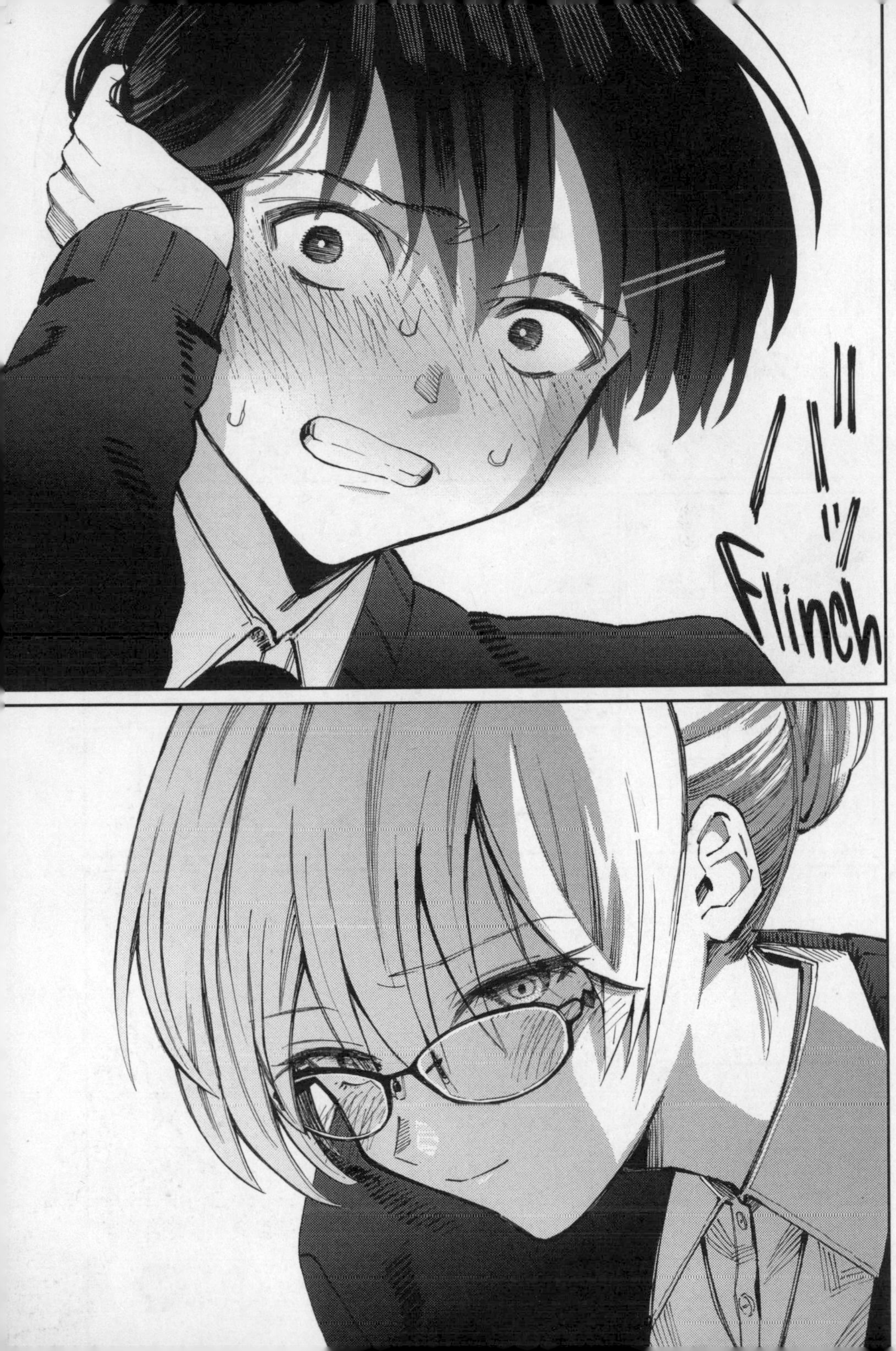
Flinch

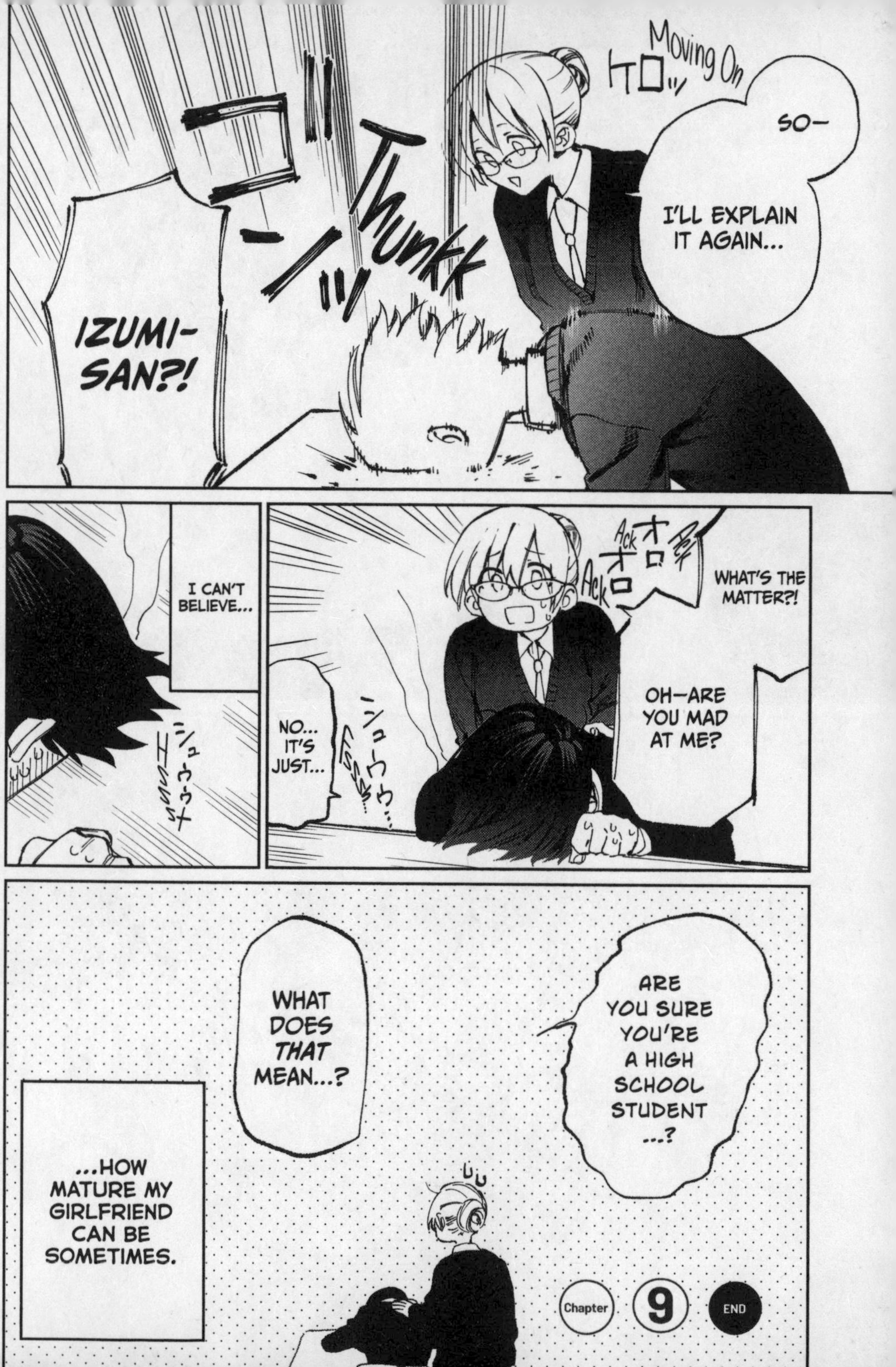

Moving On
SO—
I'LL EXPLAIN IT AGAIN...
Thunkk
IZUMI-SAN?!
Ack Ack
WHAT'S THE MATTER?!
OH—ARE YOU MAD AT ME?
NO... IT'S JUST...
Fsss
I CAN'T BELIEVE...
Hsss
ARE YOU SURE YOU'RE A HIGH SCHOOL STUDENT ...?
WHAT DOES THAT MEAN...?
...HOW MATURE MY GIRLFRIEND CAN BE SOMETIMES.
Chapter 9 END

Yesss!!
Year 1 Class 2 Seat 12 Shikimori
Rank Overall (5) Overall (3)
Year 12th 16th
Class 3rd 5th
Year 1 Class 2 Seat 1 Izumi
Rank Overall (5) Overall (3)
Year 5th 8th
Class 2nd 2nd
Yesss!! I won—er...

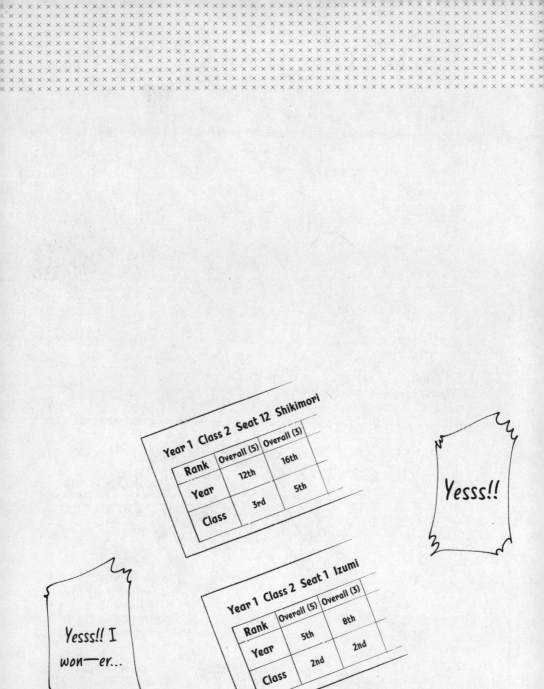

SHIKIMORI'S
Not just a cutie

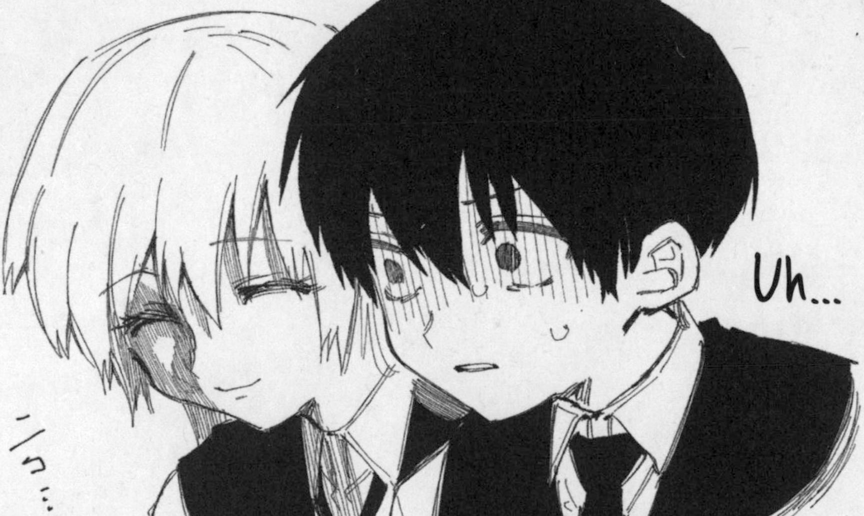
Uh...
BEAM...

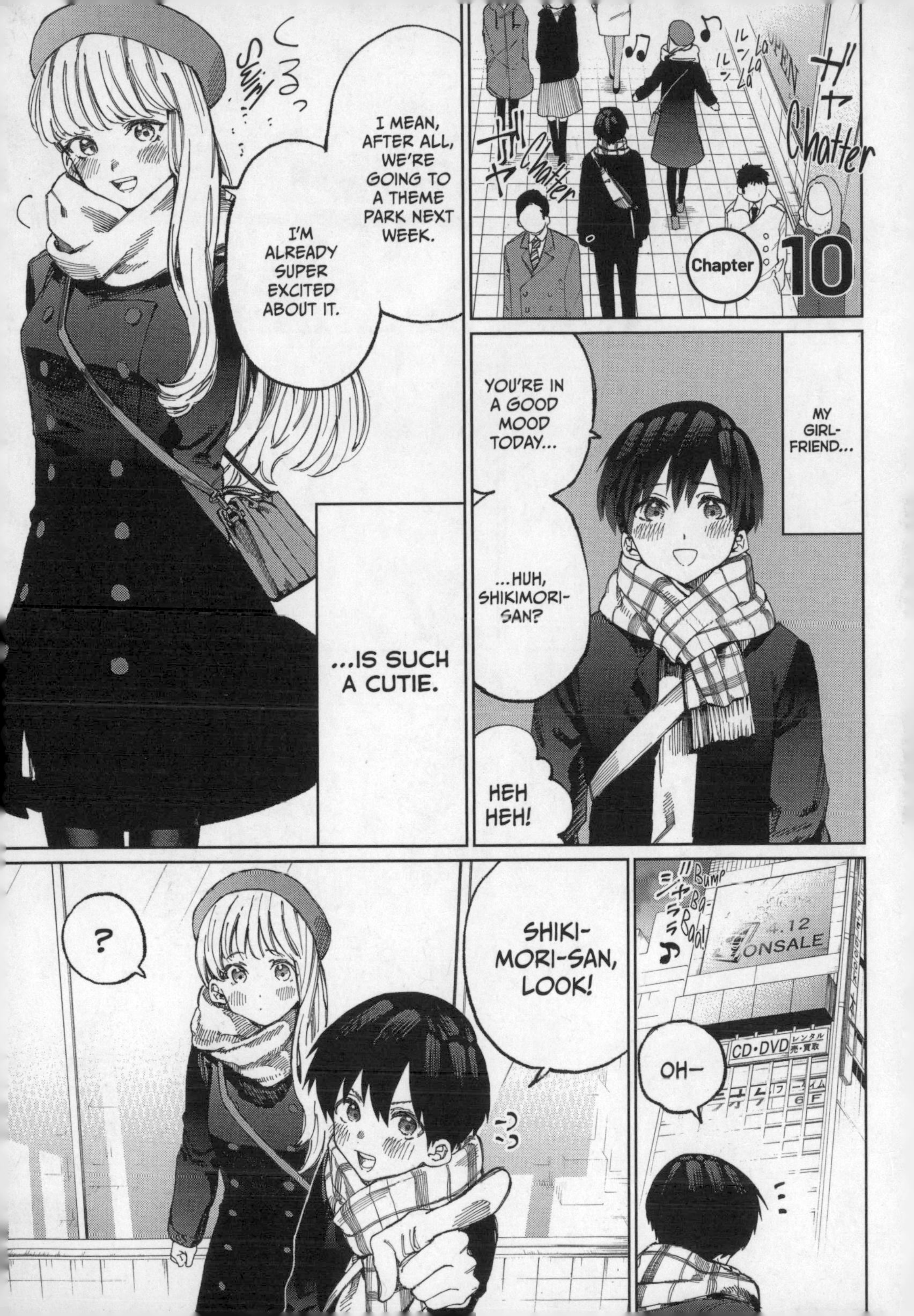

La La
Chatter
Chatter
Chapter 10
MY GIRL-FRIEND...
YOU'RE IN A GOOD MOOD TODAY...
...HUH, SHIKIMORI-SAN?
HEH HEH!
Swirl
I MEAN, AFTER ALL, WE'RE GOING TO A THEME PARK NEXT WEEK.
I'M ALREADY SUPER EXCITED ABOUT IT.
...IS SUCH A CUTIE.
Bump Ba-Baa!
4.12 ON SALE
CD・DVD
レンタル 売・買取
OH—
SHIKI-MORI-SAN, LOOK!
?

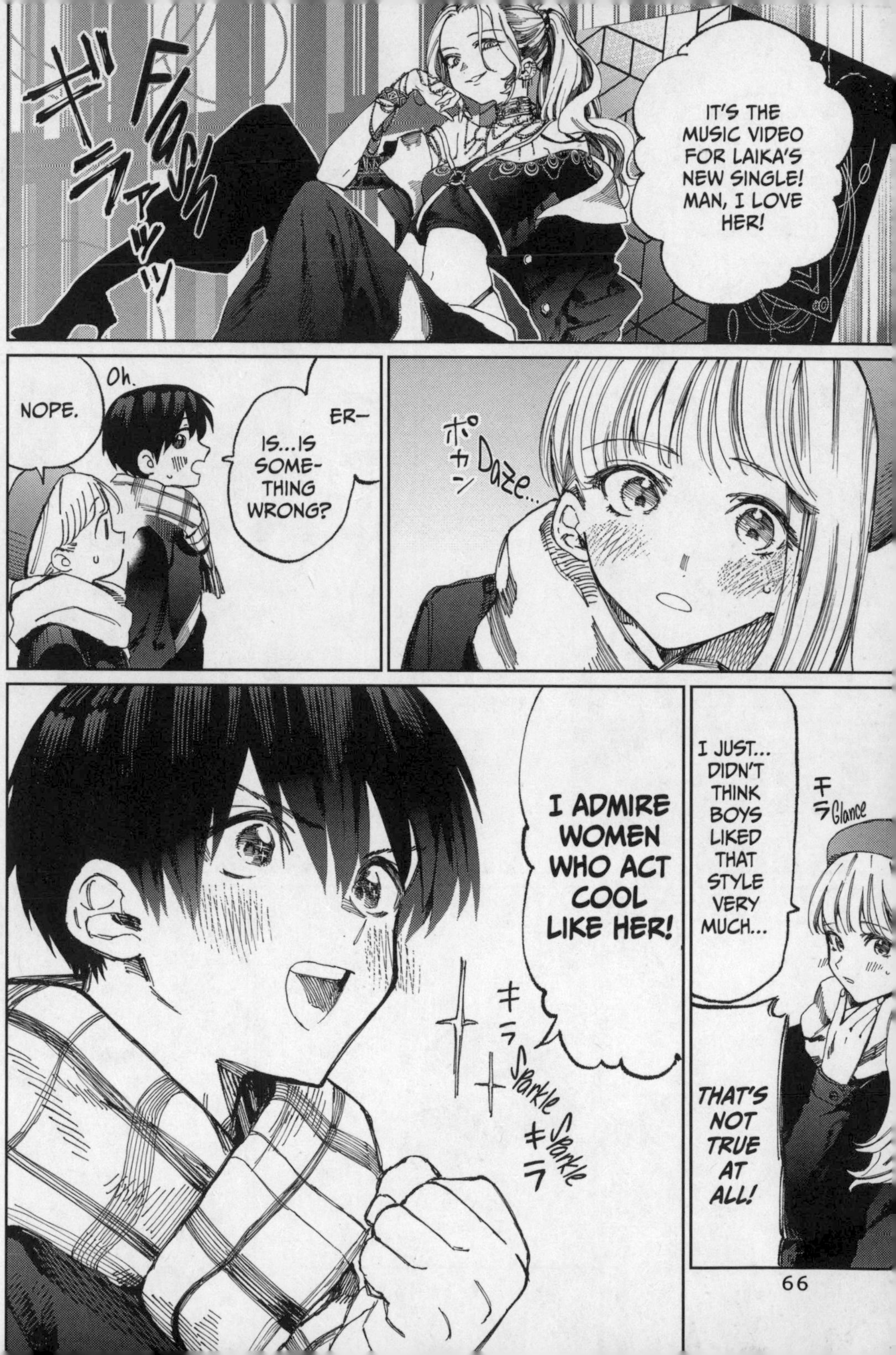
IT'S THE MUSIC VIDEO FOR LAIKA'S NEW SINGLE! MAN, I LOVE HER!
ギラァッッ Flash
ポカン Daze...
ER—
IS...IS SOMETHING WRONG?
Oh.
NOPE.
チラ Glance
I JUST... DIDN'T THINK BOYS LIKED THAT STYLE VERY MUCH...
THAT'S NOT TRUE AT ALL!
I ADMIRE WOMEN WHO ACT COOL LIKE HER!
キラ Sparkle
キラ Sparkle

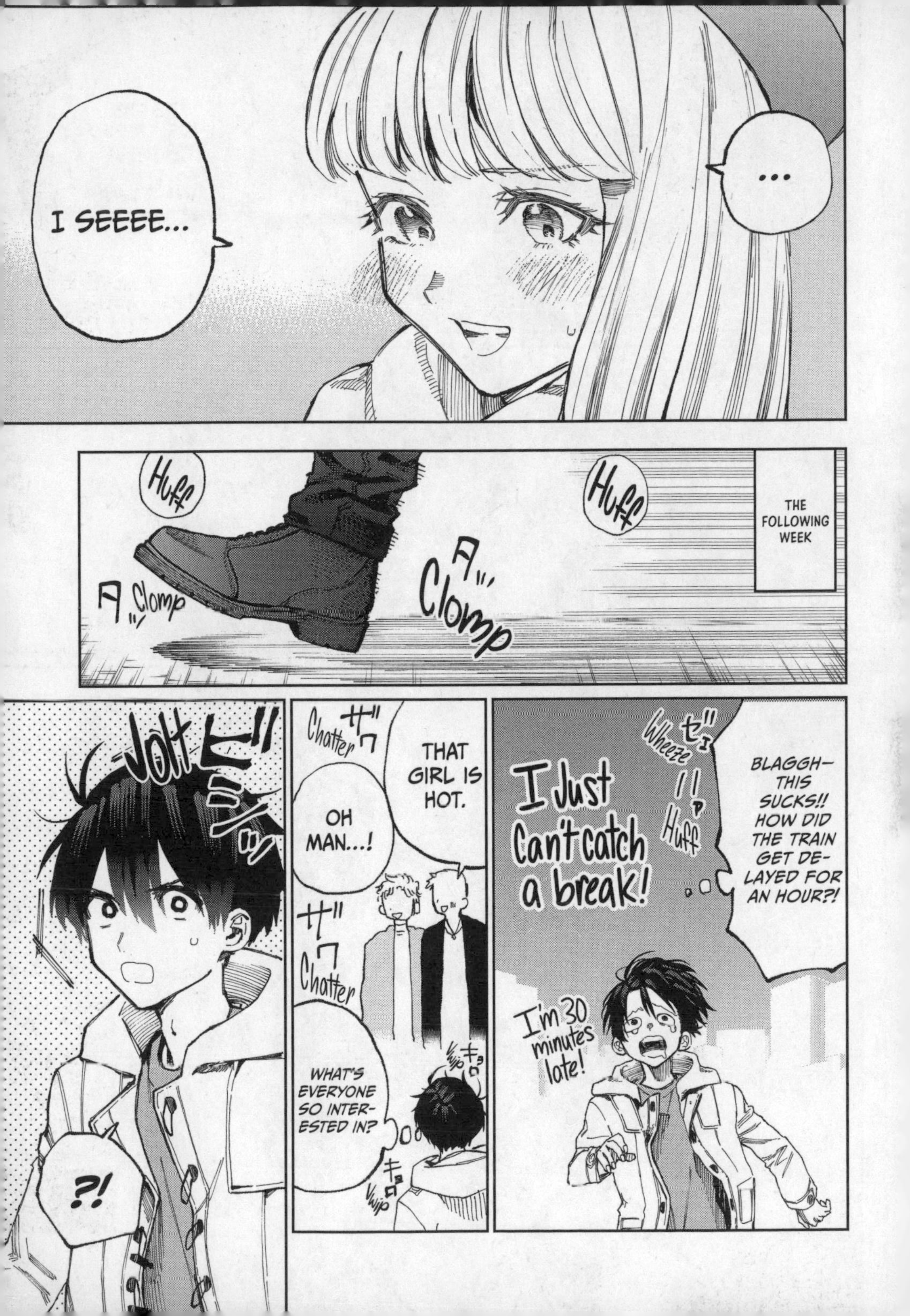
...
I SEEEE...
THE FOLLOWING WEEK
Huff
Clomp
Huff
Clomp
BLAGGH—THIS SUCKS!! HOW DID THE TRAIN GET DE-LAYED FOR AN HOUR?!
Wheeze
Huff
I Just Can't catch a break!
I'm 30 minutes late!
THAT GIRL IS HOT.
Chatter
OH MAN...!
Chatter
Whip
WHAT'S EVERYONE SO INTER-ESTED IN?
Whip
Jolt
?!

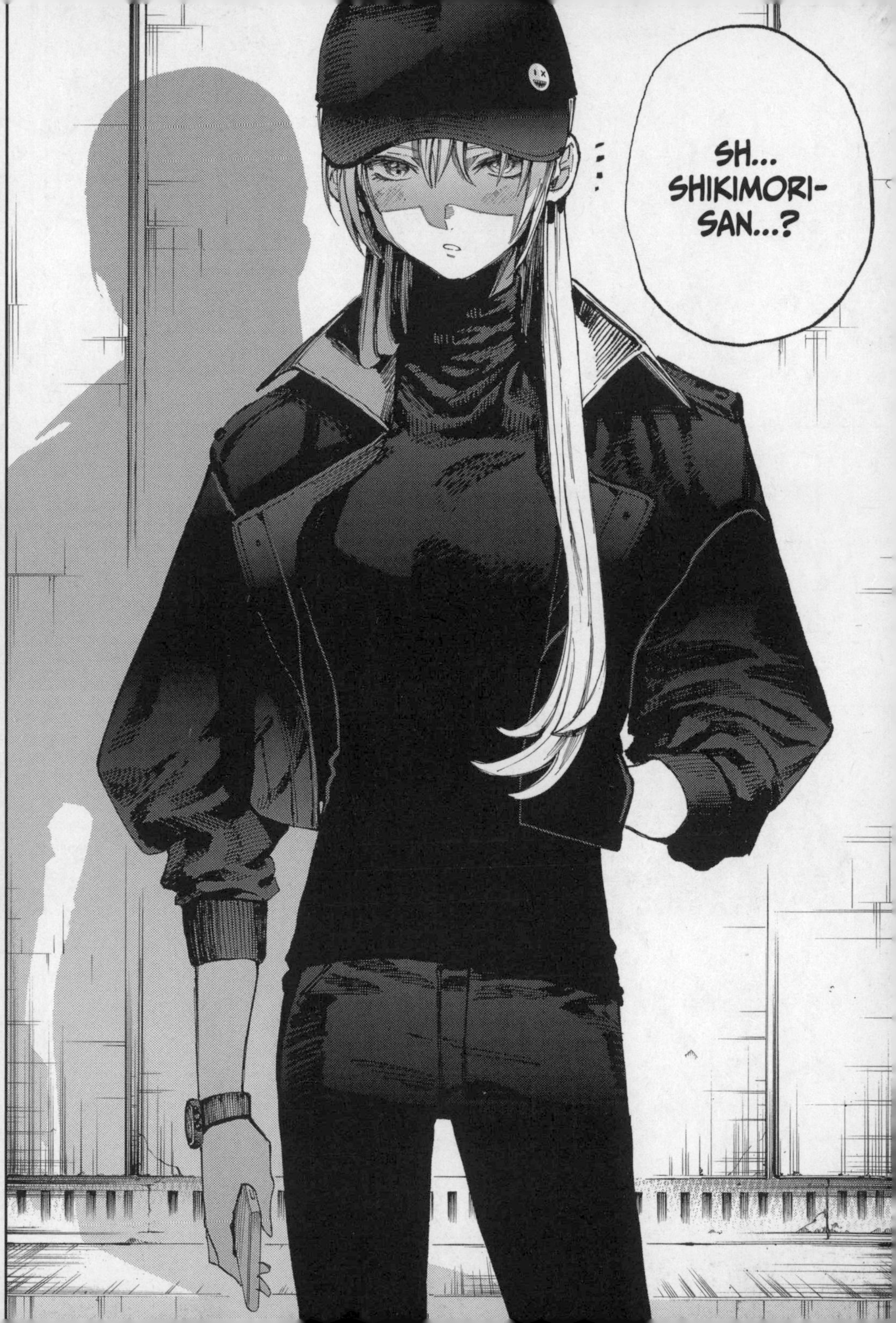
SH... SHIKIMORI-SAN...?

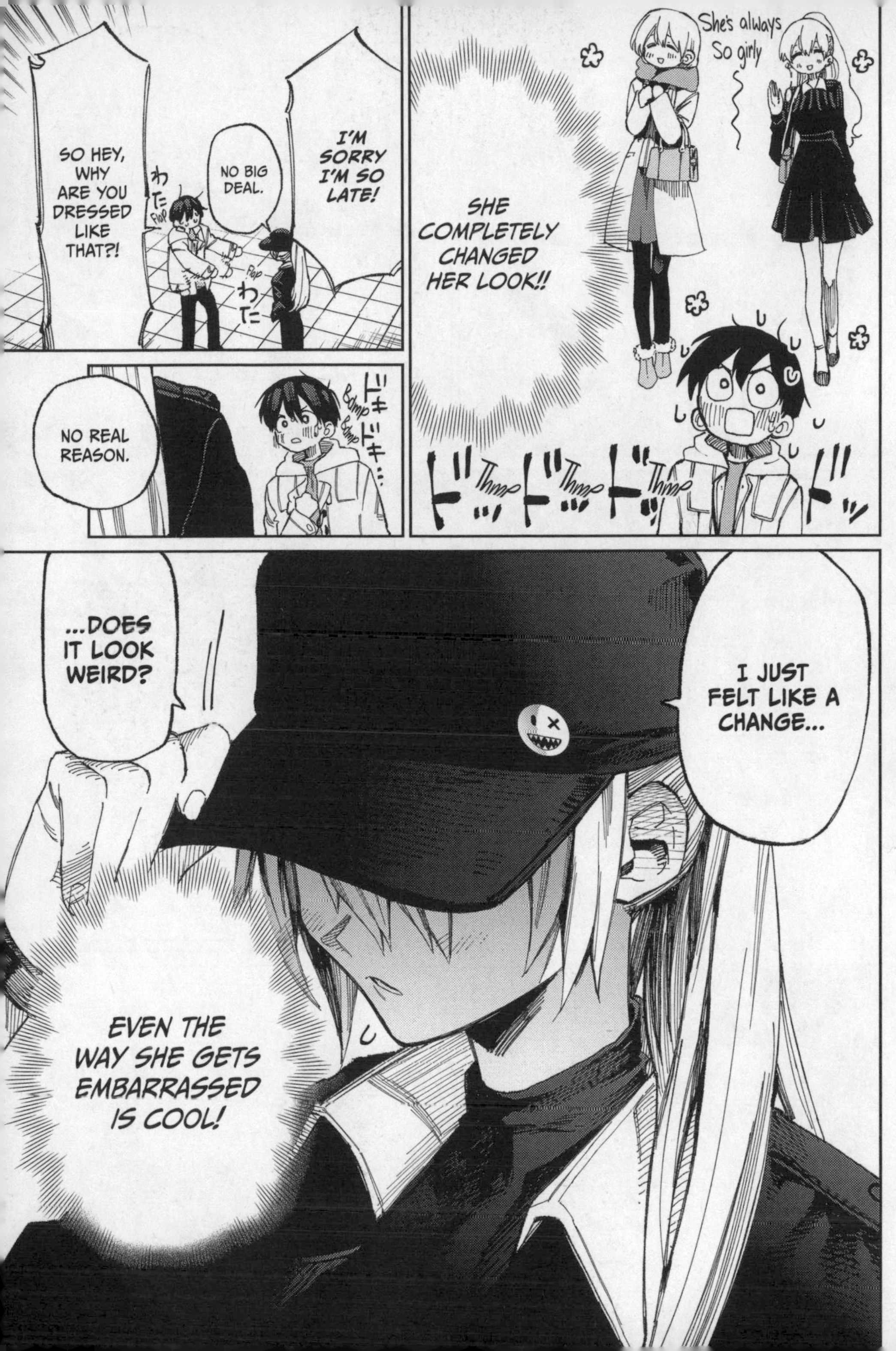
She's always So girly
SHE COMPLETELY CHANGED HER LOOK!!
ドッ Thmp ドッ Thmp ドッ Thmp ドッ
I'M SORRY I'M SO LATE!
NO BIG DEAL.
わた Flop わた Flop
SO HEY, WHY ARE YOU DRESSED LIKE THAT?!
ドキドキ Bdmp Bdmp
NO REAL REASON.
I JUST FELT LIKE A CHANGE...
...DOES IT LOOK WEIRD?
EVEN THE WAY SHE GETS EMBARRASSED IS COOL!

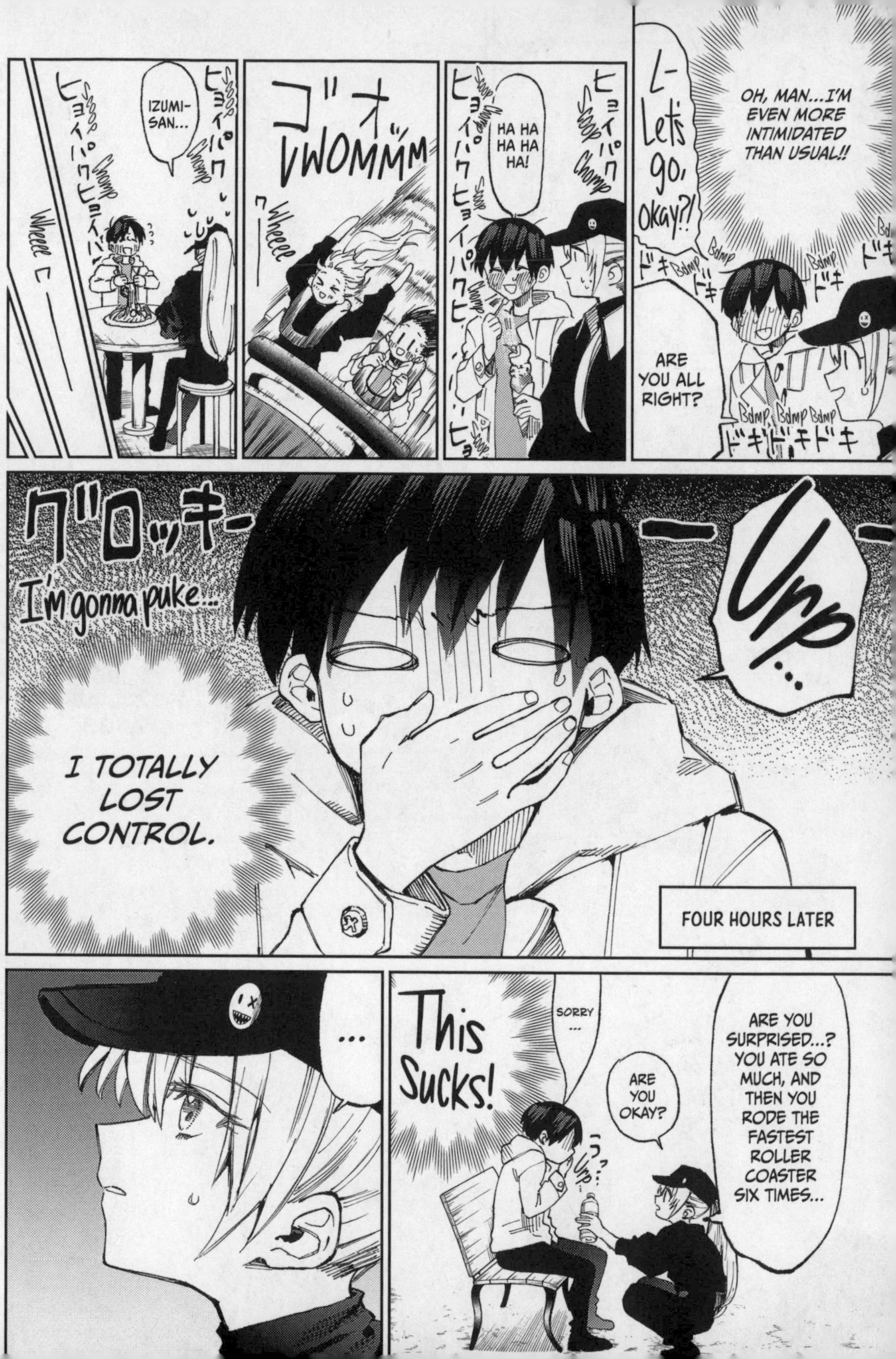

ム-
Let's go, okay?!
OH, MAN...I'M EVEN MORE INTIMIDATED THAN USUAL!!
ドキ Bdmp
ARE YOU ALL RIGHT?
ドキドキドキ Bdmp Bdmp Bdmp
ヒョイパク Scoop Chomp
HA HA HA HA HA!
ゴオッ VWOMMM
ワー Wheeee
IZUMI-SAN...
ヒョイパク Scoop Chomp
ワー Wheeee
Urp...
グロッキー
I'm gonna puke...
I TOTALLY LOST CONTROL.
FOUR HOURS LATER
ARE YOU SURPRISED...? YOU ATE SO MUCH, AND THEN YOU RODE THE FASTEST ROLLER COASTER SIX TIMES...
SORRY ...
ARE YOU OKAY?
This Sucks!
Urp...
...

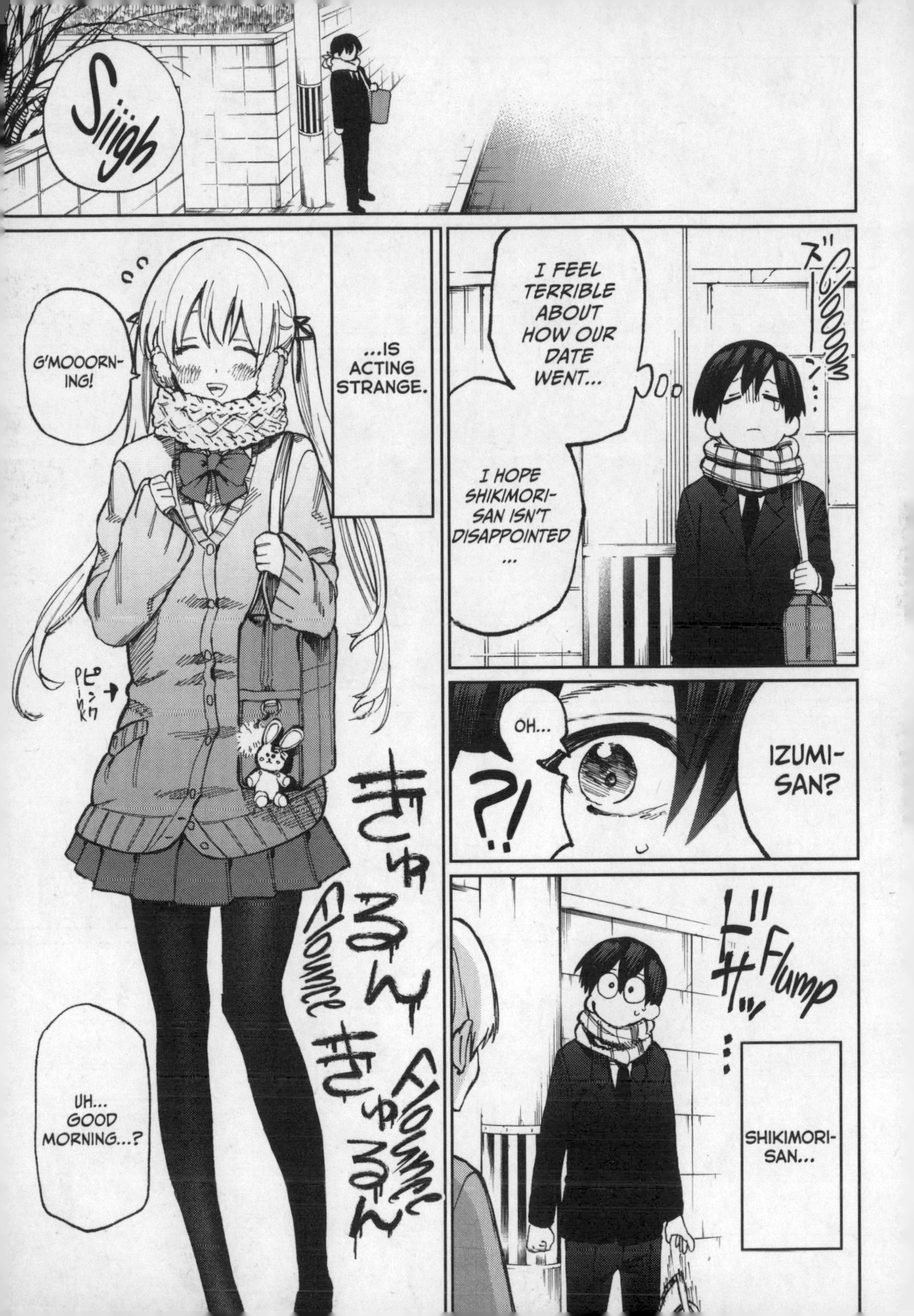
Siiigh
Gloooom
I FEEL TERRIBLE ABOUT HOW OUR DATE WENT...
I HOPE SHIKIMORI-SAN ISN'T DISAPPOINTED...
IZUMI-SAN?
OH...
?!
Flump
...
SHIKIMORI-SAN...
...IS ACTING STRANGE.
G'MOOORNING!
Pink
Flounce
Flounce
UH... GOOD MORNING...?

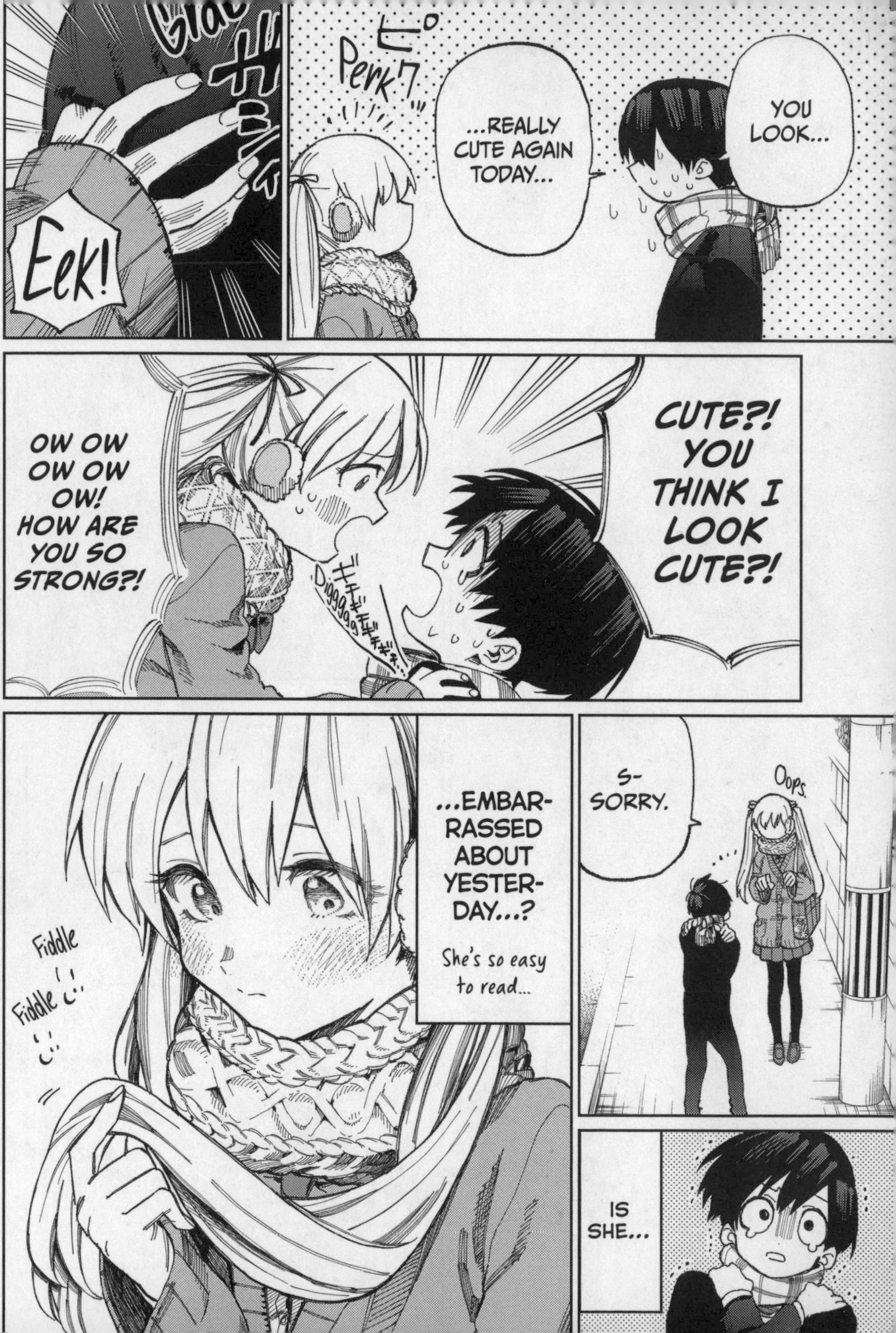
YOU LOOK...
...REALLY CUTE AGAIN TODAY...
Perk
Eek!
CUTE?! YOU THINK I LOOK CUTE?!
Digggggg
OW OW OW OW OW! HOW ARE YOU SO STRONG?!
Oops.
S- SORRY.
IS SHE...
...EMBARRASSED ABOUT YESTERDAY...?
She's so easy to read...
Fiddle
Fiddle

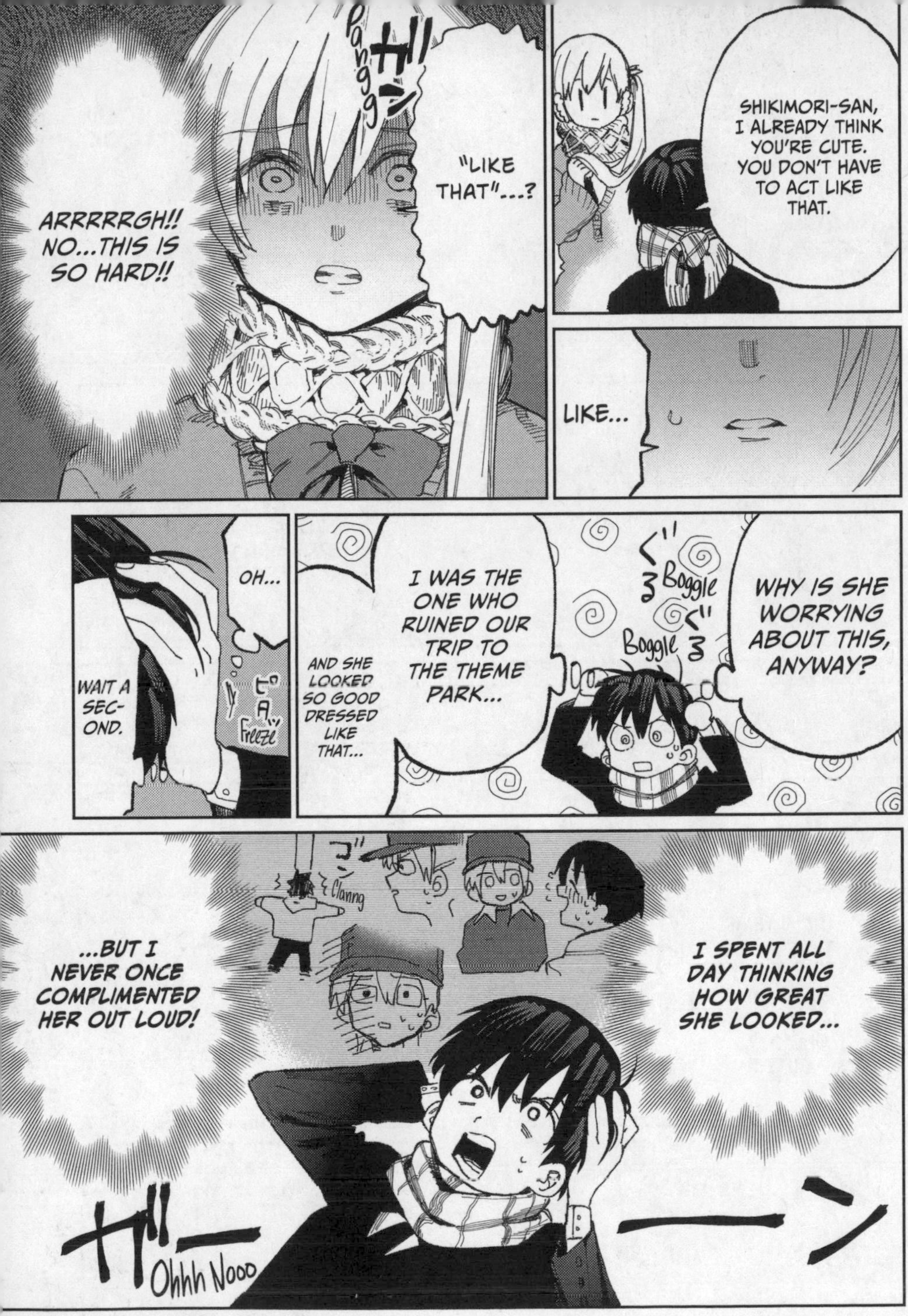
SHIKIMORI-SAN, I ALREADY THINK YOU'RE CUTE. YOU DON'T HAVE TO ACT LIKE THAT.
LIKE...
Pangg
"LIKE THAT"...?
ARRRRGH!! NO...THIS IS SO HARD!!
WHY IS SHE WORRYING ABOUT THIS, ANYWAY?
Boggle
Boggle
I WAS THE ONE WHO RUINED OUR TRIP TO THE THEME PARK...
AND SHE LOOKED SO GOOD DRESSED LIKE THAT...
OH...
Freeze
WAIT A SEC-OND.
I SPENT ALL DAY THINKING HOW GREAT SHE LOOKED...
Clanng
...BUT I NEVER ONCE COMPLIMENTED HER OUT LOUD!
Ohhh Nooo

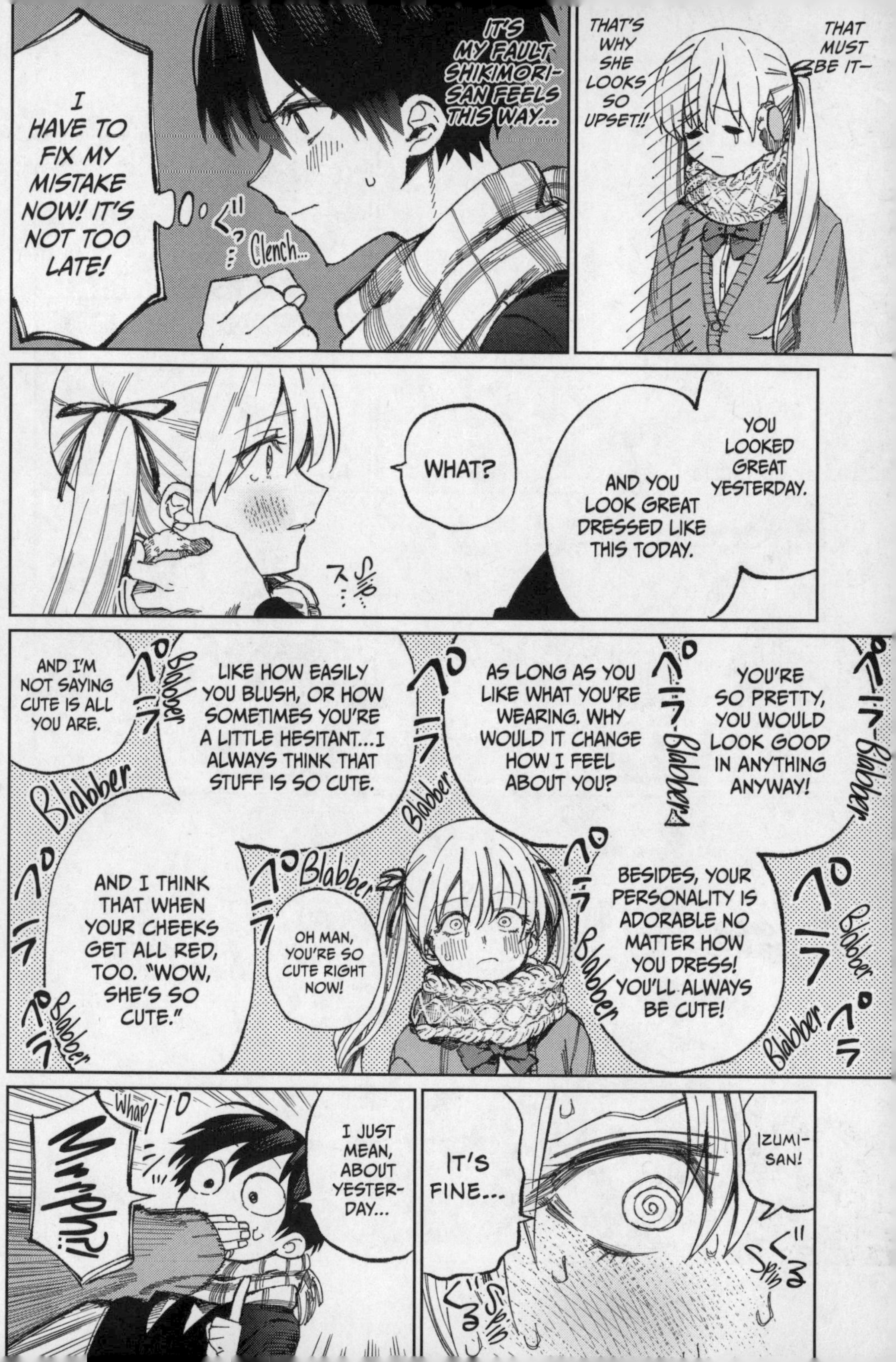
THAT MUST BE IT—
THAT'S WHY SHE LOOKS SO UPSET!!
IT'S MY FAULT SHIKIMORI-SAN FEELS THIS WAY...
I HAVE TO FIX MY MISTAKE NOW! IT'S NOT TOO LATE!
Clench...
YOU LOOKED GREAT YESTERDAY.
AND YOU LOOK GREAT DRESSED LIKE THIS TODAY.
WHAT?
Slip
YOU'RE SO PRETTY, YOU WOULD LOOK GOOD IN ANYTHING ANYWAY!
Blabber
AS LONG AS YOU LIKE WHAT YOU'RE WEARING. WHY WOULD IT CHANGE HOW I FEEL ABOUT YOU?
Blabber
LIKE HOW EASILY YOU BLUSH, OR HOW SOMETIMES YOU'RE A LITTLE HESITANT...I ALWAYS THINK THAT STUFF IS SO CUTE.
Blabber
AND I'M NOT SAYING CUTE IS ALL YOU ARE.
Blabber
Blabber
BESIDES, YOUR PERSONALITY IS ADORABLE NO MATTER HOW YOU DRESS! YOU'LL ALWAYS BE CUTE!
Blabber
Blabber
OH MAN, YOU'RE SO CUTE RIGHT NOW!
Blabber
AND I THINK THAT WHEN YOUR CHEEKS GET ALL RED, TOO. "WOW, SHE'S SO CUTE."
Blabber
IZUMI-SAN!
IT'S FINE...
Spin
Spin
I JUST MEAN, ABOUT YESTERDAY...
Whap!
Mrrph!?

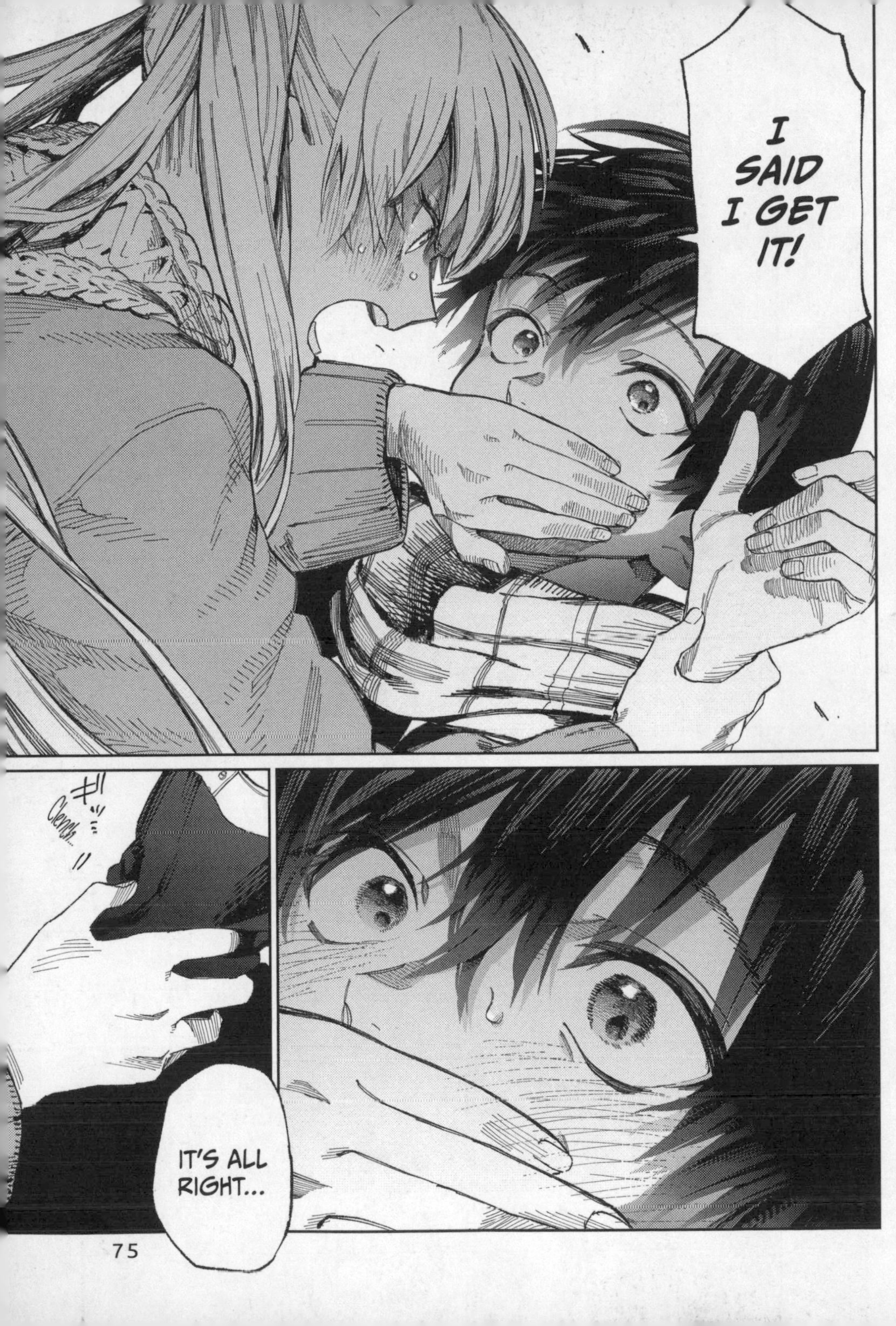
I SAID I GET IT!
Clench...
IT'S ALL RIGHT...

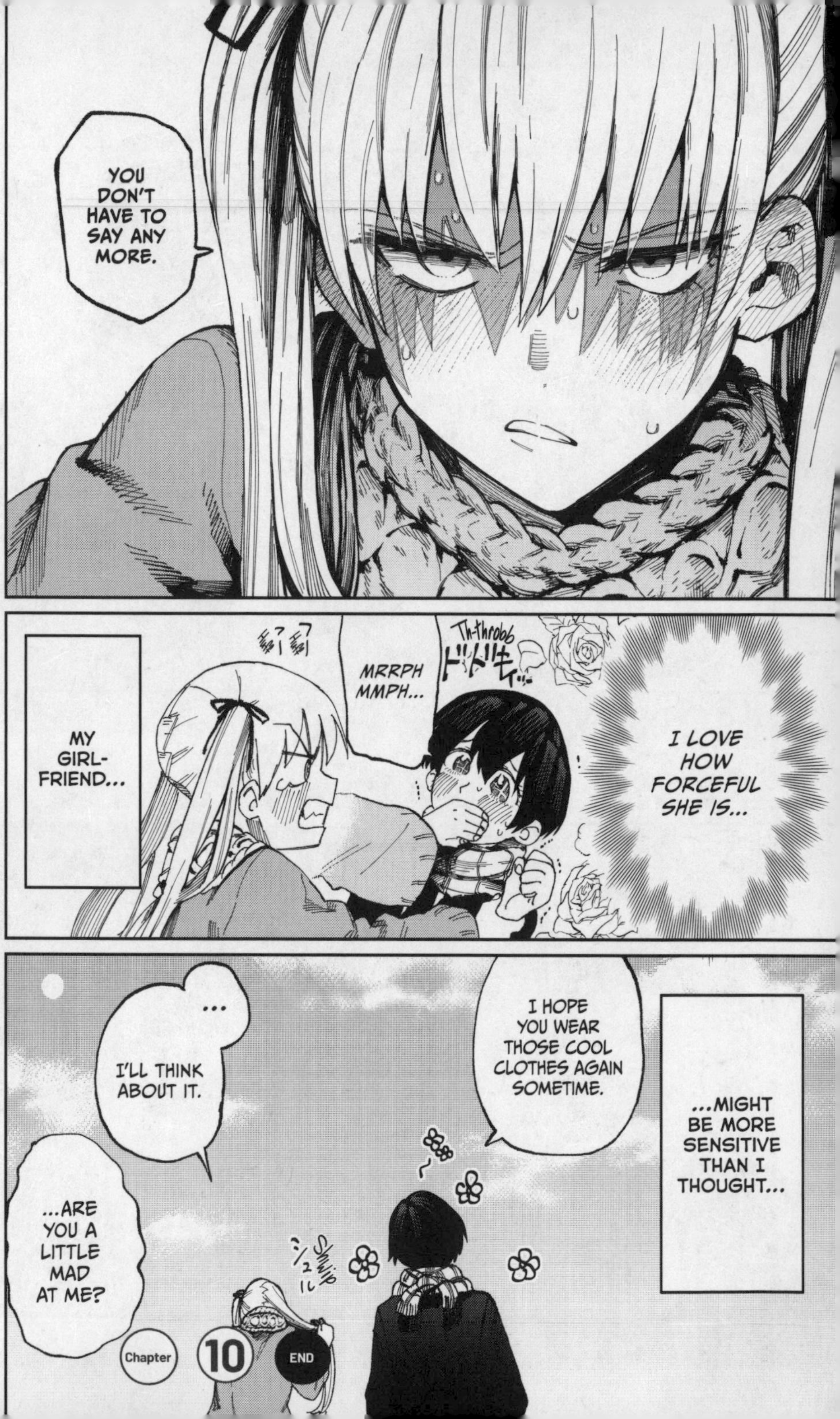
YOU DON'T HAVE TO SAY ANY MORE.
I LOVE HOW FORCEFUL SHE IS...
Th-throbb
MRRPH MMPH...
MY GIRL-FRIEND...
...MIGHT BE MORE SENSITIVE THAN I THOUGHT...
I HOPE YOU WEAR THOSE COOL CLOTHES AGAIN SOMETIME.
...
I'LL THINK ABOUT IT.
...ARE YOU A LITTLE MAD AT ME?
Chapter 10 END

SHIKIMORI'S not just a cutie

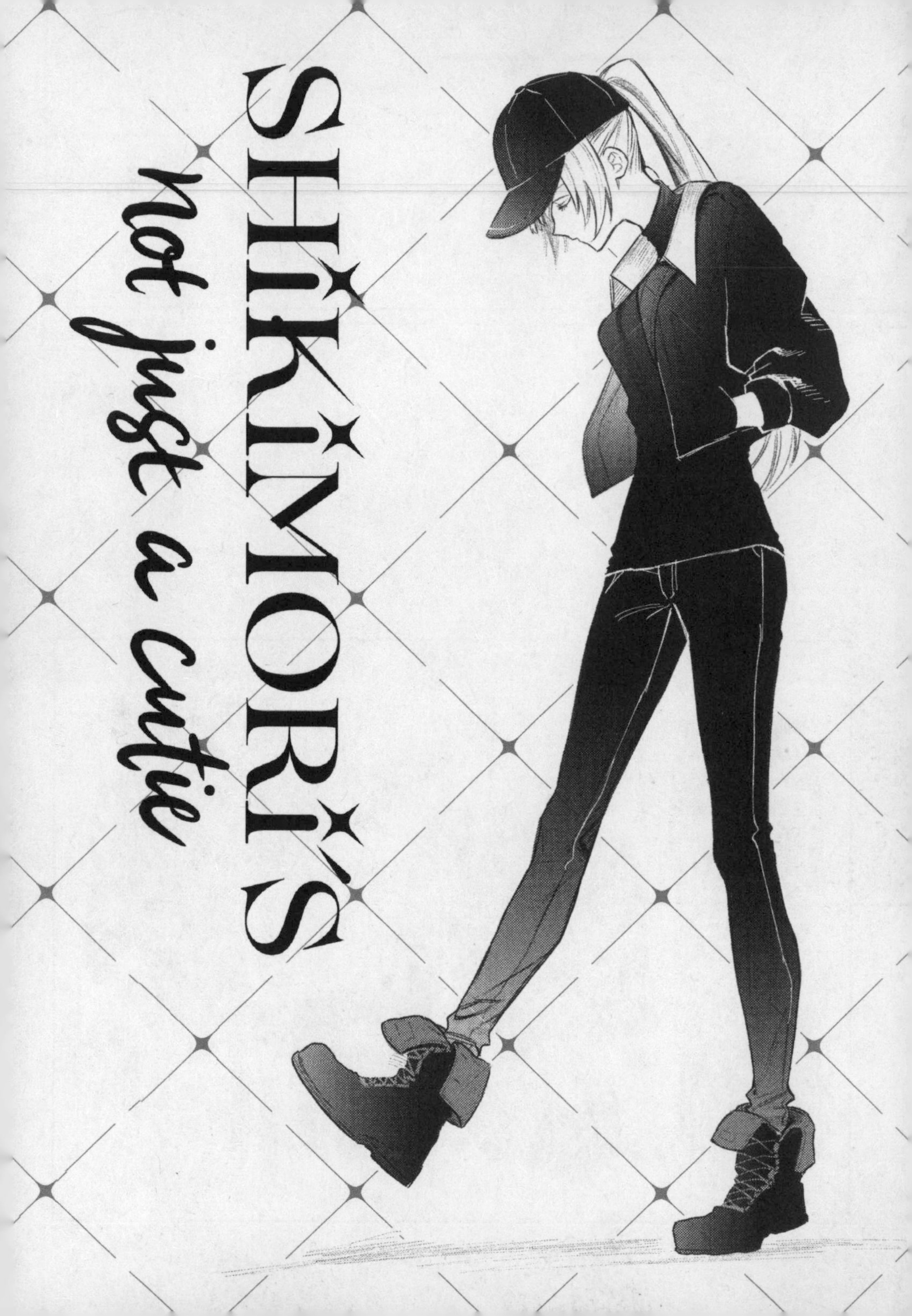
SHIKIMORI'S
not just a cutie

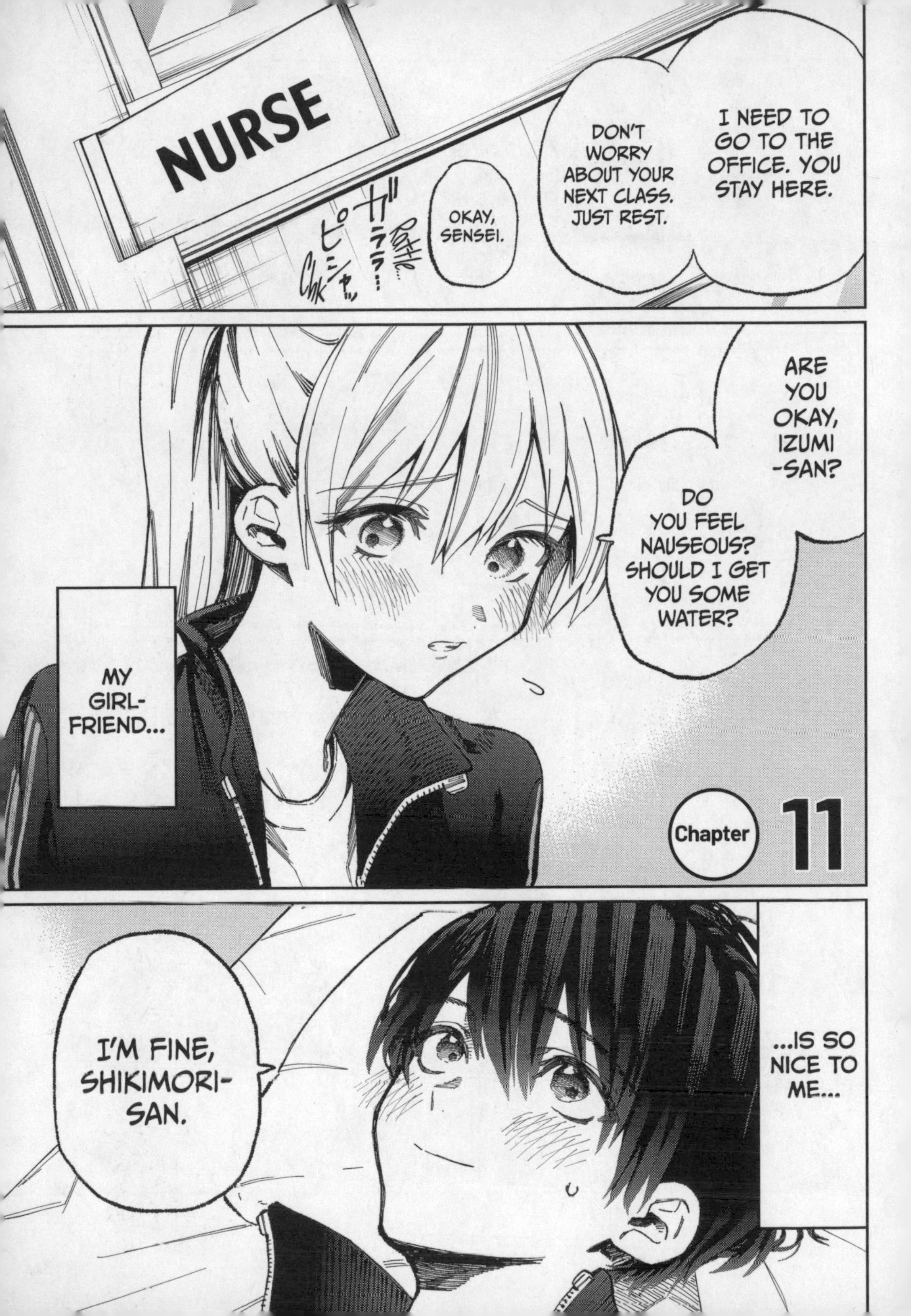
I NEED TO GO TO THE OFFICE. YOU STAY HERE.
DON'T WORRY ABOUT YOUR NEXT CLASS. JUST REST.
OKAY, SENSEI.
ガラララ… Rattle...
ピシャッ Chk
NURSE
ARE YOU OKAY, IZUMI-SAN?
DO YOU FEEL NAUSEOUS? SHOULD I GET YOU SOME WATER?
MY GIRLFRIEND...
Chapter 11
...IS SO NICE TO ME...
I'M FINE, SHIKIMORI-SAN.

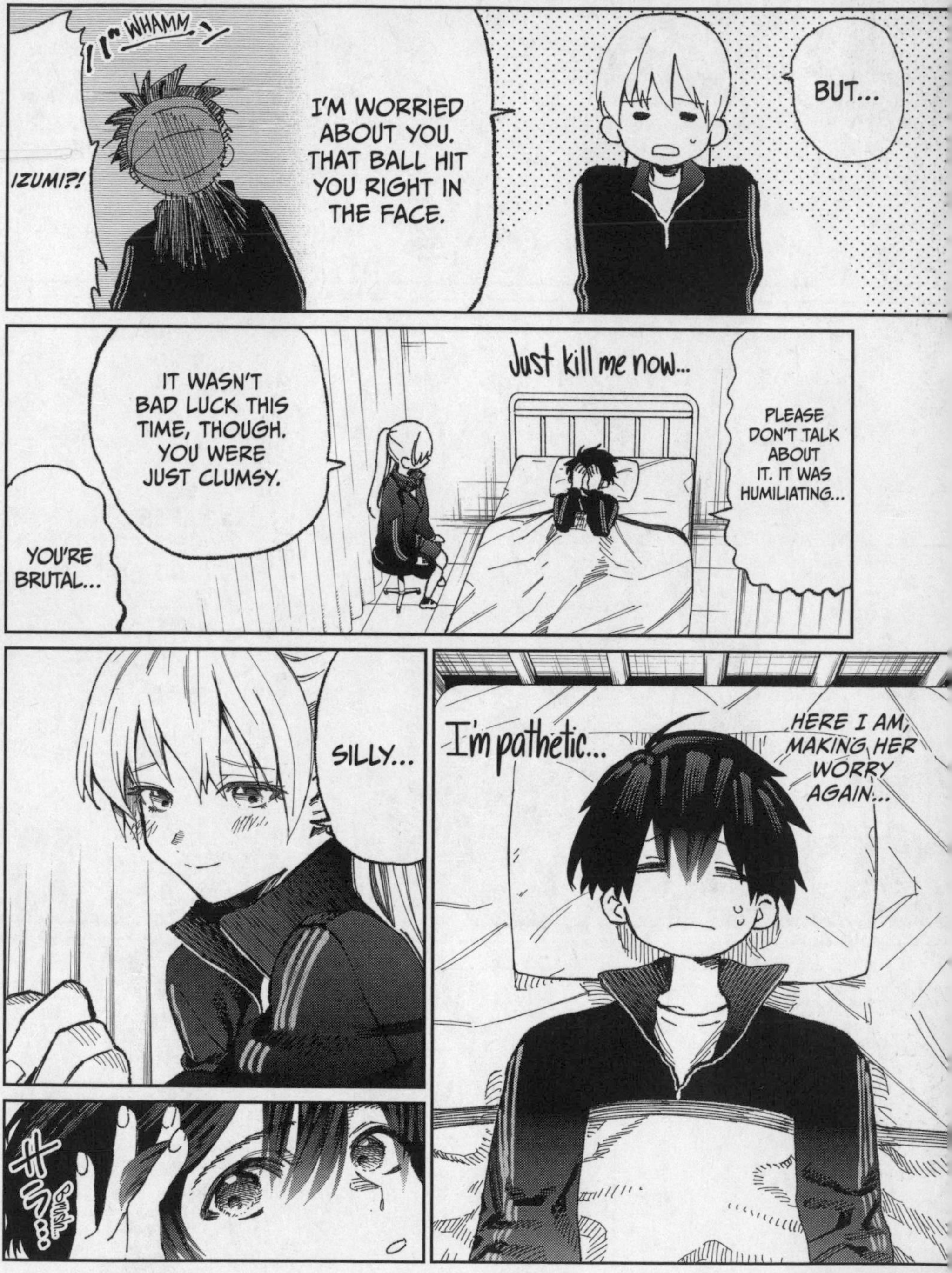
BUT...
I'M WORRIED ABOUT YOU. THAT BALL HIT YOU RIGHT IN THE FACE.
WHAMM
IZUMI?!
PLEASE DON'T TALK ABOUT IT. IT WAS HUMILIATING...
Just kill me now...
IT WASN'T BAD LUCK THIS TIME, THOUGH. YOU WERE JUST CLUMSY.
YOU'RE BRUTAL...
HERE I AM, MAKING HER WORRY AGAIN...
I'm pathetic...
SILLY...
Brush...

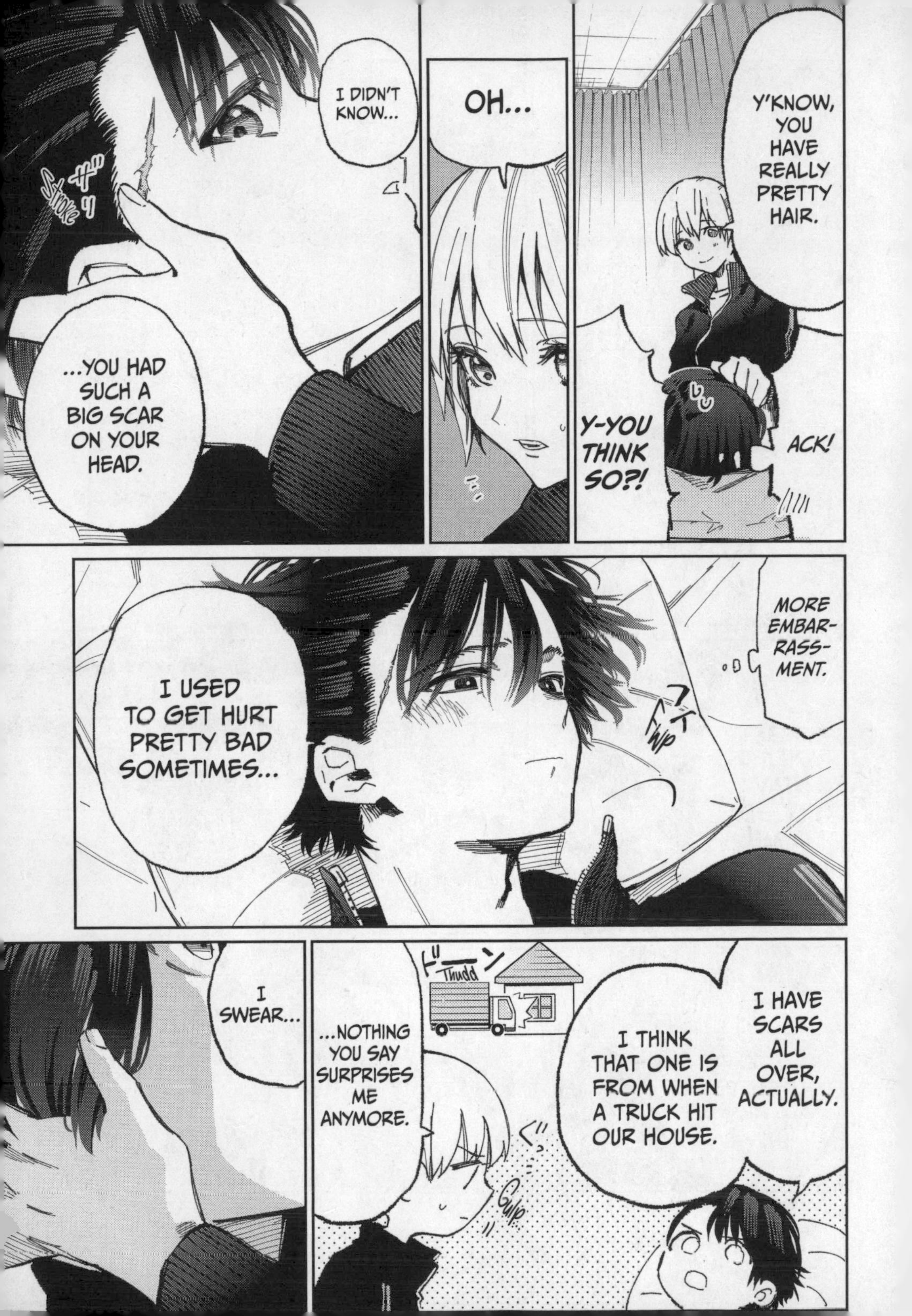
Y'KNOW, YOU HAVE REALLY PRETTY HAIR.
ACK!
Y-YOU THINK SO?!
OH...
I DIDN'T KNOW...
...YOU HAD SUCH A BIG SCAR ON YOUR HEAD.
Stroke
MORE EMBARRASSMENT.
Fwip
I USED TO GET HURT PRETTY BAD SOMETIMES...
I HAVE SCARS ALL OVER, ACTUALLY.
I THINK THAT ONE IS FROM WHEN A TRUCK HIT OUR HOUSE.
Thudd
Gulp
...NOTHING YOU SAY SURPRISES ME ANYMORE.
I SWEAR...

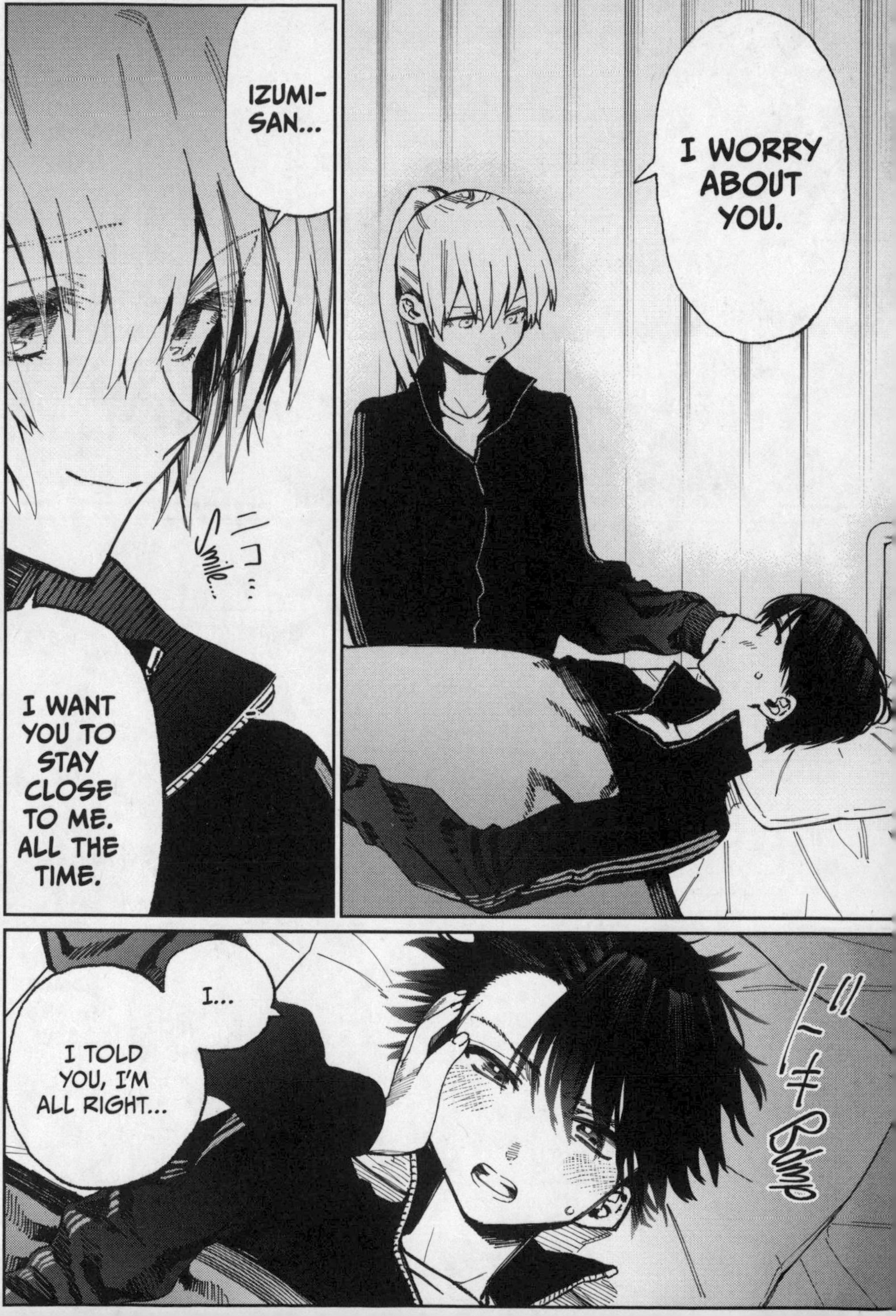
I WORRY ABOUT YOU.
IZUMI-SAN...
ニコ…
Smile...
I WANT YOU TO STAY CLOSE TO ME. ALL THE TIME.
ドキ
Bdmp
I...
I TOLD YOU, I'M ALL RIGHT...

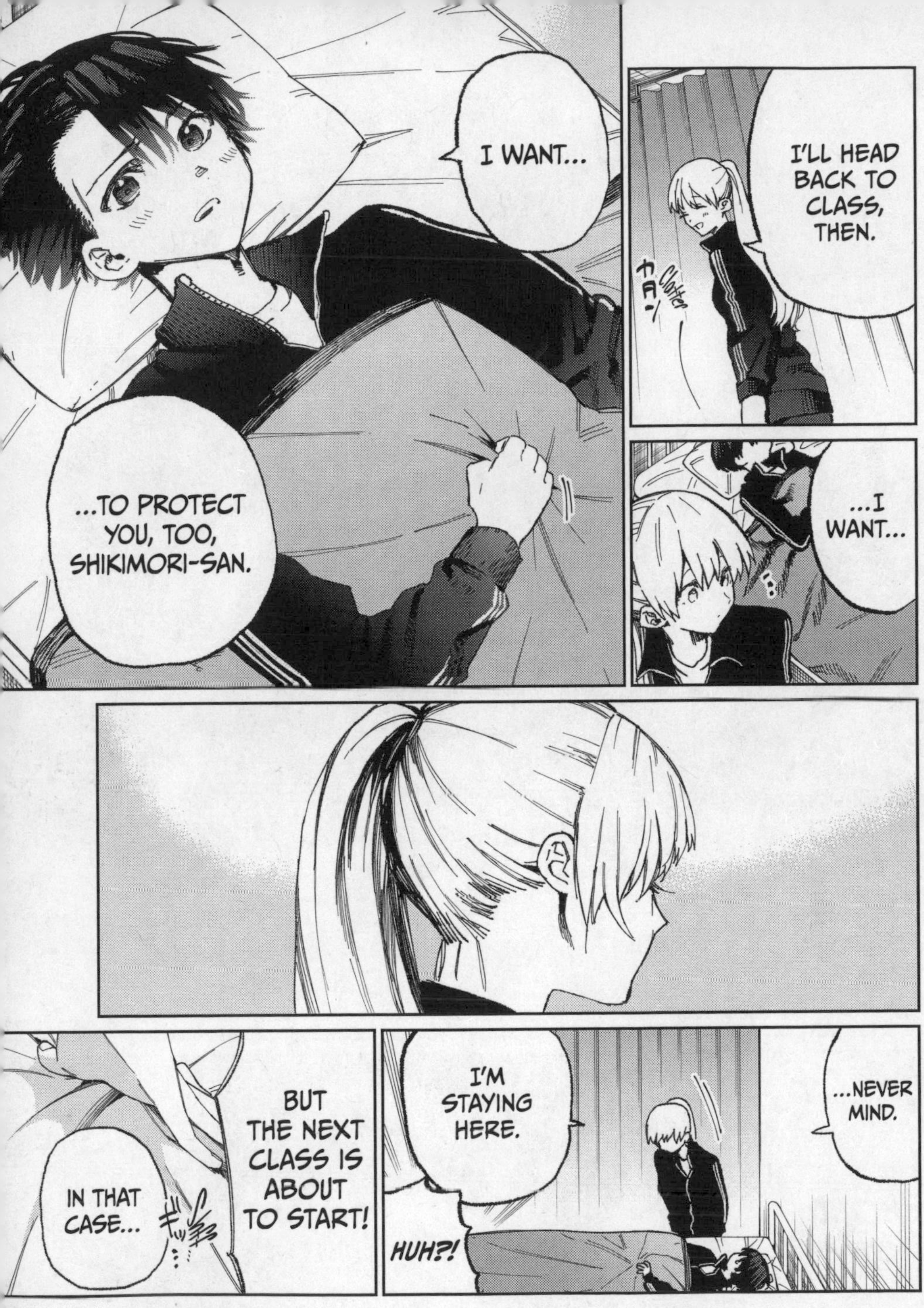
I'LL HEAD BACK TO CLASS, THEN.
カタン
Clatter
...I WANT...
I WANT...
...TO PROTECT YOU, TOO, SHIKIMORI-SAN.
...NEVER MIND.
I'M STAYING HERE.
HUH?!
BUT THE NEXT CLASS IS ABOUT TO START!
IN THAT CASE...

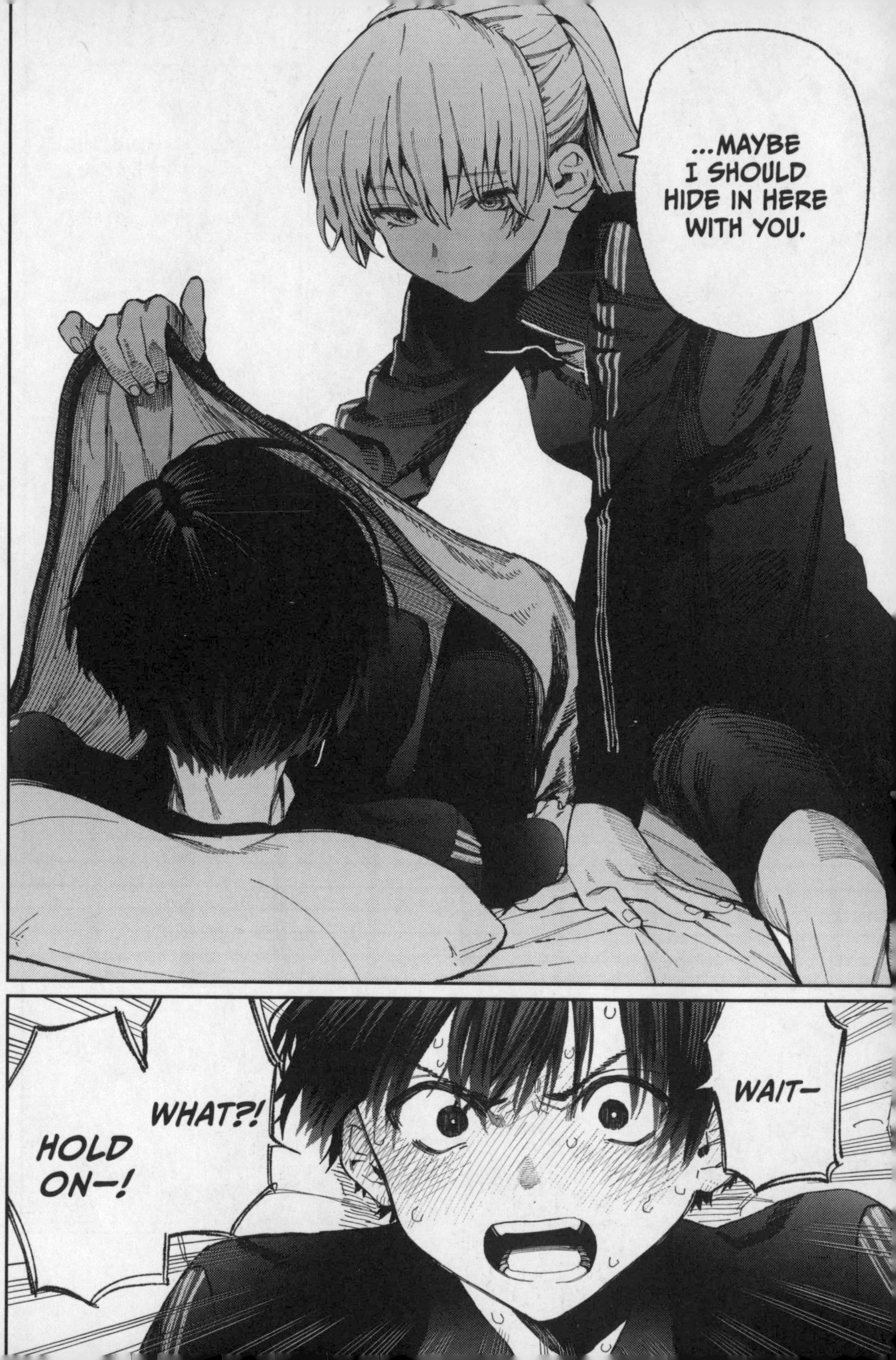
...MAYBE I SHOULD HIDE IN HERE WITH YOU.
WAIT–
WHAT?!
HOLD ON–!

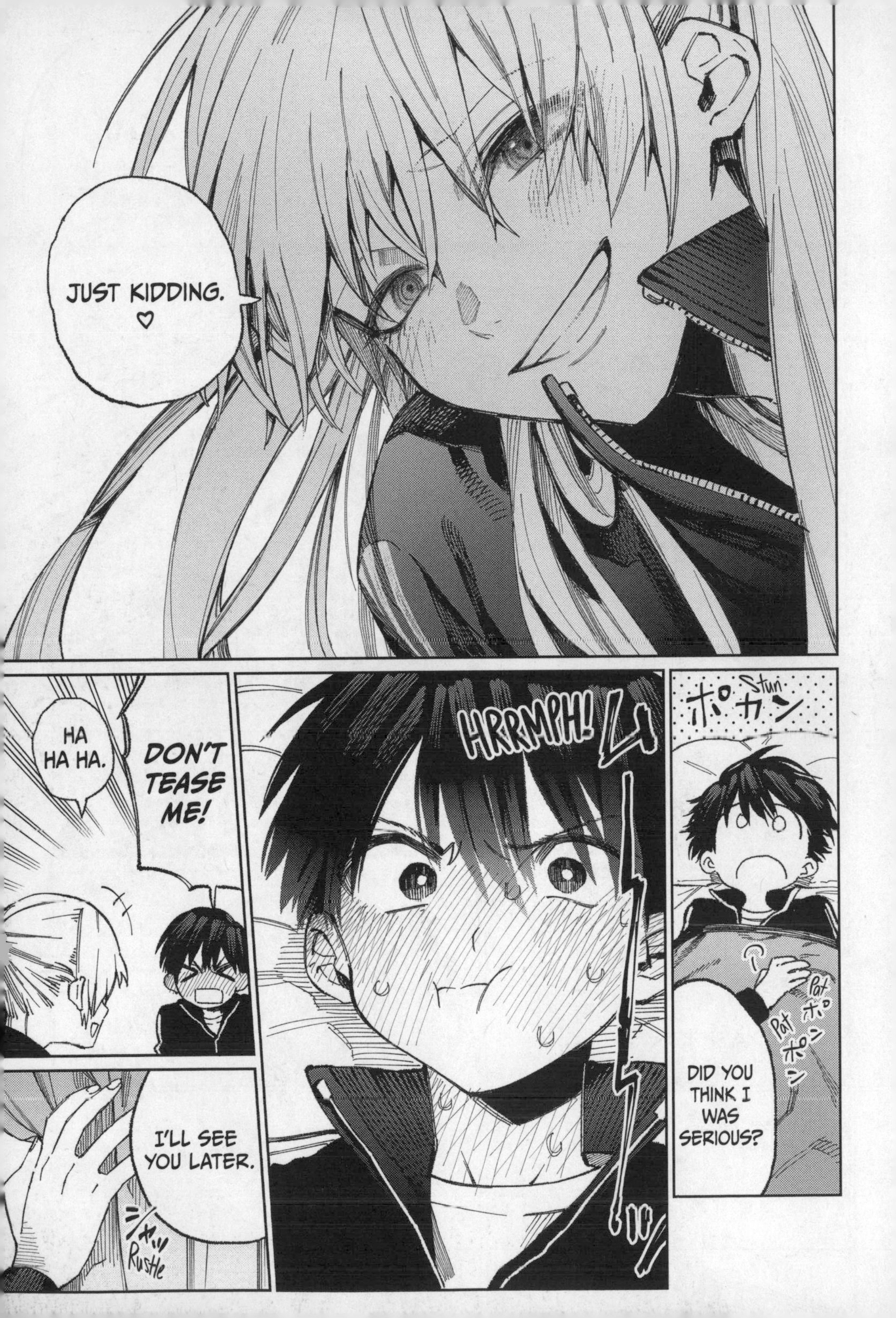
JUST KIDDING. ♡
ポカン
Stun
DID YOU THINK I WAS SERIOUS?
Pat Pat
HRRMPH!
HA HA HA.
DON'T TEASE ME!
I'LL SEE YOU LATER.
Rustle

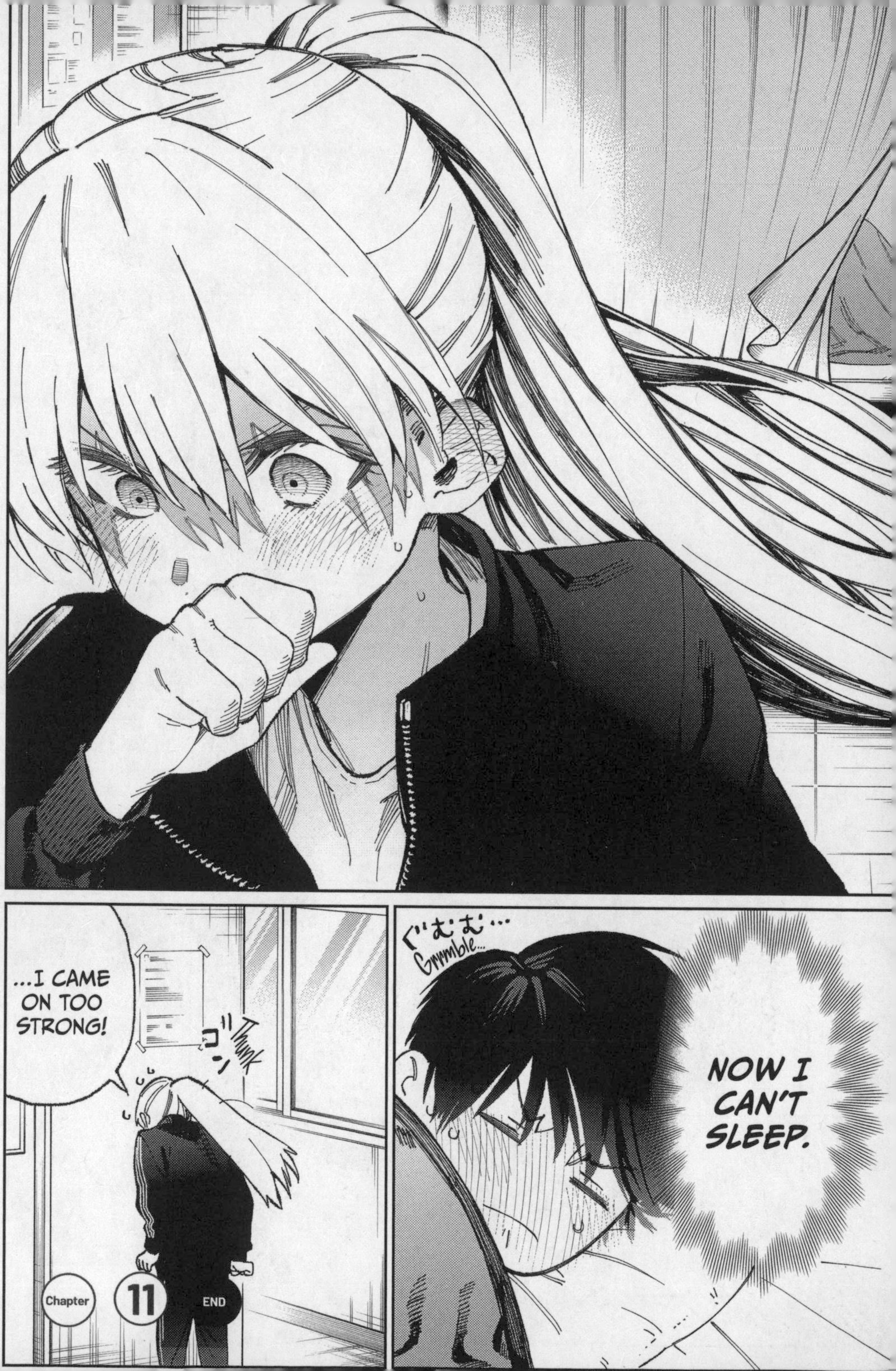
ぐむむ…
Grrmble…
NOW I CAN'T SLEEP.
...I CAME ON TOO STRONG!
ゴン
Thunk
Chapter 11 END

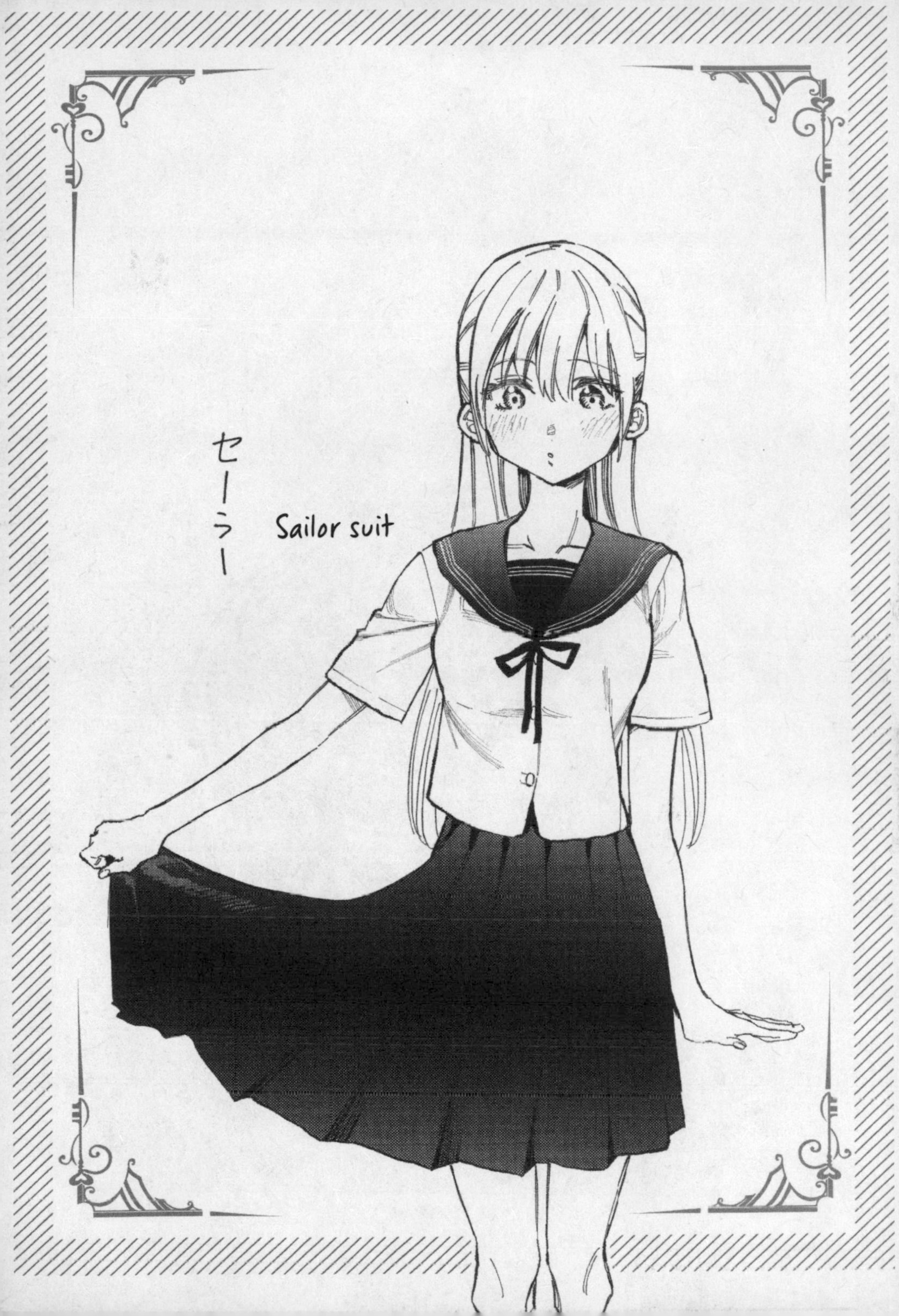
セーラー
Sailor suit

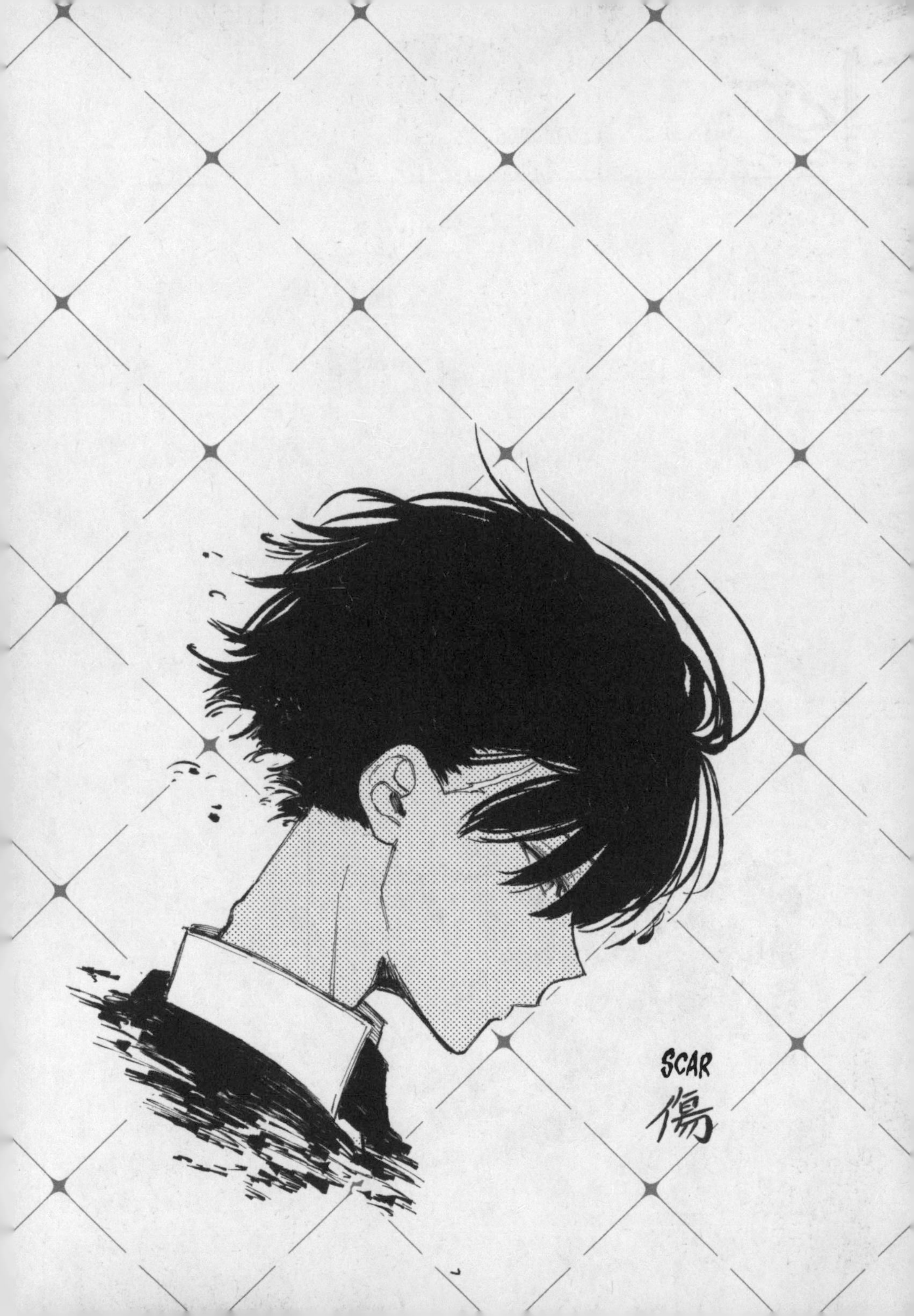
SCAR
傷

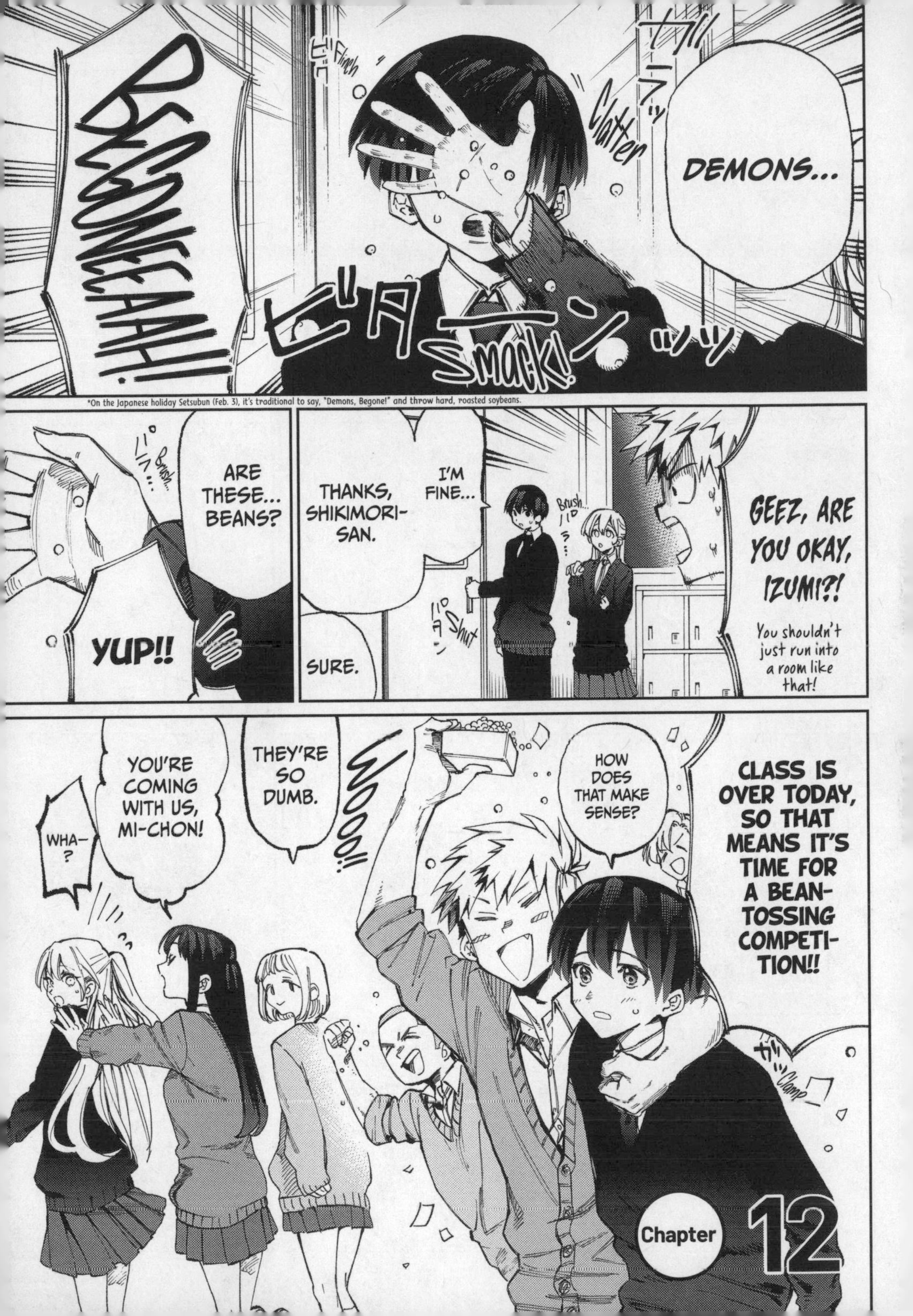
DEMONS...
Clatter
Flinch
SMACK!
BEGONEEAAH!*
GEEZ, ARE YOU OKAY, IZUMI?!
You shouldn't just run into a room like that!
Brush...
I'M FINE...
THANKS, SHIKIMORI-SAN.
SURE.
Shut
ARE THESE... BEANS?
Brush...
YUP!!
CLASS IS OVER TODAY, SO THAT MEANS IT'S TIME FOR A BEAN-TOSSING COMPETITION!!
Clamp
HOW DOES THAT MAKE SENSE?
WOOOO!!
THEY'RE SO DUMB.
YOU'RE COMING WITH US, MI-CHON!
WHA-?
Chapter 12

*On the Japanese holiday Setsubun (Feb. 3), it's traditional to say, "Demons, Begone!" and throw hard, roasted soybeans.

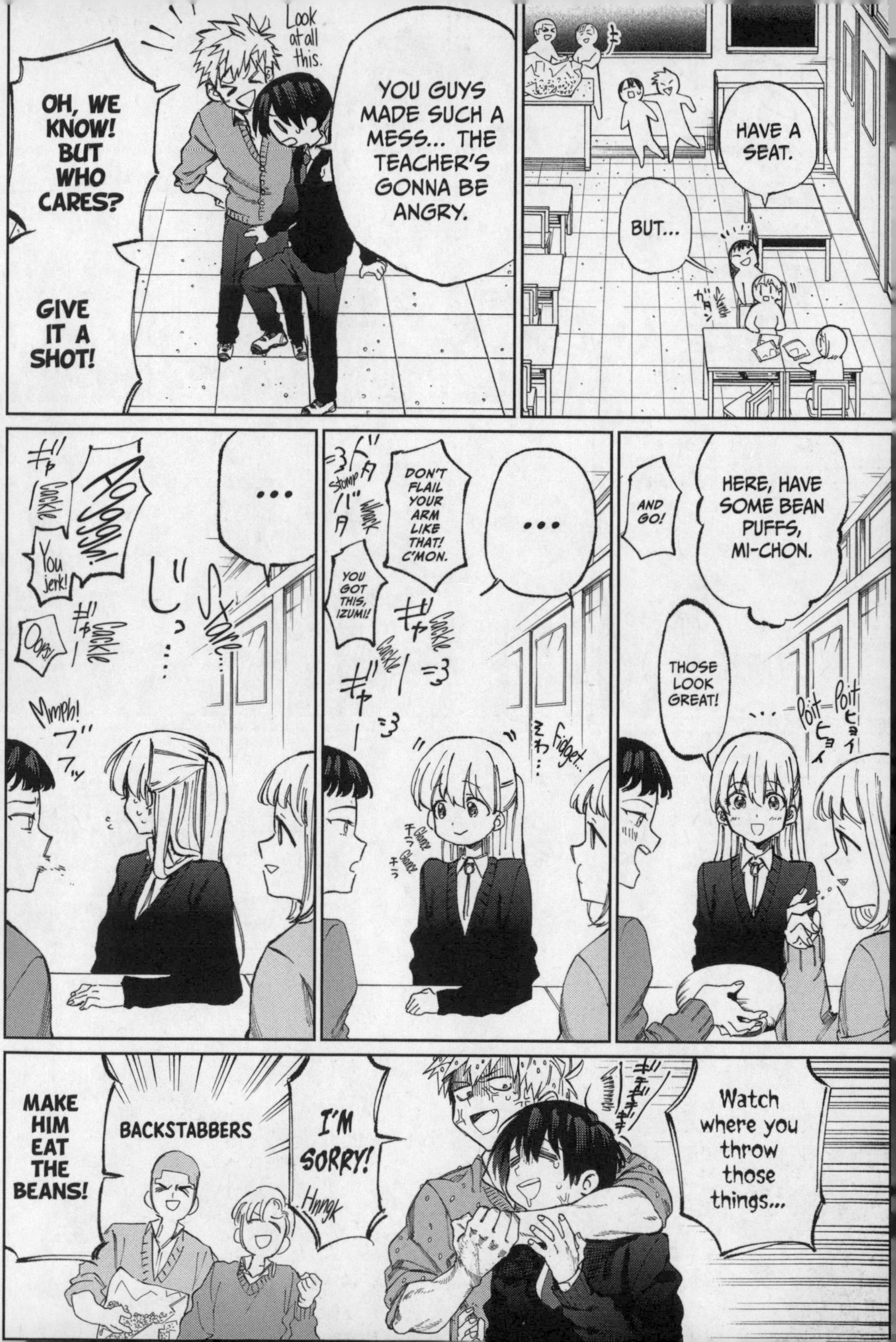
HAVE A SEAT.
BUT...
YOU GUYS MADE SUCH A MESS... THE TEACHER'S GONNA BE ANGRY.
Look at all this.
OH, WE KNOW! BUT WHO CARES?
GIVE IT A SHOT!
HERE, HAVE SOME BEAN PUFFS, MI-CHON.
AND GO!
THOSE LOOK GREAT!
Poit Poit
...
...
DON'T FLAIL YOUR ARM LIKE THAT! C'MON.
stomp
Whack
YOU GOT THIS, IZUMI!
Cackle
Cackle
Fidget...
Glance Glance
...
Agggh!
Cackle
You jerk!
Cackle
Oops!
Stare...
Mmph!
Watch where you throw those things...
I'M SORRY!
Hnngk
BACKSTABBERS
MAKE HIM EAT THE BEANS!

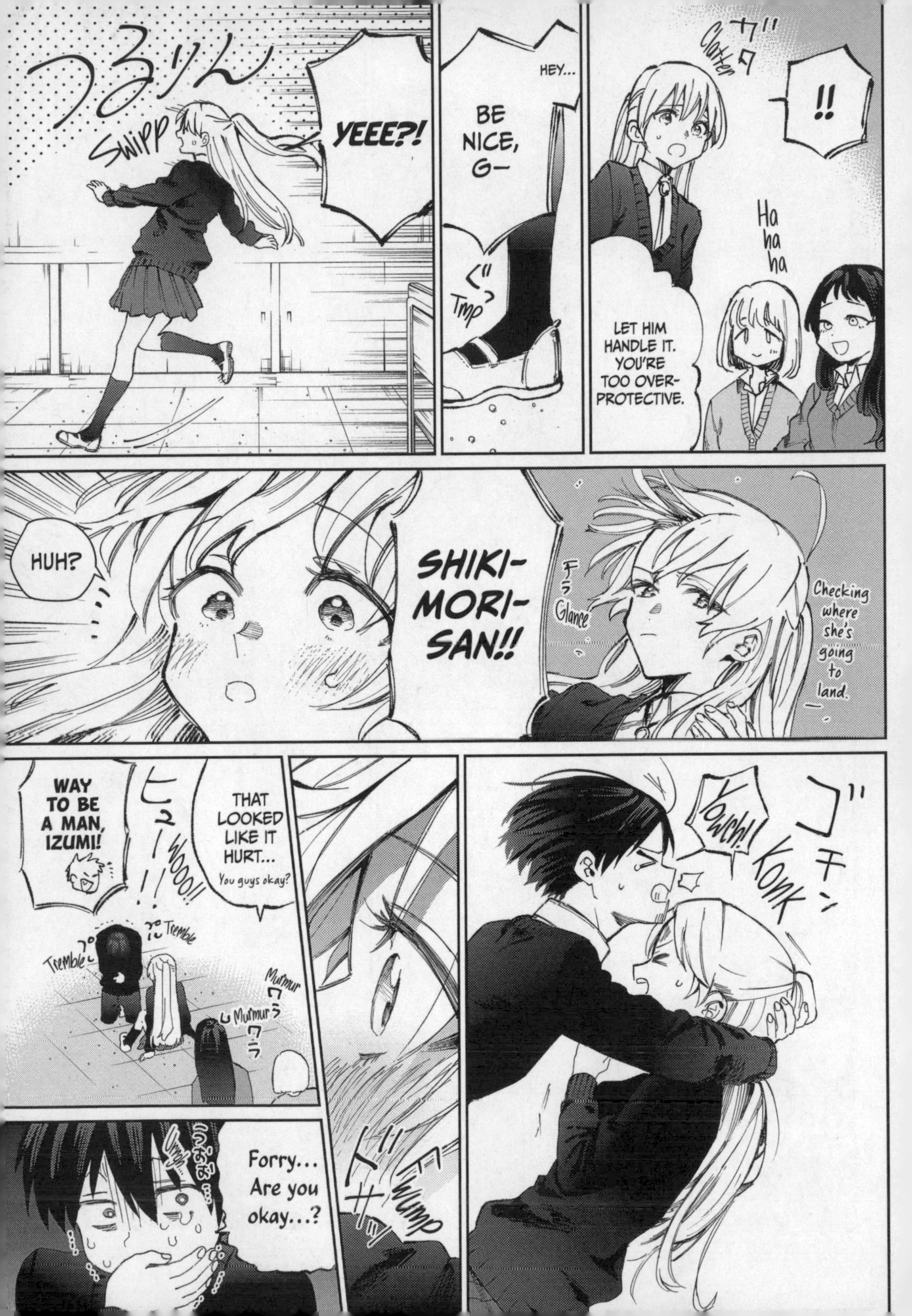

Clatter
!!
Ha ha ha
LET HIM HANDLE IT. YOU'RE TOO OVER-PROTECTIVE.
HEY...
BE NICE, G—
Tmp
YEEE?!
つるりん
Swipp
Glance
Checking where she's going to land.
SHIKI-MORI-SAN!!
HUH?
ゴチン
Youch!
Konk
Wump
THAT LOOKED LIKE IT HURT...
You guys okay?
Wooo!!
WAY TO BE A MAN, IZUMI!
Tremble
Tremble
Murmur
Murmur
Forry... Are you okay...?

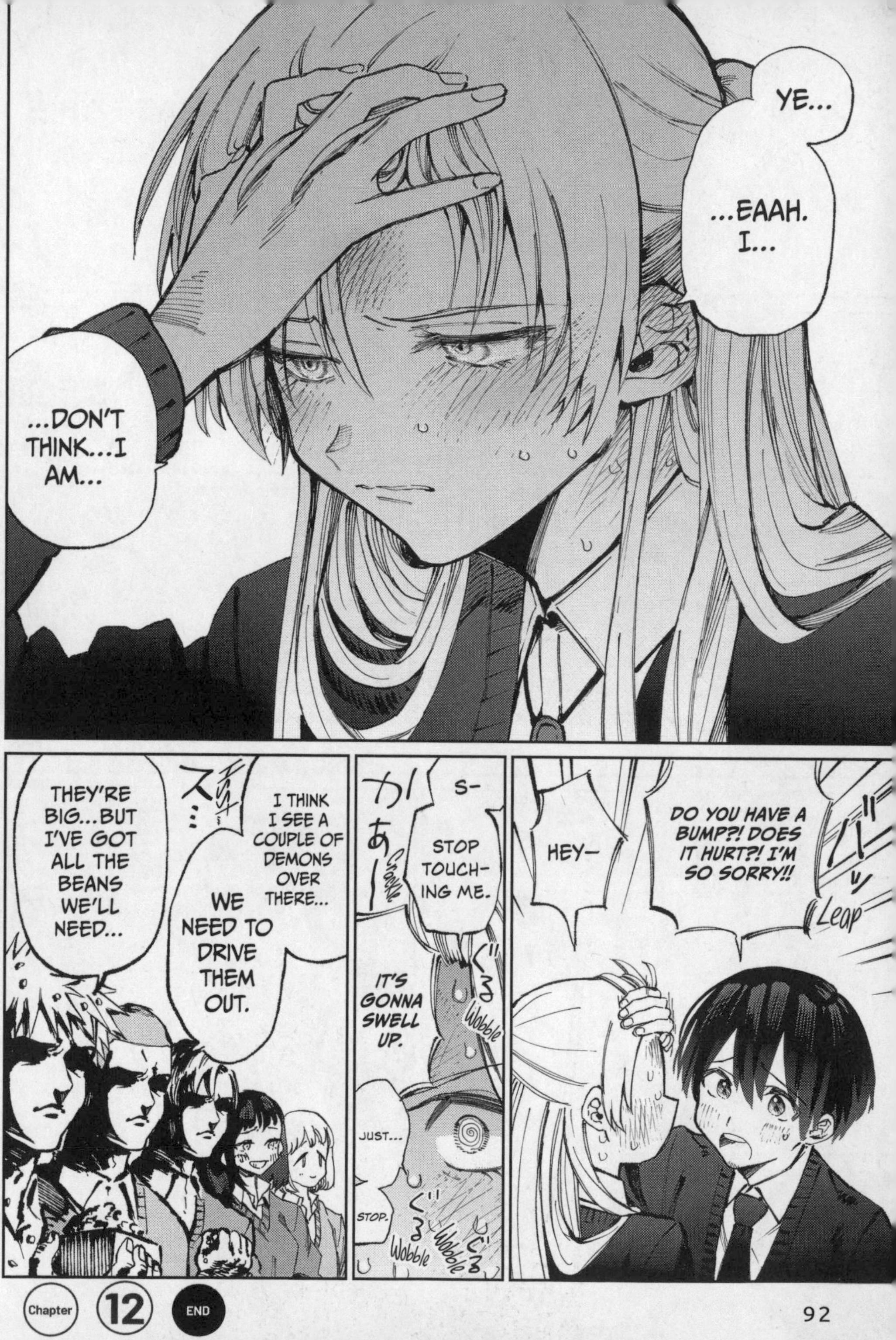

YE...
...EAAH. I...
...DON'T THINK...I AM...
Leap
DO YOU HAVE A BUMP?! DOES IT HURT?! I'M SO SORRY!!
HEY—
S-
STOP TOUCHING ME.
Crackle
IT'S GONNA SWELL UP.
Wobble
JUST...
STOP.
Wobble
Wobble
I THINK I SEE A COUPLE OF DEMONS OVER THERE...
WE NEED TO DRIVE THEM OUT.
Fist
THEY'RE BIG...BUT I'VE GOT ALL THE BEANS WE'LL NEED...

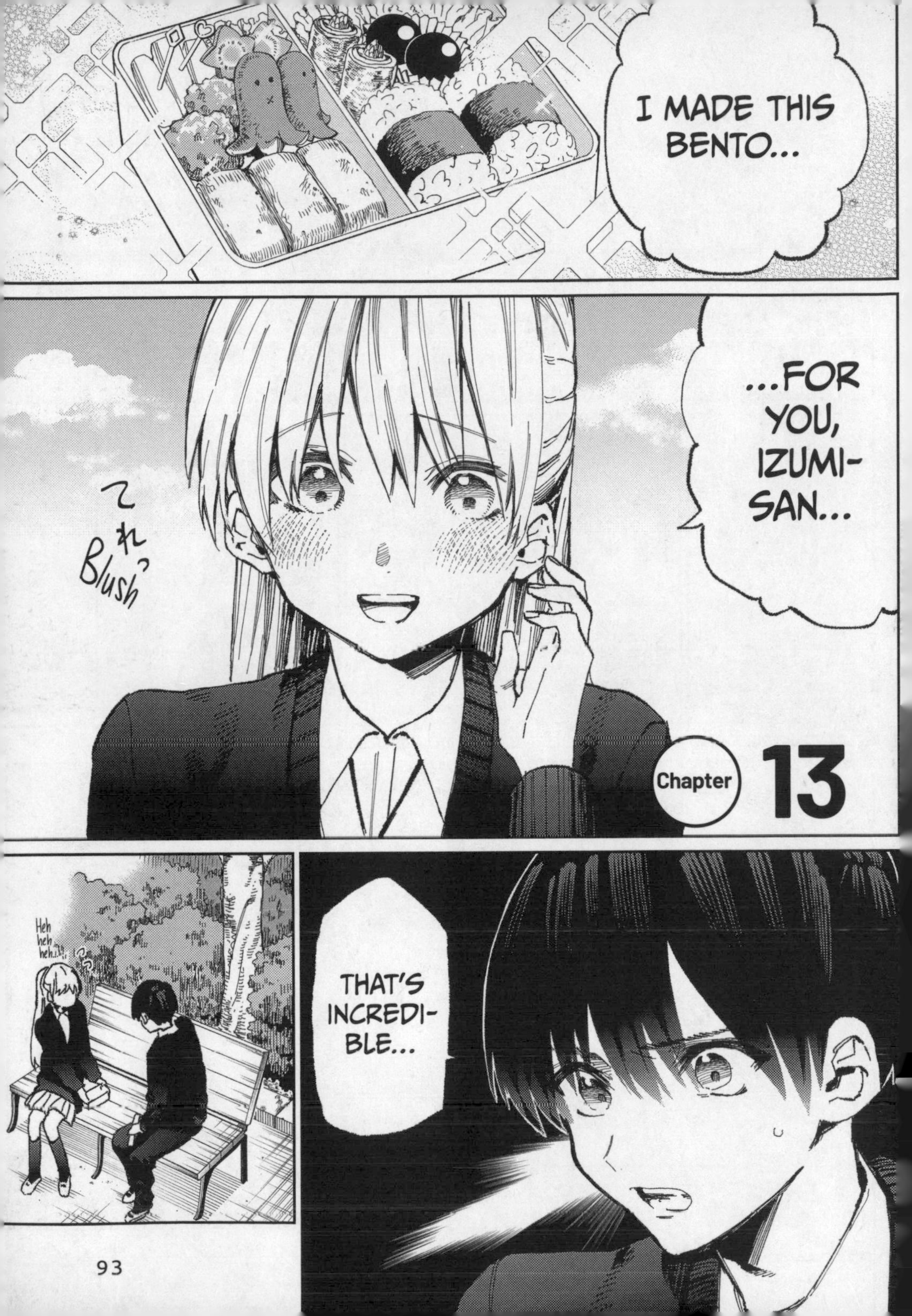
I MADE THIS BENTO...
...FOR YOU, IZUMI-SAN...
Blush
Chapter 13
THAT'S INCREDI-BLE...
Heh heh heh...

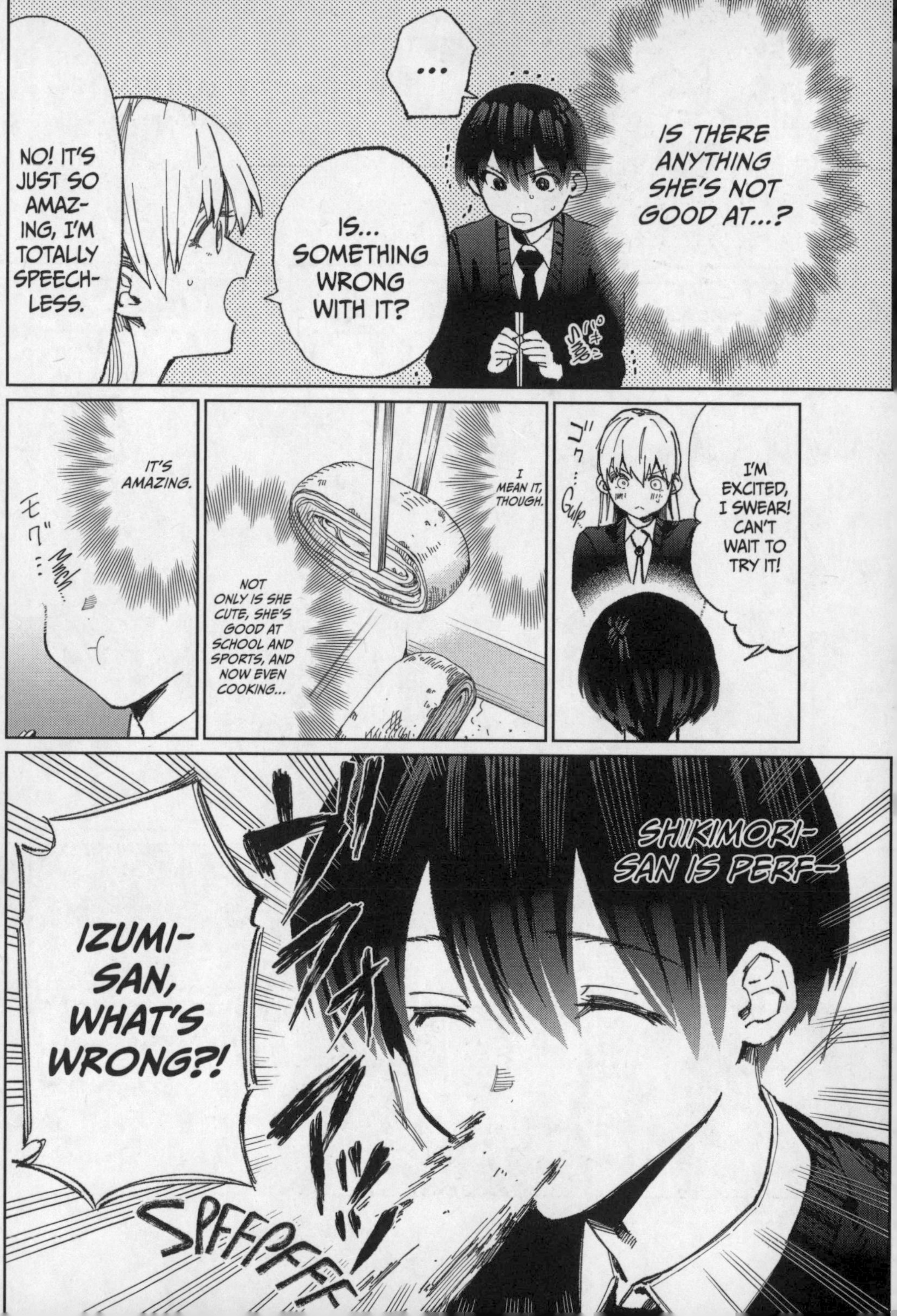
IS THERE ANYTHING SHE'S NOT GOOD AT...?
...
IS... SOMETHING WRONG WITH IT?
NO! IT'S JUST SO AMAZ-ING, I'M TOTALLY SPEECH-LESS.
Gulp
I'M EXCITED, I SWEAR! CAN'T WAIT TO TRY IT!
I MEAN IT, THOUGH.
NOT ONLY IS SHE CUTE, SHE'S GOOD AT SCHOOL AND SPORTS, AND NOW EVEN COOKING...
IT'S AMAZING.
Munch
SHIKIMORI-SAN IS PERF—
IZUMI-SAN, WHAT'S WRONG?!
SPFFPFFF

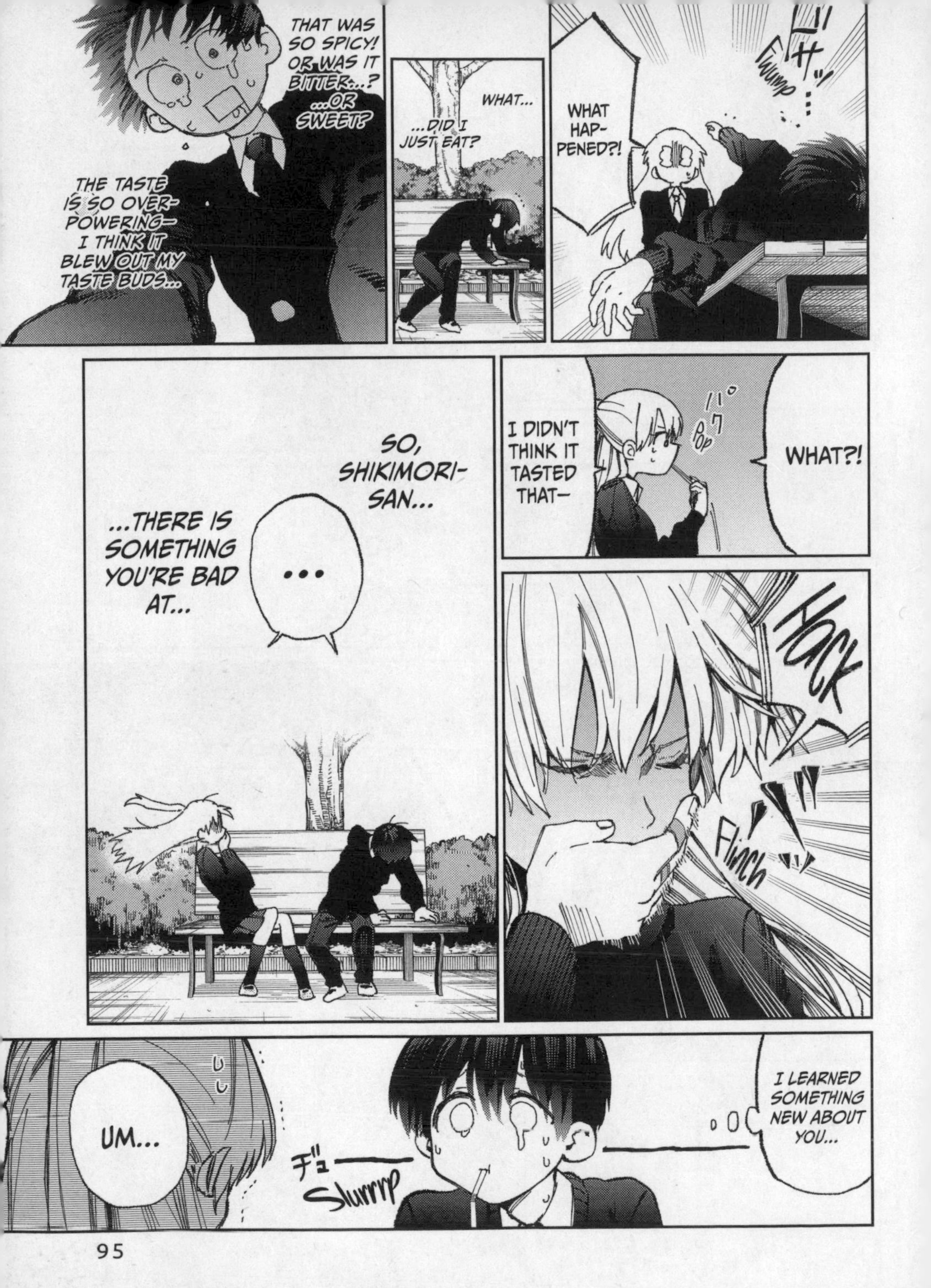
ピシャッ
Fwump
WHAT HAP-PENED?!
WHAT...
...DID I JUST EAT?
THAT WAS SO SPICY! OR WAS IT BITTER...? ...OR SWEET?
THE TASTE IS SO OVER-POWERING— I THINK IT BLEW OUT MY TASTE BUDS...
WHAT?!
パク
Pop
I DIDN'T THINK IT TASTED THAT—
HACK
Flinch
SO, SHIKIMORI-SAN...
...
...THERE IS SOMETHING YOU'RE BAD AT...
I LEARNED SOMETHING NEW ABOUT YOU...
ジュー
Slurrrp
UM...

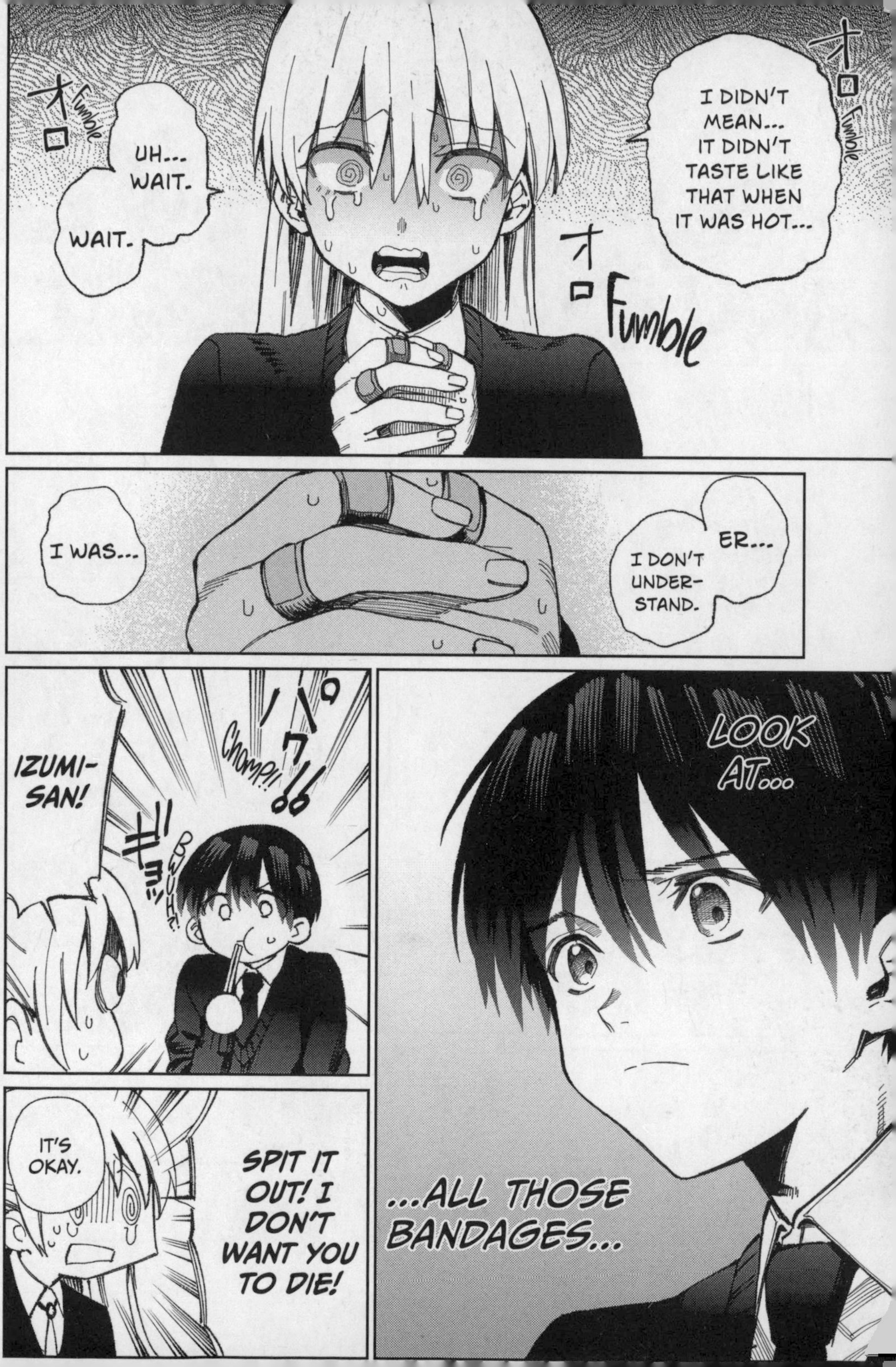

オロ Fumble
I DIDN'T MEAN... IT DIDN'T TASTE LIKE THAT WHEN IT WAS HOT...
オロ Fumble
UH... WAIT.
WAIT.
オロ Fumble
ER... I DON'T UNDER-STAND.
I WAS...
LOOK AT...
...ALL THOSE BANDAGES...
パクッ Chomp!!
ギョッ BWUH?!
IZUMI-SAN!
SPIT IT OUT! I DON'T WANT YOU TO DIE!
IT'S OKAY.

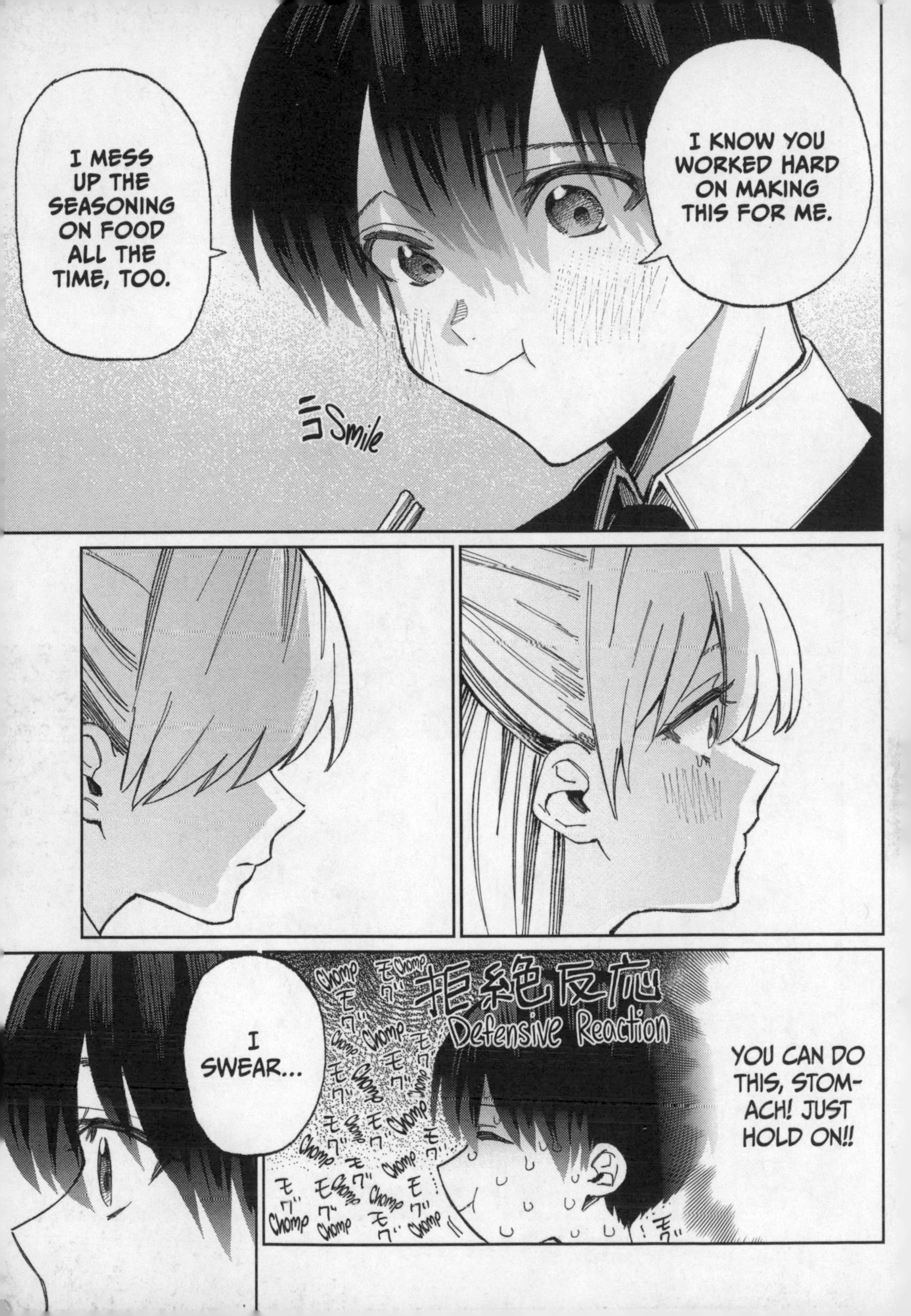
I KNOW YOU WORKED HARD ON MAKING THIS FOR ME.
I MESS UP THE SEASONING ON FOOD ALL THE TIME, TOO.
ニコ Smile
YOU CAN DO THIS, STOMACH! JUST HOLD ON!!
拒絶反応
Defensive Reaction
モグ Chomp
モグ Chomp
モグ Chomp
モグ Chomp
モグ Chomp
モグ Chomp
モグ Chomp
モグ Chomp
モグ Chomp
モグ Chomp
モグ
I SWEAR...

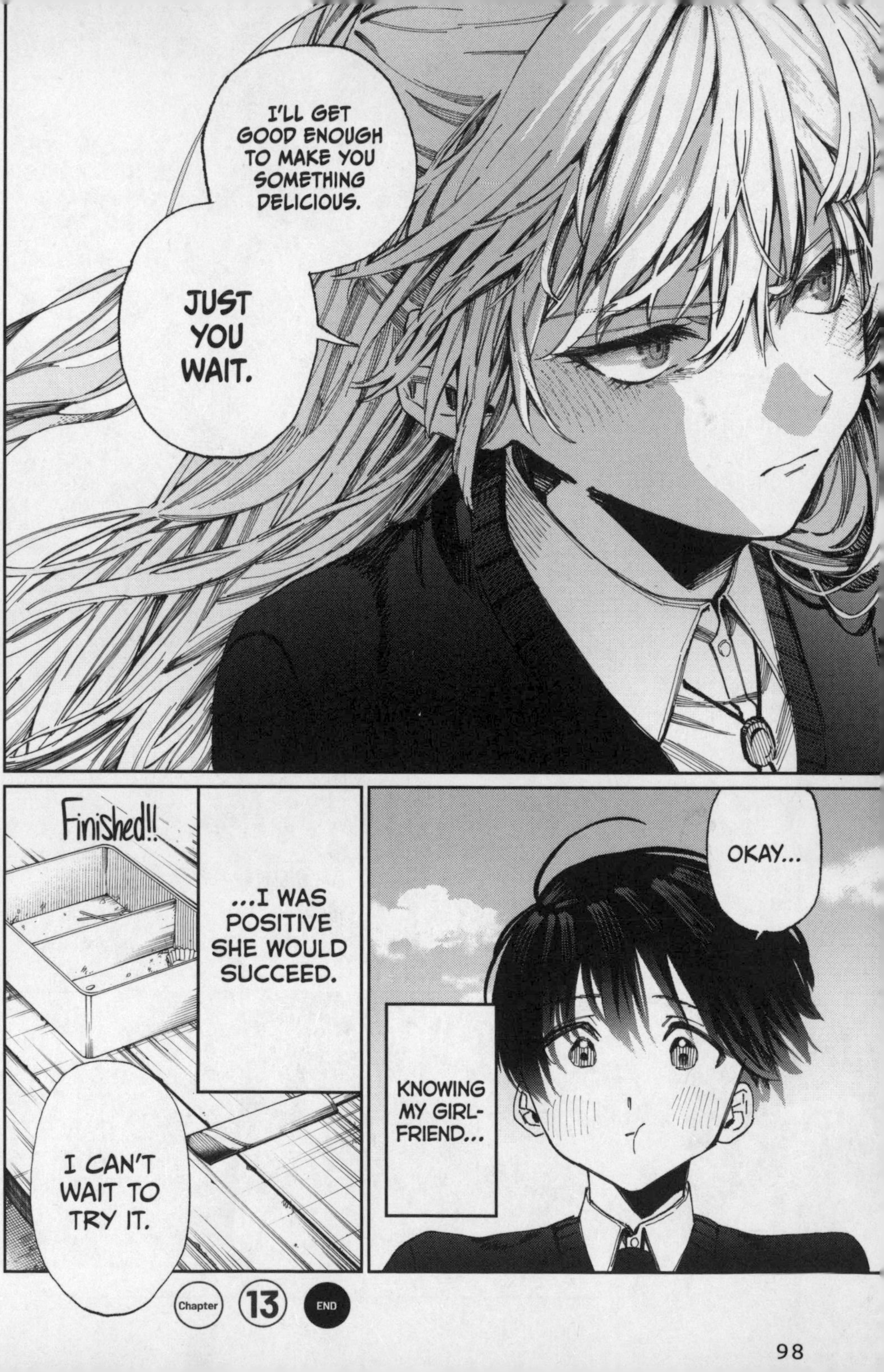
I'LL GET GOOD ENOUGH TO MAKE YOU SOMETHING DELICIOUS.
JUST YOU WAIT.
OKAY...
KNOWING MY GIRL-FRIEND...
...I WAS POSITIVE SHE WOULD SUCCEED.
Finished!!
I CAN'T WAIT TO TRY IT.

Chapter 13 END

"To taste"?
What does that
even mean...?

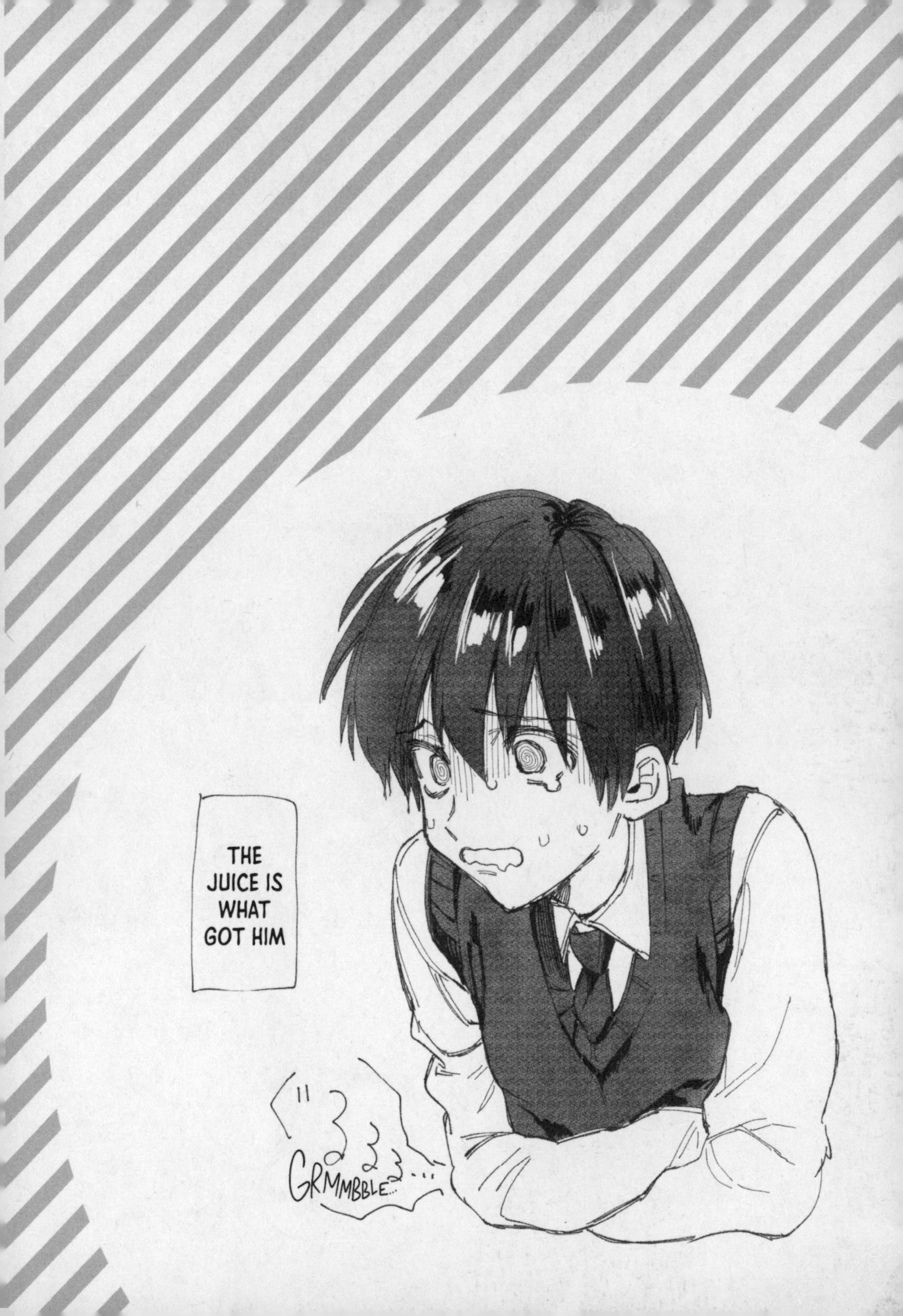
THE JUICE IS WHAT GOT HIM
GRMMBBLE...

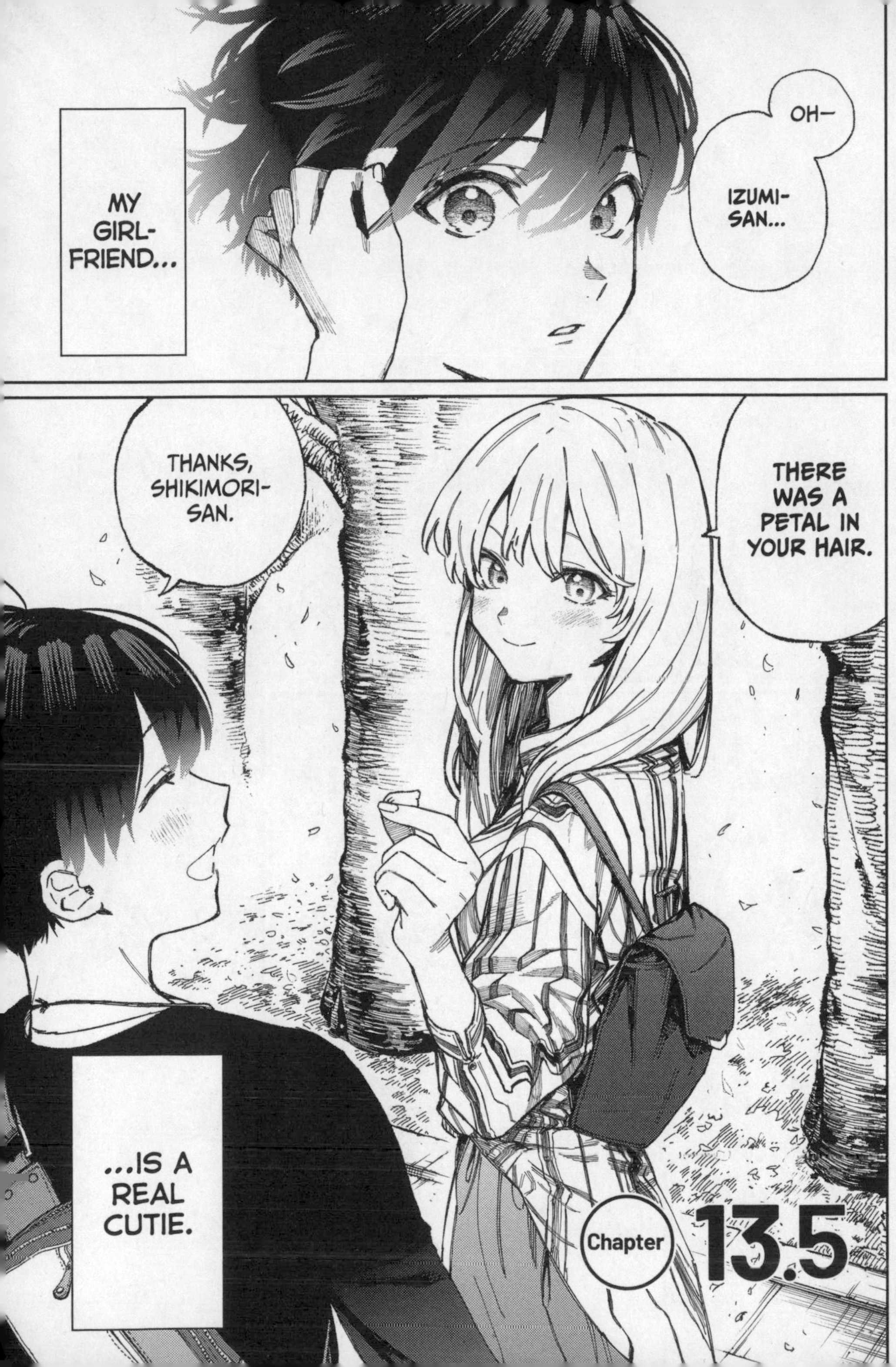
OH—
IZUMI-SAN...
MY GIRL-FRIEND...
THERE WAS A PETAL IN YOUR HAIR.
THANKS, SHIKIMORI-SAN.
...IS A REAL CUTIE.
Chapter 13.5

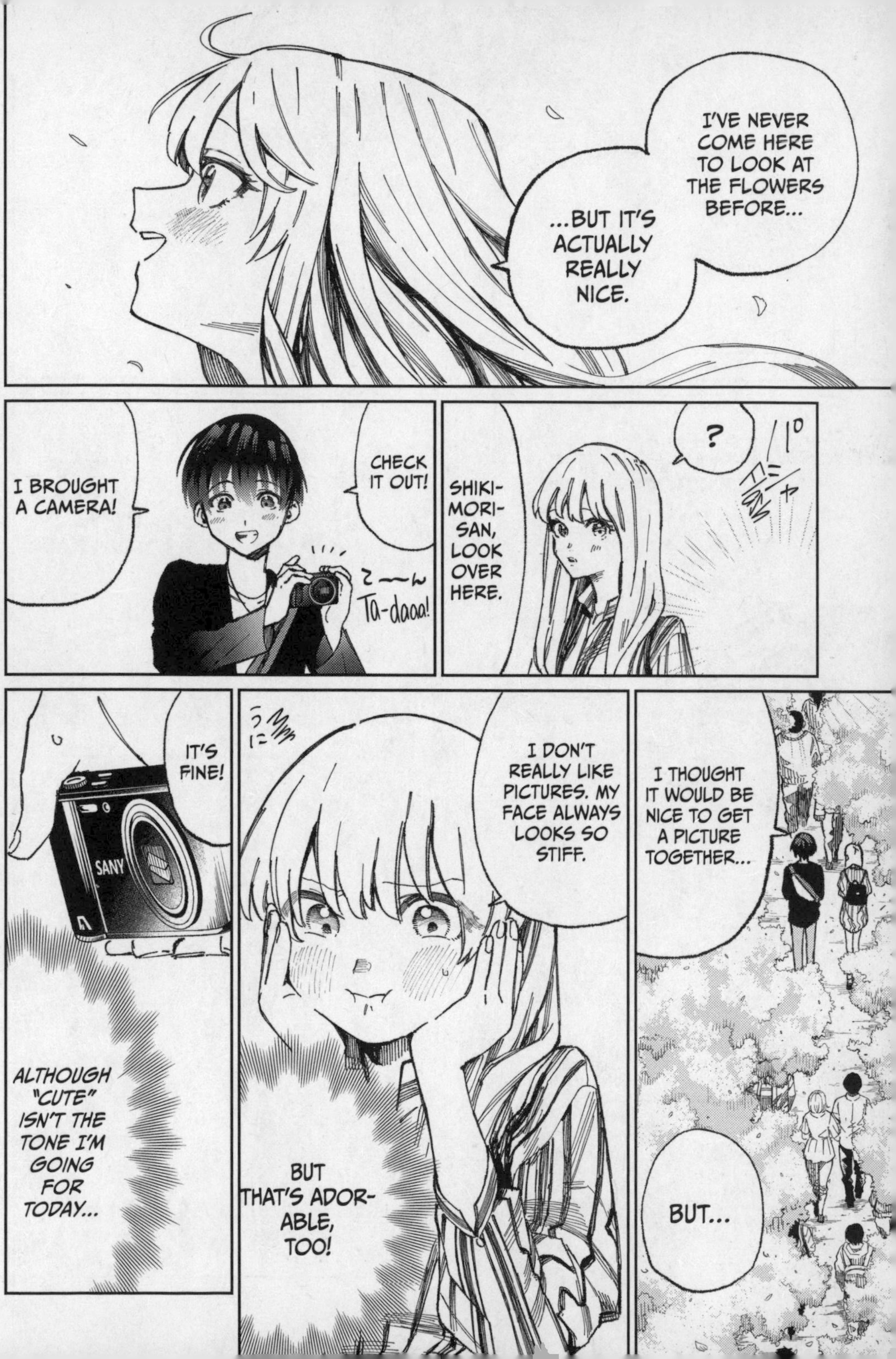
I'VE NEVER COME HERE TO LOOK AT THE FLOWERS BEFORE...
...BUT IT'S ACTUALLY REALLY NICE.
?
パ
FLASH
SHIKI-MORI-SAN, LOOK OVER HERE.
CHECK IT OUT!
I BROUGHT A CAMERA!
Ta-daaa!
I THOUGHT IT WOULD BE NICE TO GET A PICTURE TOGETHER...
BUT...
I DON'T REALLY LIKE PICTURES. MY FACE ALWAYS LOOKS SO STIFF.
Mmm
BUT THAT'S ADOR-ABLE, TOO!
IT'S FINE!
SANY
ALTHOUGH "CUTE" ISN'T THE TONE I'M GOING FOR TODAY...

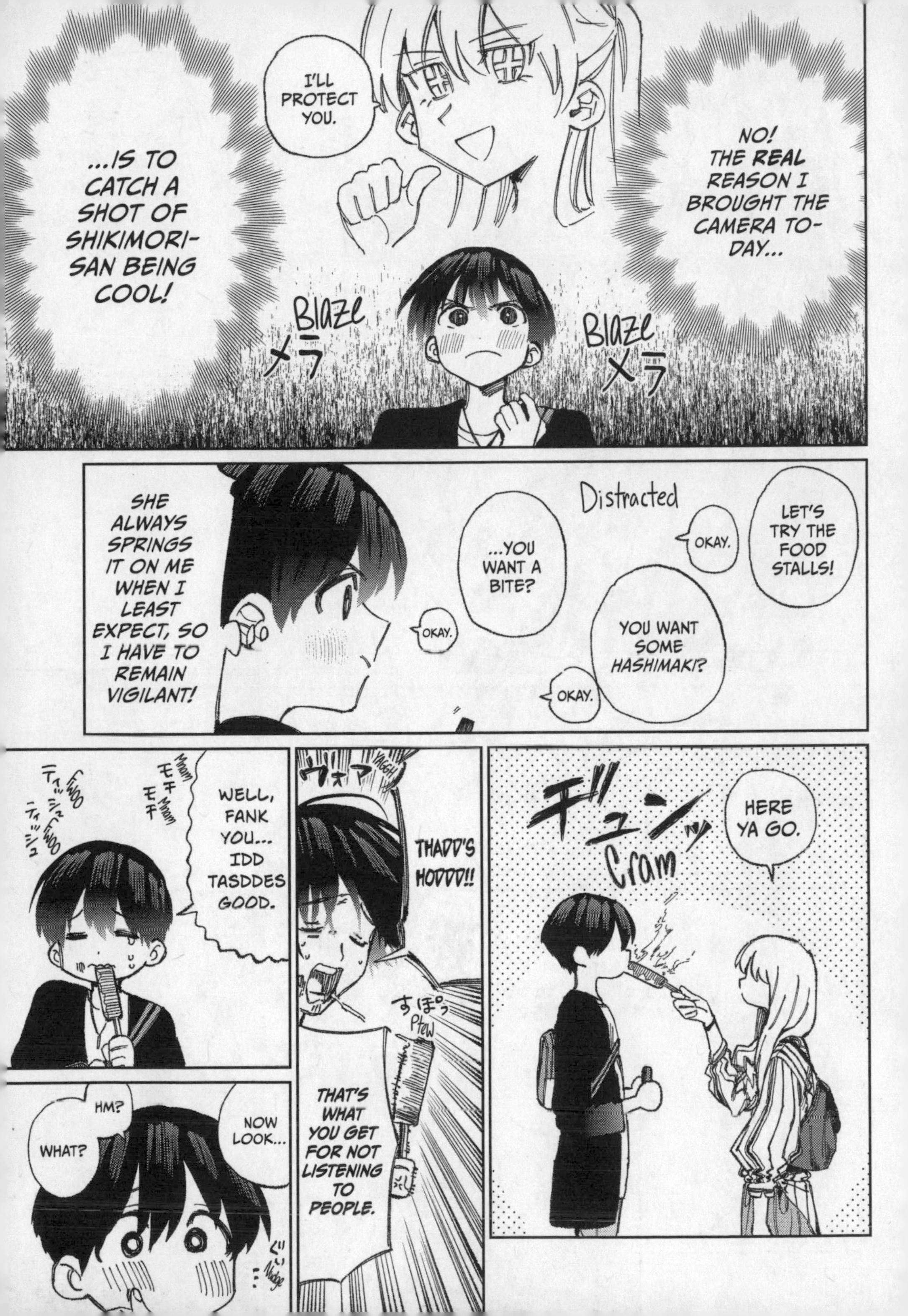
I'LL PROTECT YOU.
NO! THE REAL REASON I BROUGHT THE CAMERA TO-DAY...
...IS TO CATCH A SHOT OF SHIKIMORI-SAN BEING COOL!
Blaze メラ
Blaze メラ
LET'S TRY THE FOOD STALLS!
Distracted
OKAY.
...YOU WANT A BITE?
OKAY.
YOU WANT SOME HASHIMAKI?
OKAY.
SHE ALWAYS SPRINGS IT ON ME WHEN I LEAST EXPECT, SO I HAVE TO REMAIN VIGILANT!
HERE YA GO.
Cram
YAGGH
THADD'S HODDD!!
Ptew
THAT'S WHAT YOU GET FOR NOT LISTENING TO PEOPLE.
Mnom Mnom
Fwoo Fwoo
WELL, FANK YOU... IDD TASDDES GOOD.
NOW LOOK...
HM?
WHAT?
Nudge

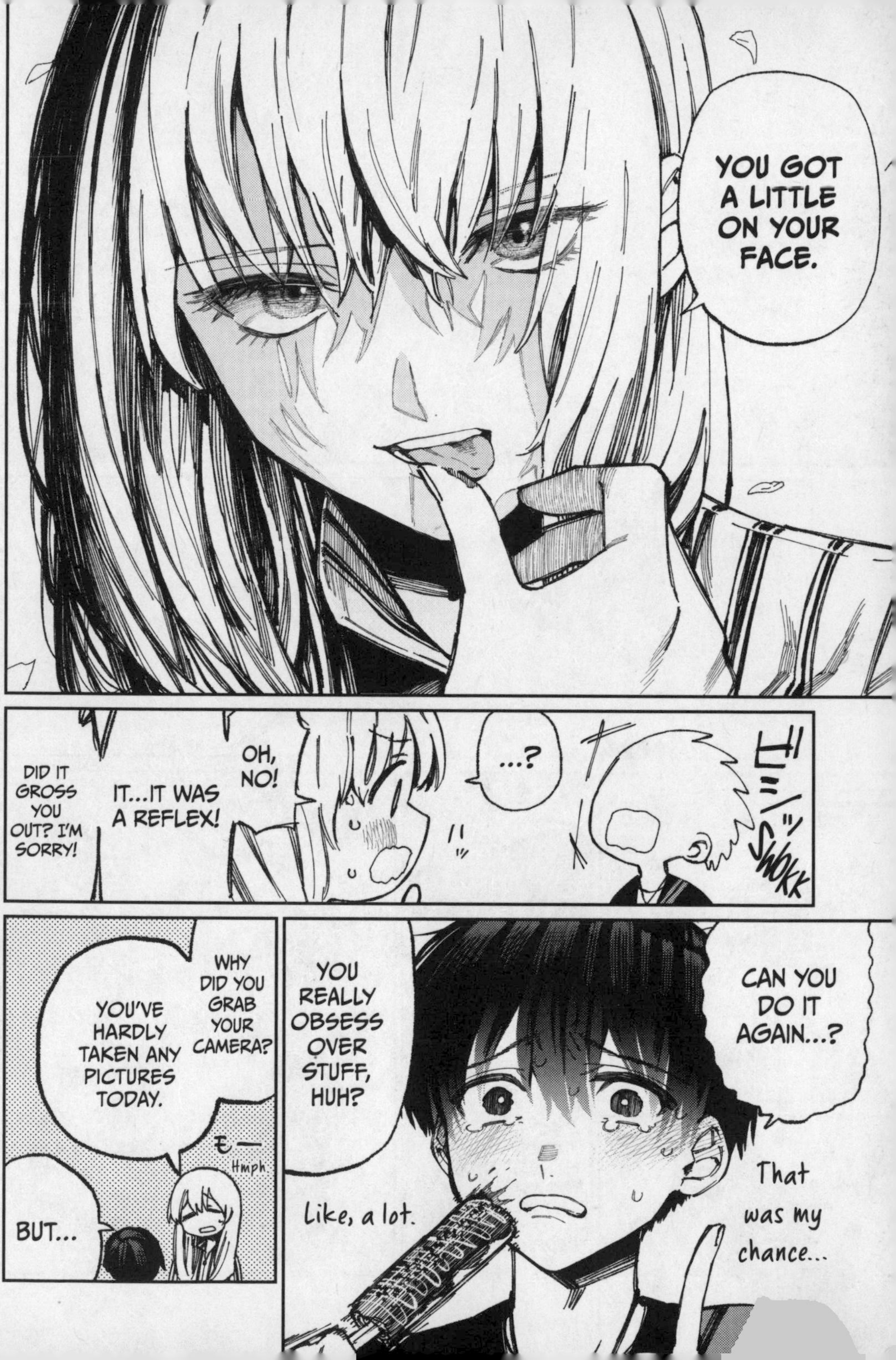
YOU GOT A LITTLE ON YOUR FACE.
SWOKK
...?
OH, NO!
IT...IT WAS A REFLEX!
DID IT GROSS YOU OUT? I'M SORRY!
CAN YOU DO IT AGAIN...?
That was my chance...
YOU REALLY OBSESS OVER STUFF, HUH?
Like, a lot.
WHY DID YOU GRAB YOUR CAMERA?
YOU'VE HARDLY TAKEN ANY PICTURES TODAY.
モー
Hmph
BUT...

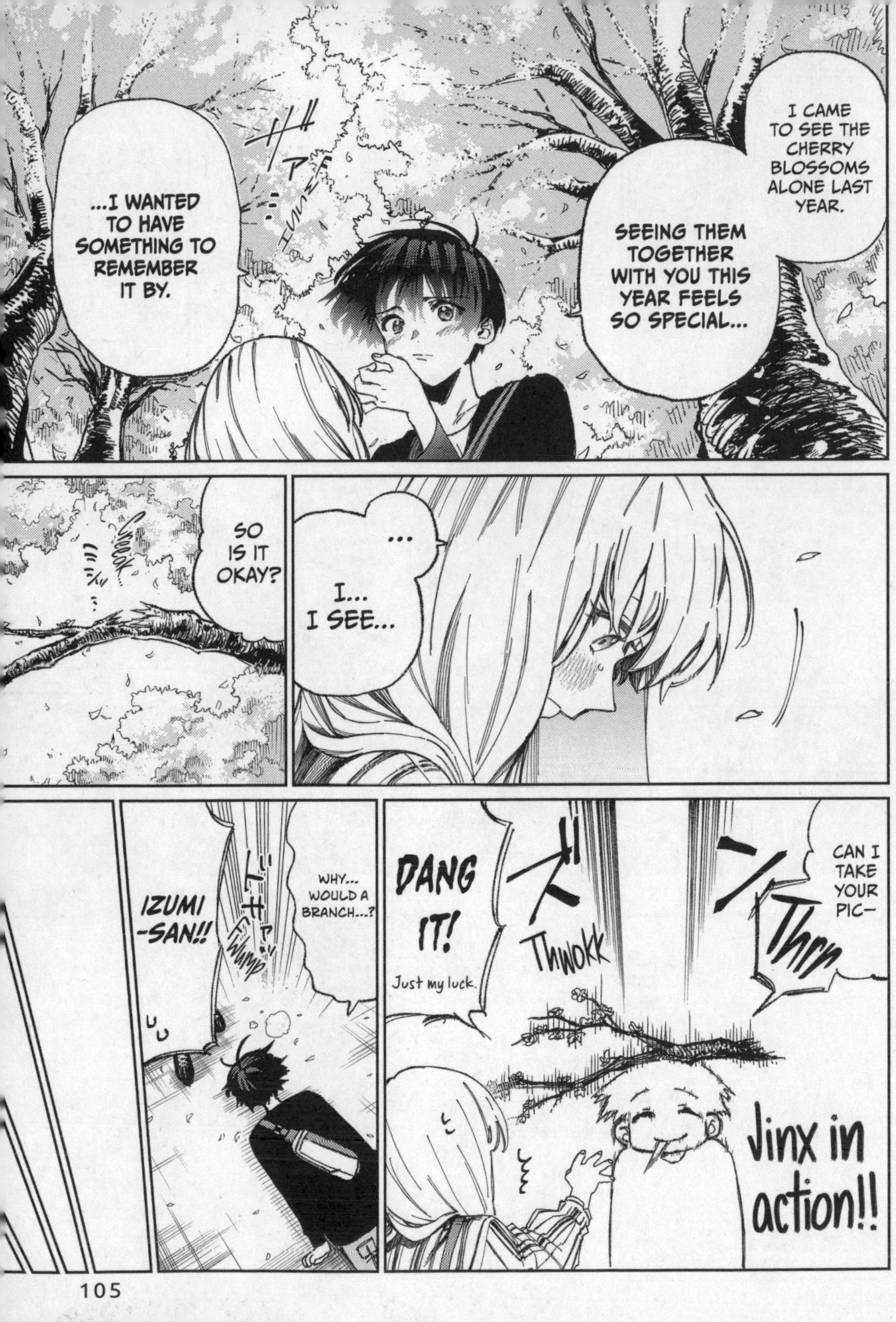
I CAME TO SEE THE CHERRY BLOSSOMS ALONE LAST YEAR.
SEEING THEM TOGETHER WITH YOU THIS YEAR FEELS SO SPECIAL...
...I WANTED TO HAVE SOMETHING TO REMEMBER IT BY.
...
I... I SEE...
SO IS IT OKAY?
Creeak
CAN I TAKE YOUR PIC—
Thrn
Thwokk
DANG IT!
Just my luck.
Jinx in action!!
WHY... WOULD A BRANCH...?
IZUMI-SAN!!
Fwump

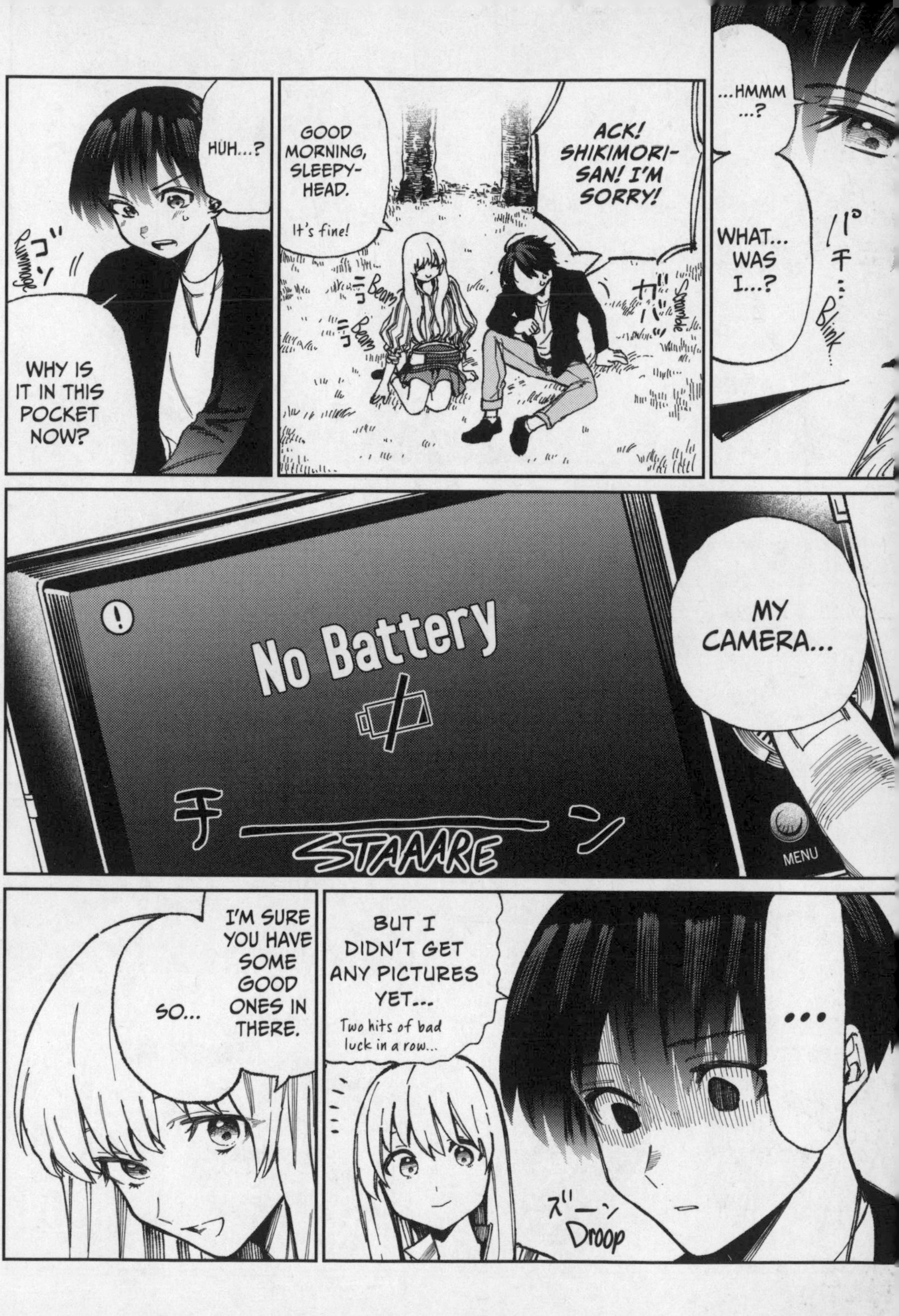
...HMMM ...?
WHAT... WAS I...?
パチ…
Blink
ACK! SHIKIMORI-SAN! I'M SORRY!
ガバッ
Scramble
GOOD MORNING, SLEEPY-HEAD.
It's fine!
ニコ
Beam
ニコ
Beam
HUH...?
WHY IS IT IN THIS POCKET NOW?
ゴソ
Rummage
MY CAMERA...
No Battery
MENU
チーーン
STAARE
...
ズーン
Droop
BUT I DIDN'T GET ANY PICTURES YET...
Two hits of bad luck in a row...
I'M SURE YOU HAVE SOME GOOD ONES IN THERE.
SO...

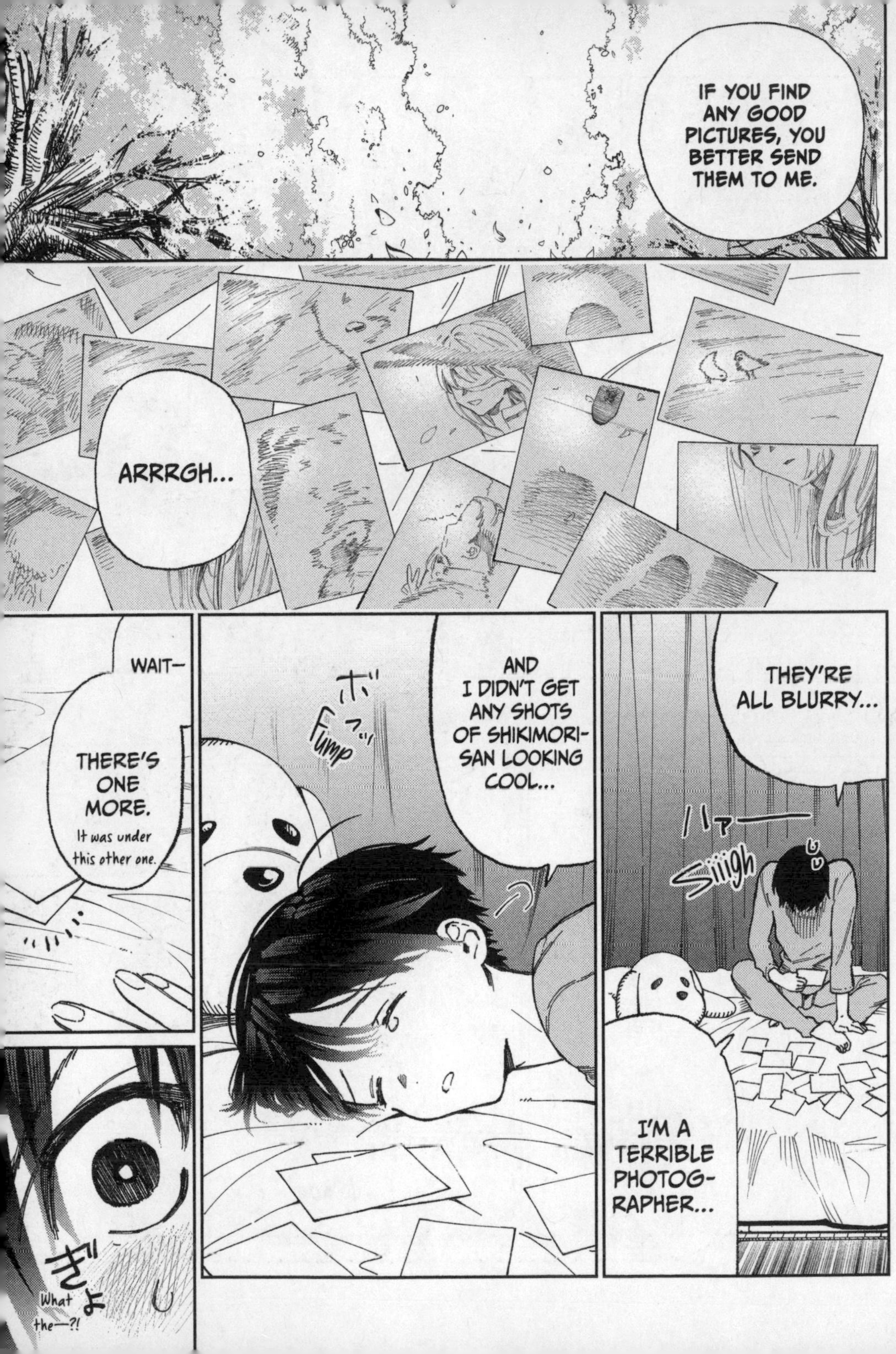
IF YOU FIND ANY GOOD PICTURES, YOU BETTER SEND THEM TO ME.
ARRRGH...
THEY'RE ALL BLURRY...
Siiigh
I'M A TERRIBLE PHOTOGRAPHER...
AND I DIDN'T GET ANY SHOTS OF SHIKIMORI-SAN LOOKING COOL...
Fump
WAIT—
THERE'S ONE MORE.
It was under this other one.
What the—?!

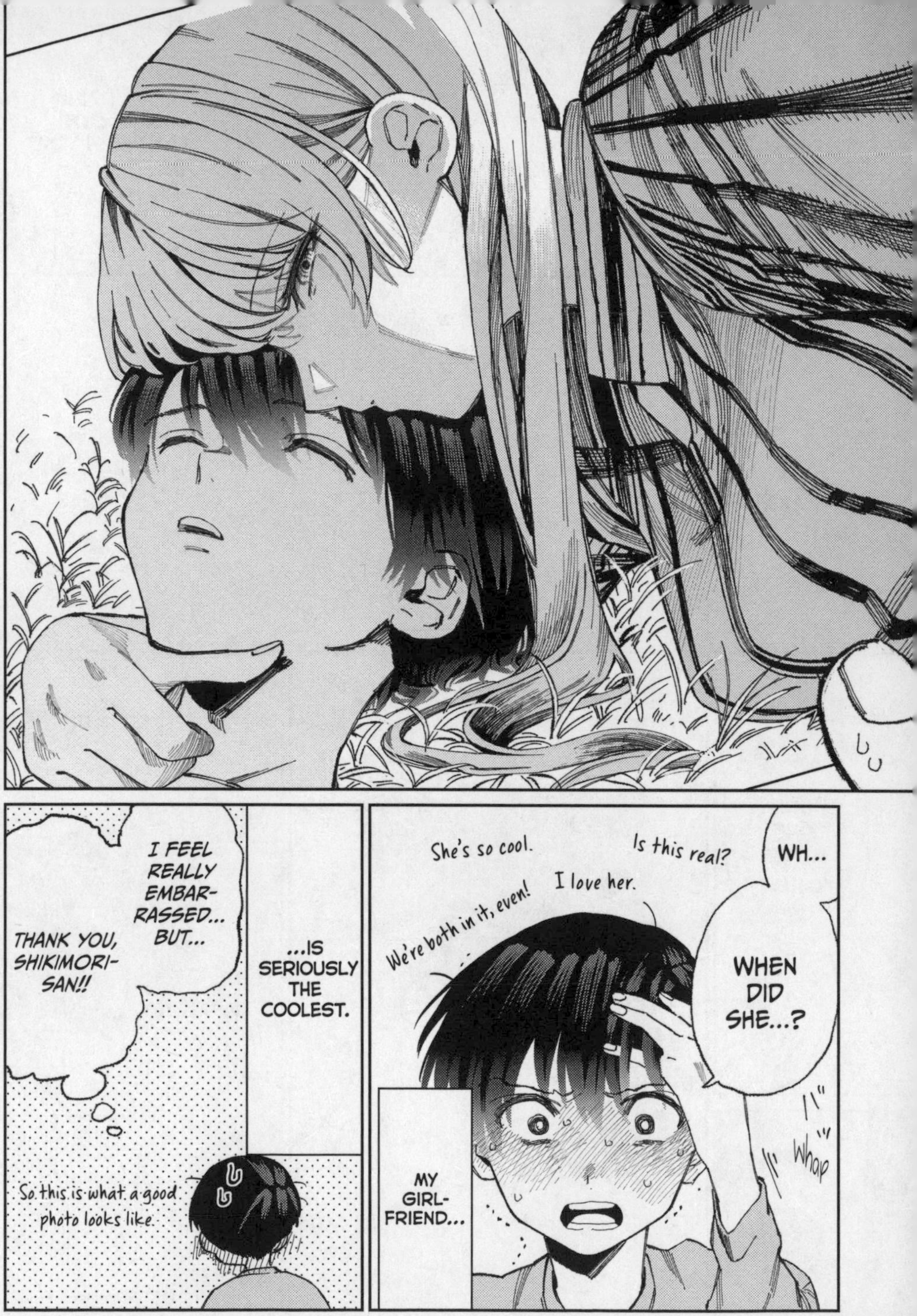
WH...
WHEN DID SHE...?
Is this real?
She's so cool.
I love her.
We're both in it, even!
Whap
MY GIRL-FRIEND...
...IS SERIOUSLY THE COOLEST.
I FEEL REALLY EMBAR-RASSED... BUT...
THANK YOU, SHIKIMORI-SAN!!
So this is what a good photo looks like.

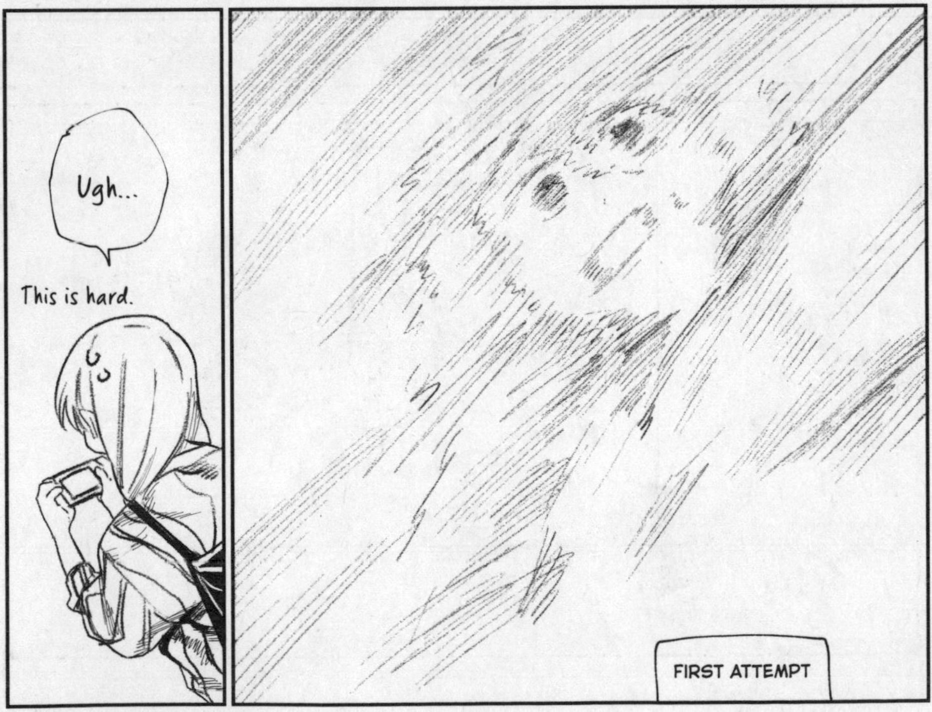
FIRST ATTEMPT
Ugh...
This is hard.

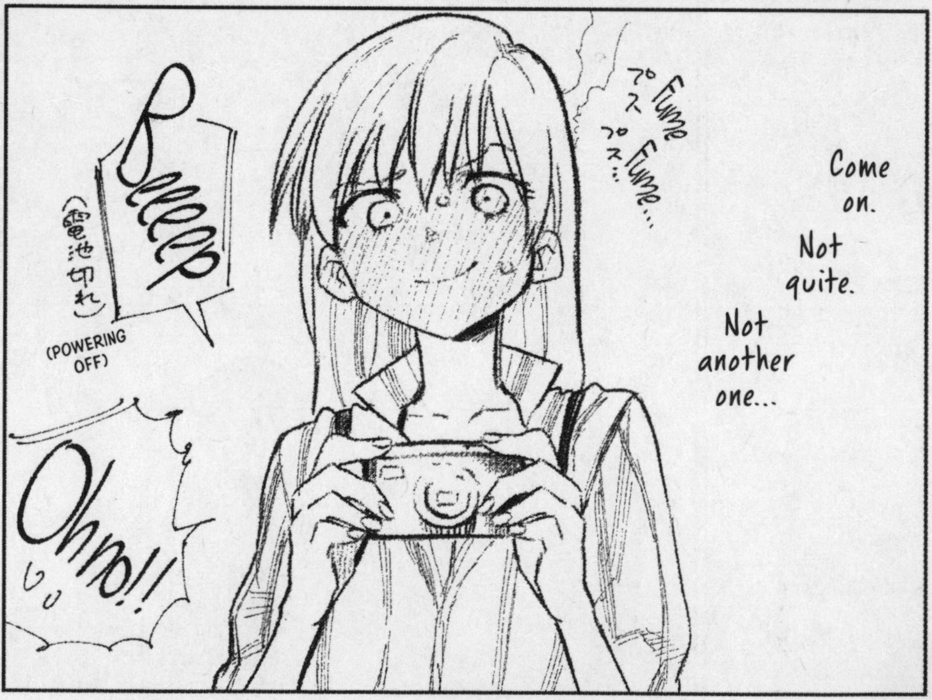
Come on.
Not quite.
Not another one...
プスプス…
Fume Fume...
Beeep
(電池切れ)
(POWERING OFF)
Ohno!!

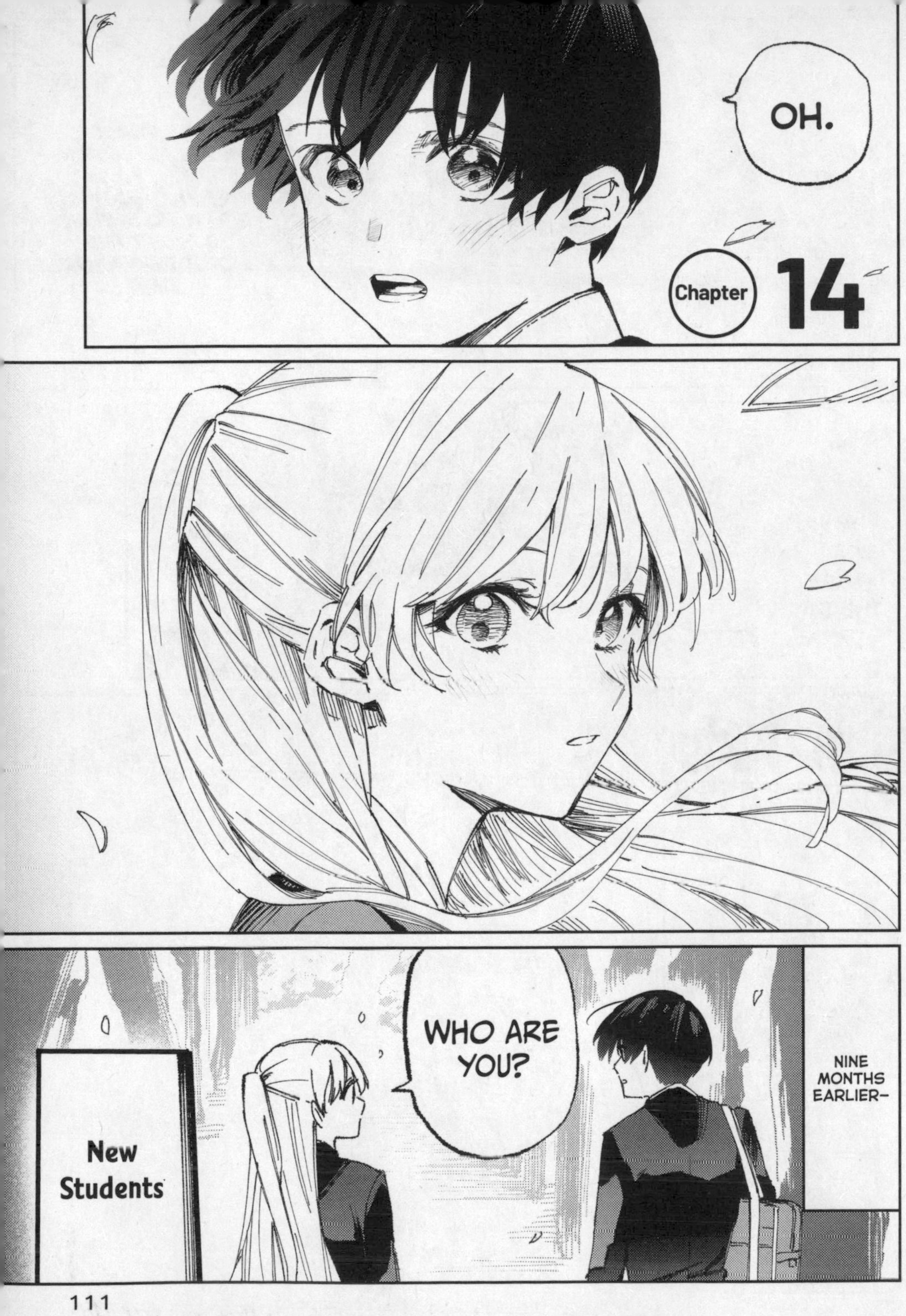
OH.
Chapter 14
NINE MONTHS EARLIER—
WHO ARE YOU?
New Students

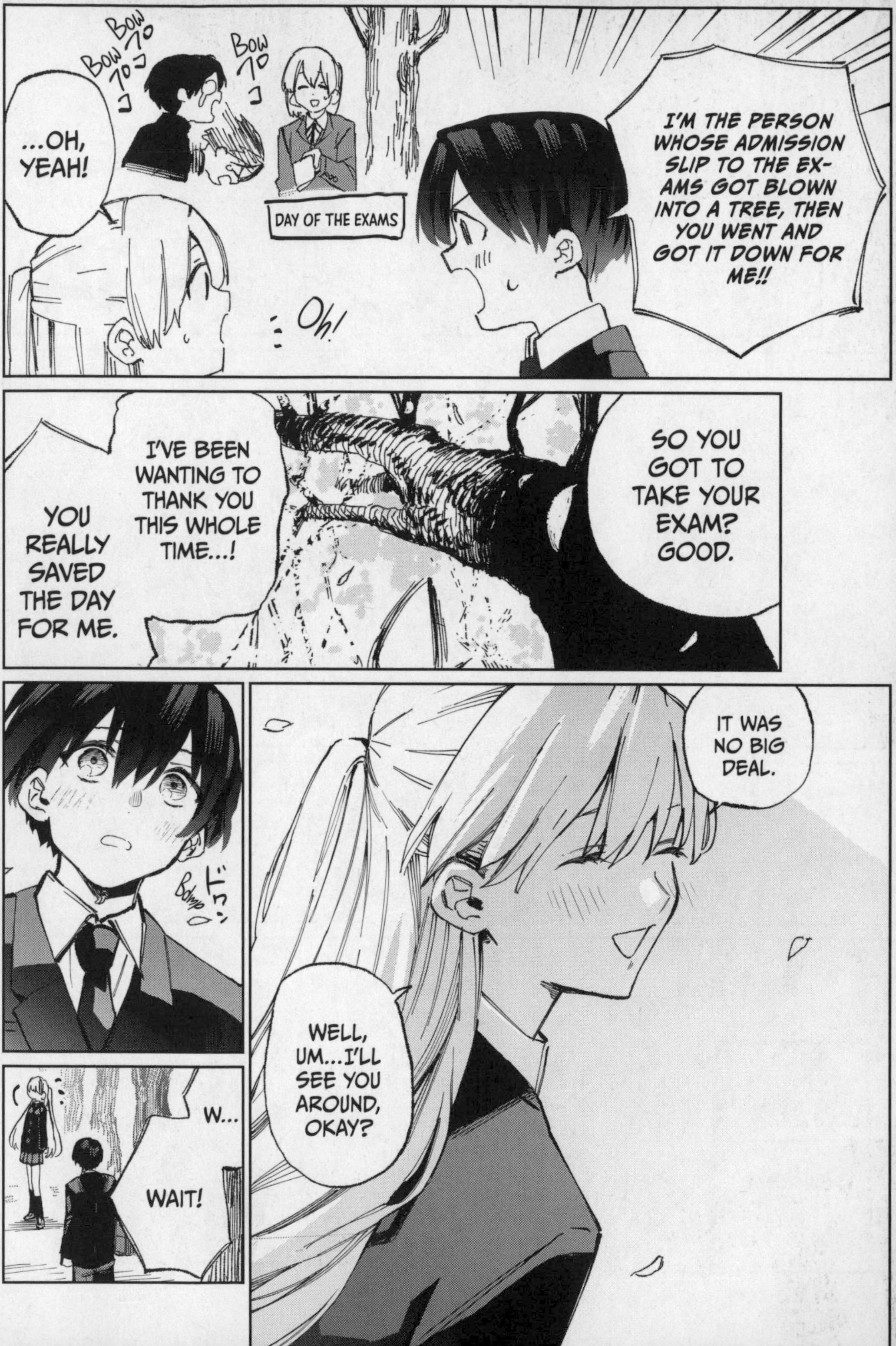
I'M THE PERSON WHOSE ADMISSION SLIP TO THE EX-AMS GOT BLOWN INTO A TREE, THEN YOU WENT AND GOT IT DOWN FOR ME!!
DAY OF THE EXAMS
Bow
Bow Bow
Oh!
...OH, YEAH!
SO YOU GOT TO TAKE YOUR EXAM? GOOD.
I'VE BEEN WANTING TO THANK YOU THIS WHOLE TIME...!
YOU REALLY SAVED THE DAY FOR ME.
IT WAS NO BIG DEAL.
WELL, UM...I'LL SEE YOU AROUND, OKAY?
W...
WAIT!

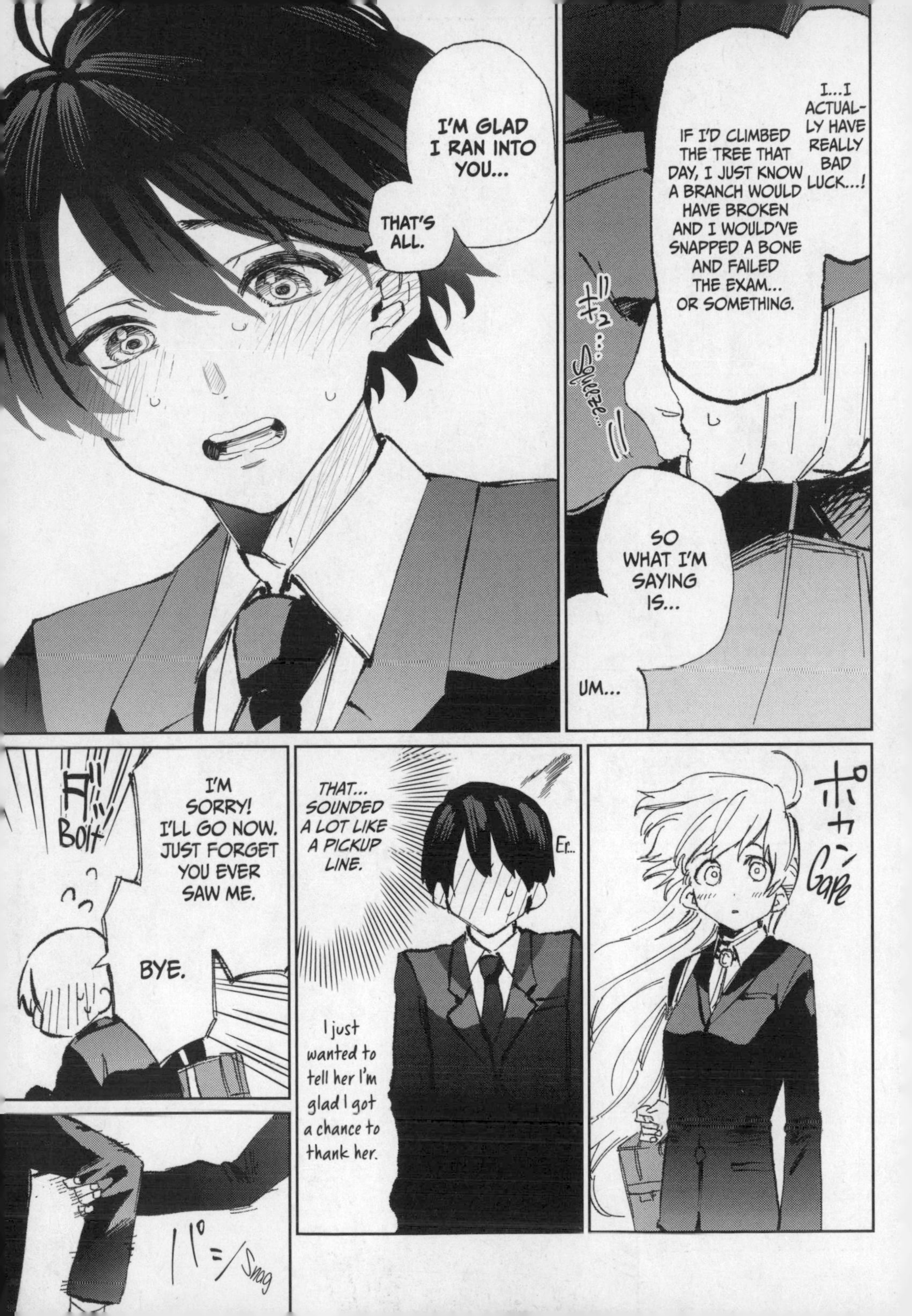
I...I ACTUAL-LY HAVE REALLY BAD LUCK...!
IF I'D CLIMBED THE TREE THAT DAY, I JUST KNOW A BRANCH WOULD HAVE BROKEN AND I WOULD'VE SNAPPED A BONE AND FAILED THE EXAM... OR SOMETHING.
Squeeze...
SO WHAT I'M SAYING IS...
UM...
I'M GLAD I RAN INTO YOU...
THAT'S ALL.
Gape
THAT... SOUNDED A LOT LIKE A PICKUP LINE.
Er...
I just wanted to tell her I'm glad I got a chance to thank her.
I'M SORRY! I'LL GO NOW. JUST FORGET YOU EVER SAW ME.
Bolt
BYE.
Snag

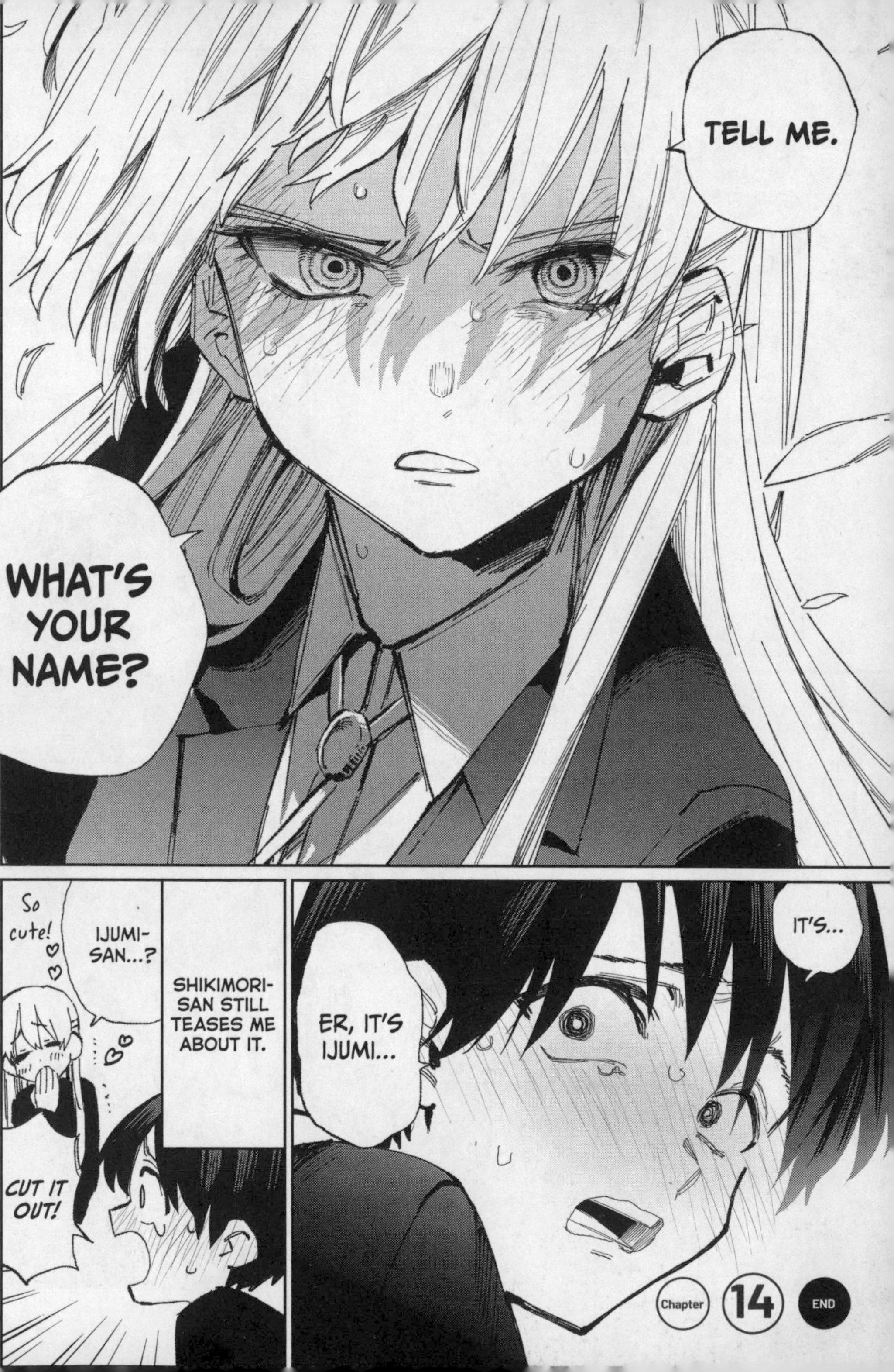
TELL ME.
WHAT'S YOUR NAME?
IT'S...
ER, IT'S IJUMI...
SHIKIMORI-SAN STILL TEASES ME ABOUT IT.
IJUMI-SAN...?
So cute!
CUT IT OUT!
Chapter 14 END

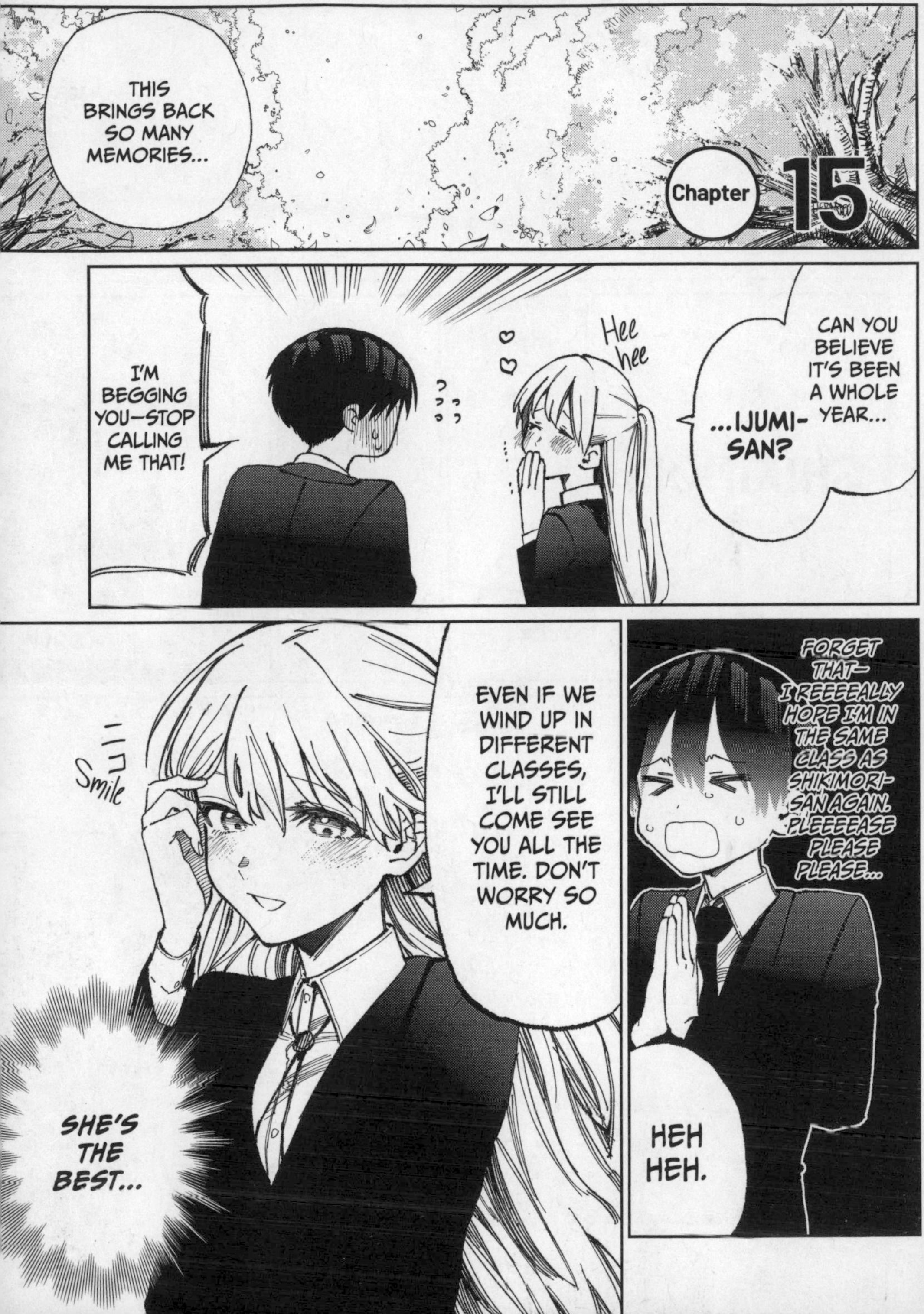
THIS BRINGS BACK SO MANY MEMORIES...
Chapter 15
CAN YOU BELIEVE IT'S BEEN A WHOLE YEAR... ...IJUMI-SAN?
Hee hee
I'M BEGGING YOU—STOP CALLING ME THAT!
FORGET THAT—I REEEEALLY HOPE I'M IN THE SAME CLASS AS SHIKIMORI-SAN AGAIN. PLEEEEASE PLEASE PLEASE...
HEH HEH.
EVEN IF WE WIND UP IN DIFFERENT CLASSES, I'LL STILL COME SEE YOU ALL THE TIME. DON'T WORRY SO MUCH.
Smile
SHE'S THE BEST...

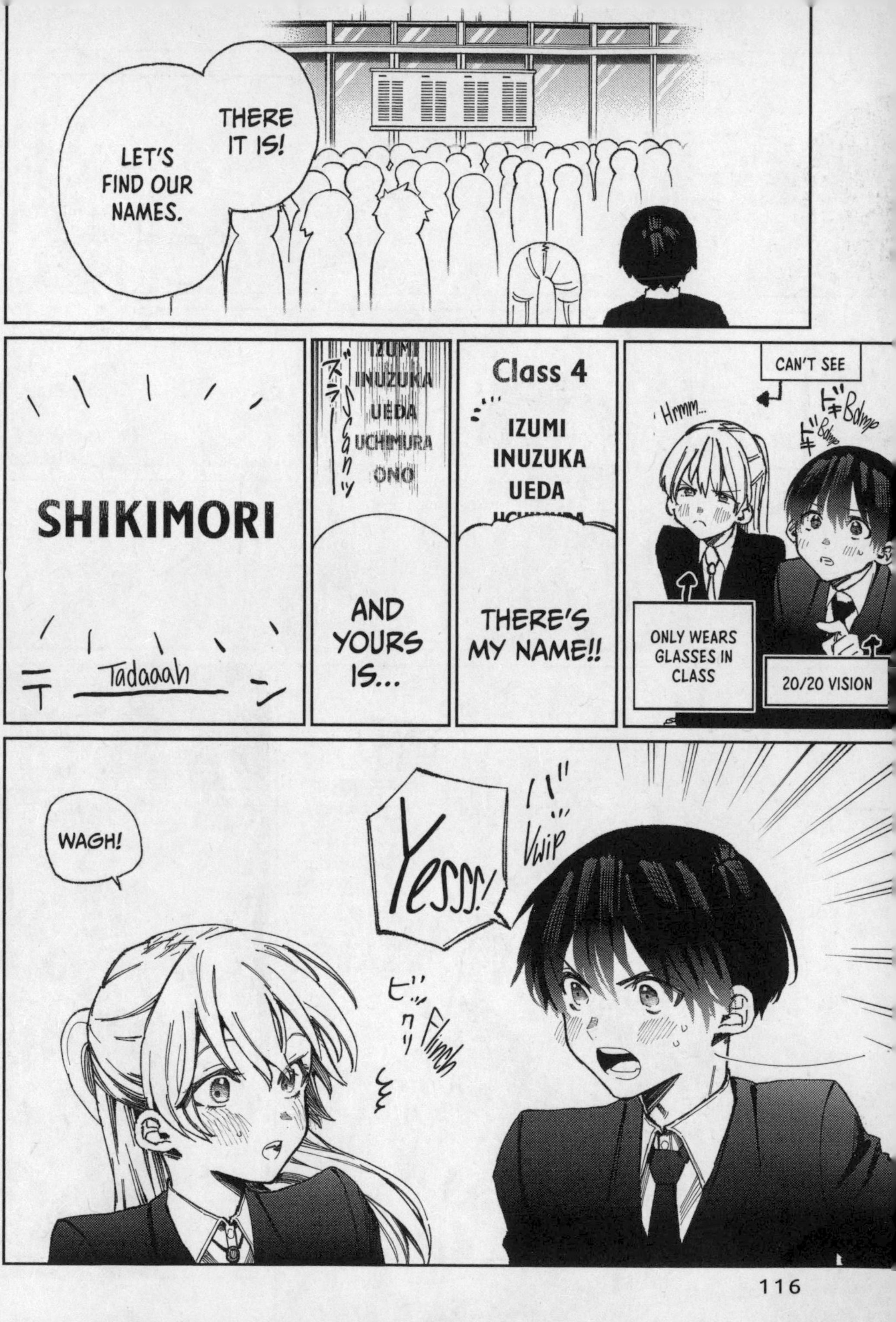
THERE IT IS!
LET'S FIND OUR NAMES.
CAN'T SEE
Bdmp
Bdmp
Hrmm...
20/20 VISION
ONLY WEARS GLASSES IN CLASS
Class 4
IZUMI
INUZUKA
UEDA
THERE'S MY NAME!!
IZUMI
INUZUKA
UEDA
UCHIMURA
ONO
AND YOURS IS...
SHIKIMORI
Tadaaah
Vwip
Yesss!
Flinch
WAGH!

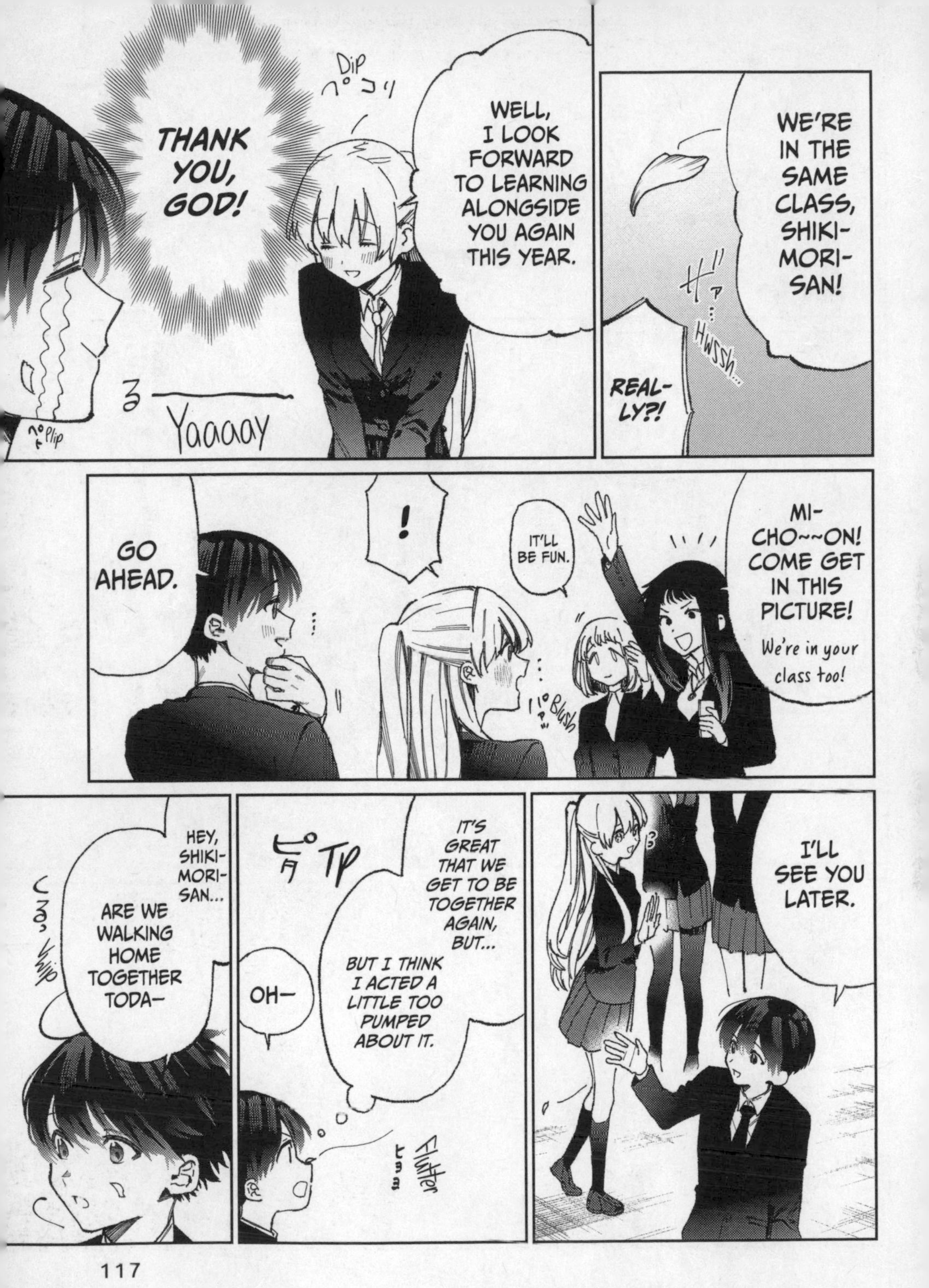
WE'RE IN THE SAME CLASS, SHIKIMORI-SAN!
Hwssh...
REALLY?!
Dip
WELL, I LOOK FORWARD TO LEARNING ALONGSIDE YOU AGAIN THIS YEAR.
THANK YOU, GOD!
Yaaaay
Plip
MI-CHO~~ON! COME GET IN THIS PICTURE!
We're in your class too!
IT'LL BE FUN.
!
Blush
GO AHEAD.
I'LL SEE YOU LATER.
IT'S GREAT THAT WE GET TO BE TOGETHER AGAIN, BUT...
Tip
BUT I THINK I ACTED A LITTLE TOO PUMPED ABOUT IT.
OH—
Flutter
HEY, SHIKIMORI-SAN...
ARE WE WALKING HOME TOGETHER TODA—
Whip

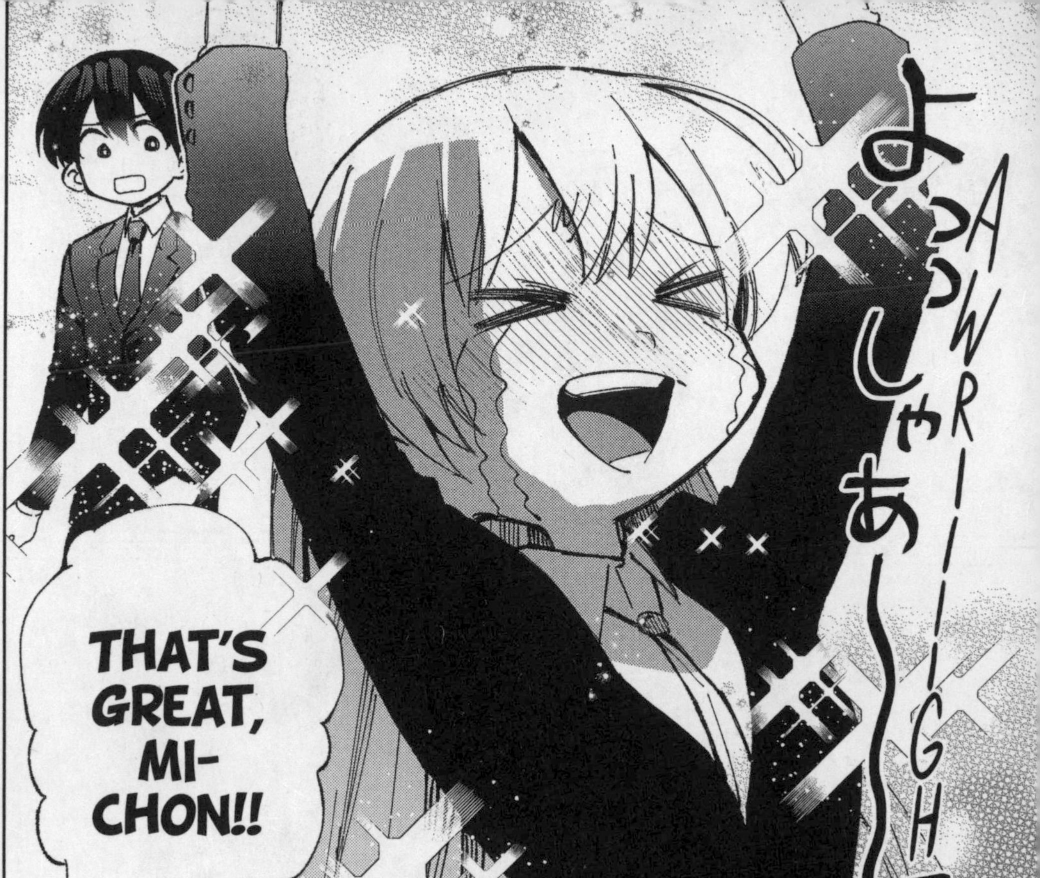
よっしゃあ～
AWRI-I-IGHT
THAT'S GREAT, MI-CHON!!
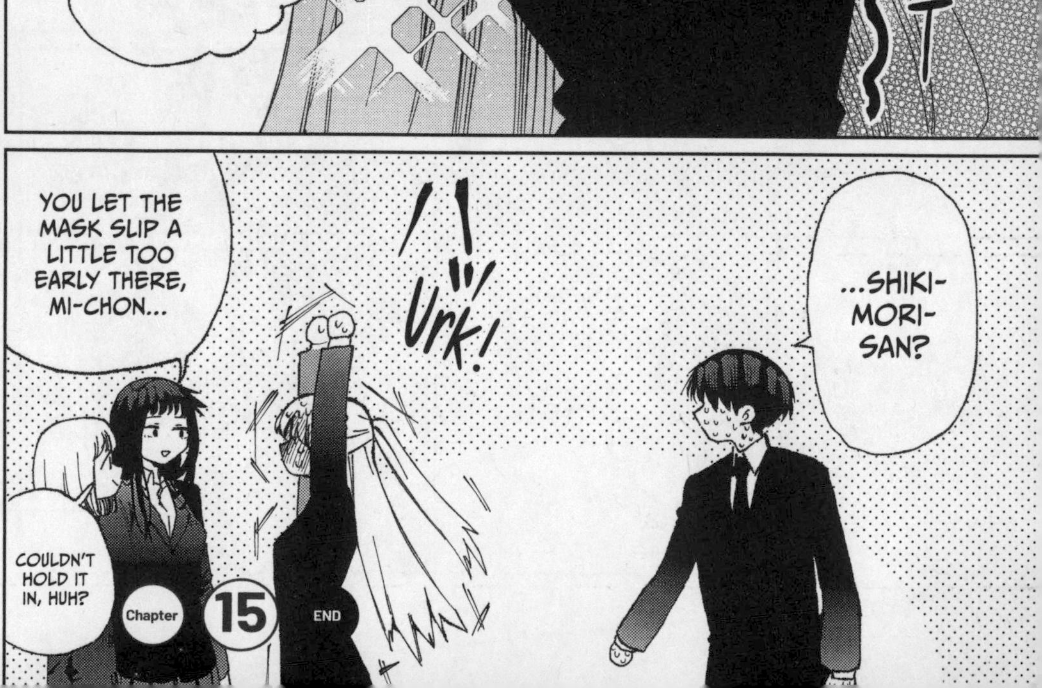
...SHIKI-MORI-SAN?
Urk!
YOU LET THE MASK SLIP A LITTLE TOO EARLY THERE, MI-CHON...
COULDN'T HOLD IT IN, HUH?
Chapter 15 END

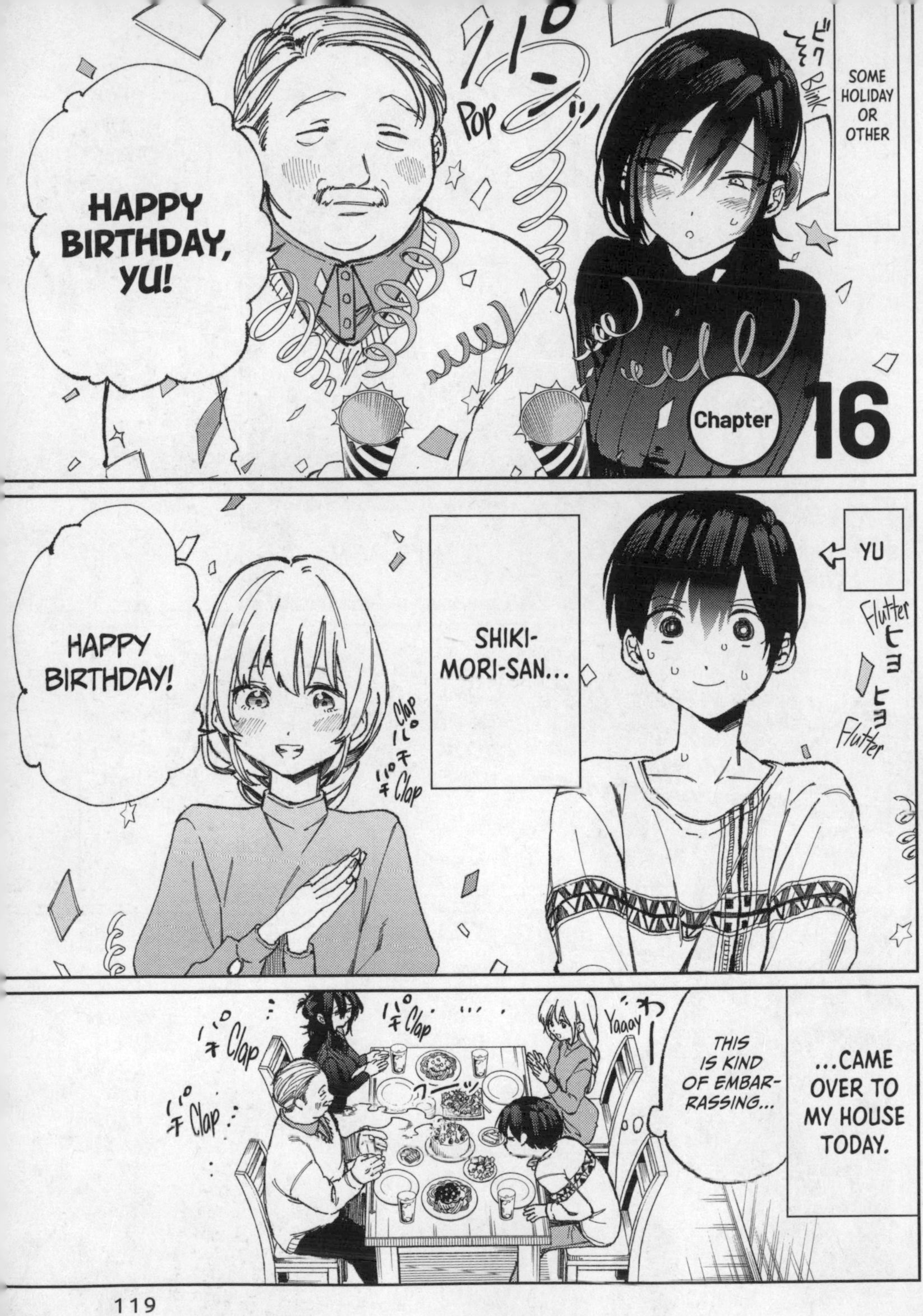

SOME HOLIDAY OR OTHER
Blink
Pop
Chapter 16
HAPPY BIRTHDAY, YU!
YU
Flutter
Flutter
SHIKI-MORI-SAN...
Clap
Clap
HAPPY BIRTHDAY!
...CAME OVER TO MY HOUSE TODAY.
THIS IS KIND OF EMBARRASSING...
Yaaay
Clap
Clap
Clap

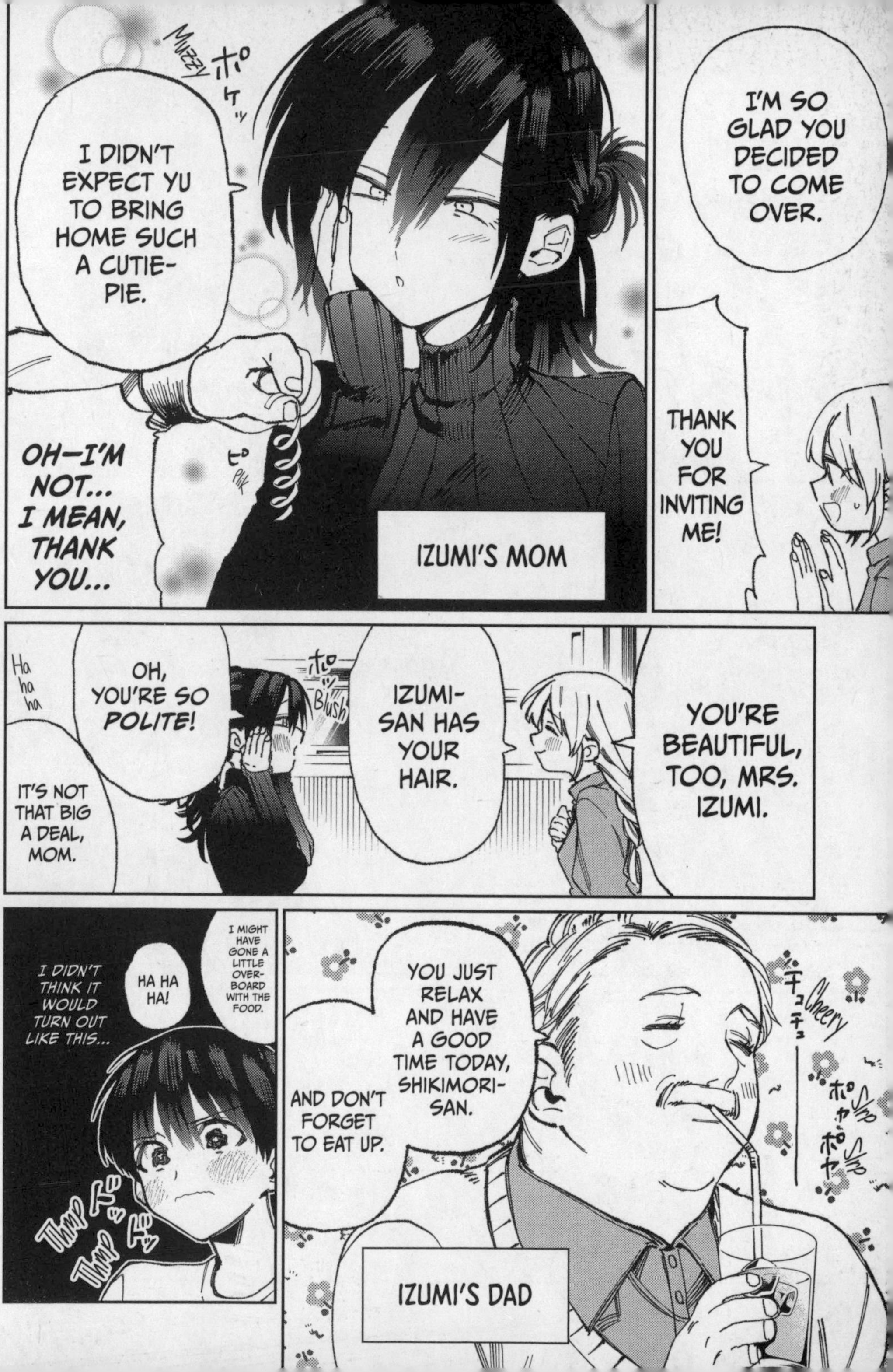
I'M SO GLAD YOU DECIDED TO COME OVER.
THANK YOU FOR INVITING ME!
Muzzy
I DIDN'T EXPECT YU TO BRING HOME SUCH A CUTIE-PIE.
IZUMI'S MOM
Plik
OH—I'M NOT... I MEAN, THANK YOU...
YOU'RE BEAUTIFUL, TOO, MRS. IZUMI.
IZUMI-SAN HAS YOUR HAIR.
Blush
OH, YOU'RE SO POLITE!
Ha ha ha
IT'S NOT THAT BIG A DEAL, MOM.
Cheery
Slrp Slrp
YOU JUST RELAX AND HAVE A GOOD TIME TODAY, SHIKIMORI-SAN.
AND DON'T FORGET TO EAT UP.
IZUMI'S DAD
I MIGHT HAVE GONE A LITTLE OVERBOARD WITH THE FOOD.
HA HA HA!
I DIDN'T THINK IT WOULD TURN OUT LIKE THIS...
Thmp Thmp

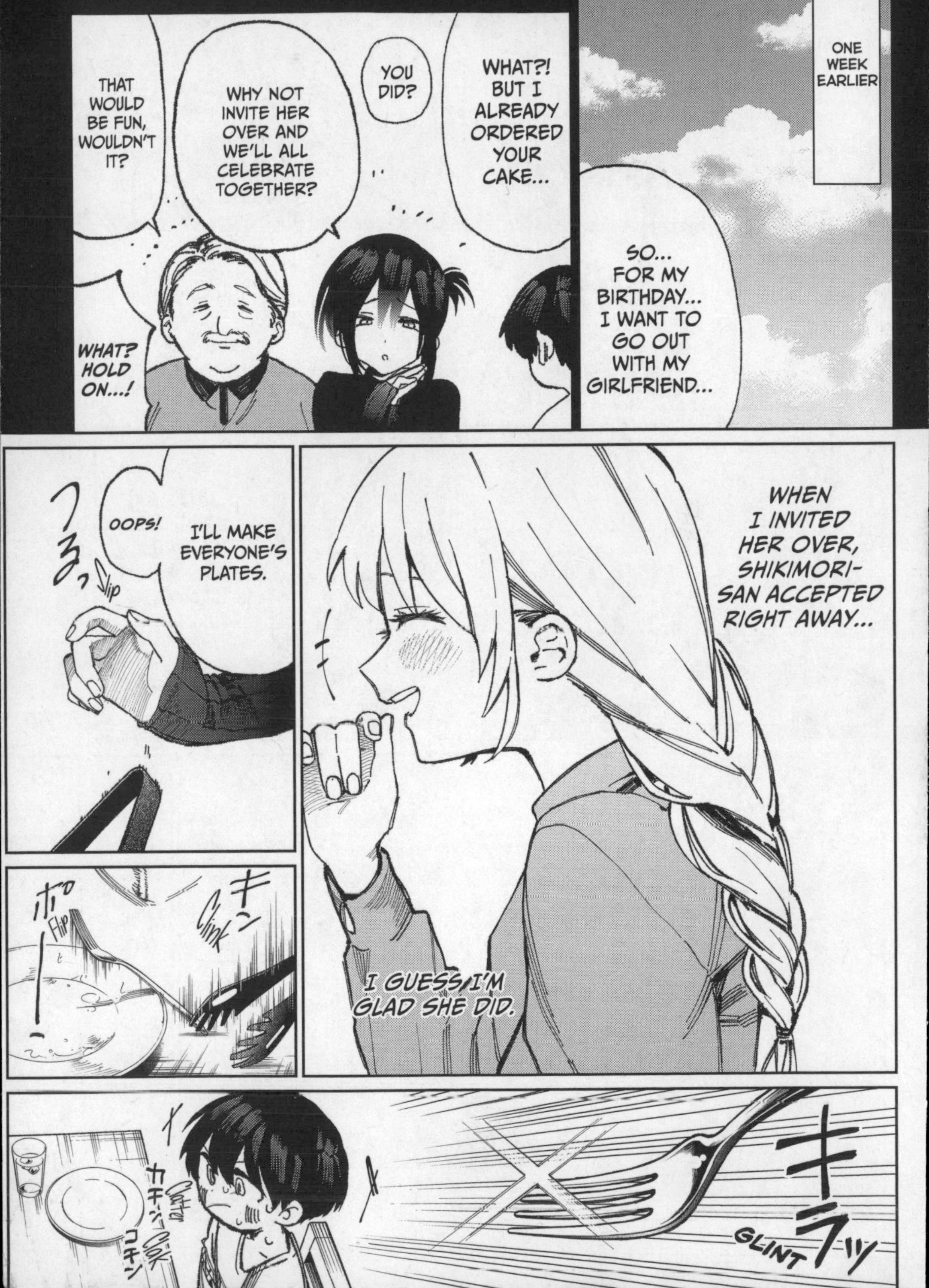

ONE WEEK EARLIER
SO... FOR MY BIRTHDAY... I WANT TO GO OUT WITH MY GIRLFRIEND...
WHAT?! BUT I ALREADY ORDERED YOUR CAKE...
YOU DID?
WHY NOT INVITE HER OVER AND WE'LL ALL CELEBRATE TOGETHER?
THAT WOULD BE FUN, WOULDN'T IT?
WHAT? HOLD ON...!
WHEN I INVITED HER OVER, SHIKIMORI-SAN ACCEPTED RIGHT AWAY...
I GUESS I'M GLAD SHE DID.
OOPS!
I'LL MAKE EVERYONE'S PLATES.
Slip
Clink
Flip
GLINT
Clatter
Clak

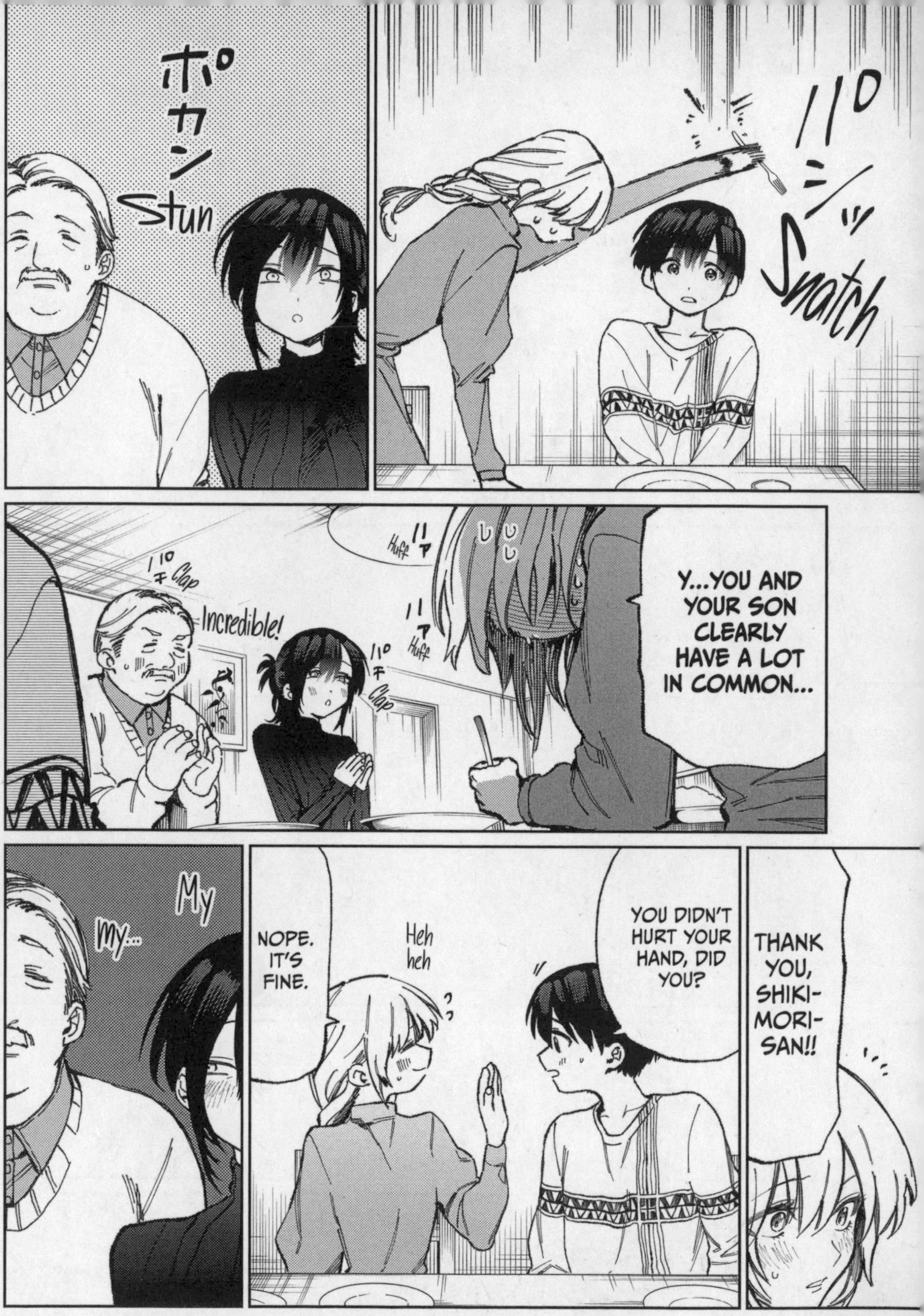

パシッ
Snatch
ポカン
Stun
Y...YOU AND YOUR SON CLEARLY HAVE A LOT IN COMMON...
ハァ Huff
ハァ Huff
パチ Clap
Incredible!
パチ Clap
THANK YOU, SHIKI-MORI-SAN!!
YOU DIDN'T HURT YOUR HAND, DID YOU?
NOPE. IT'S FINE.
Heh heh
My my...

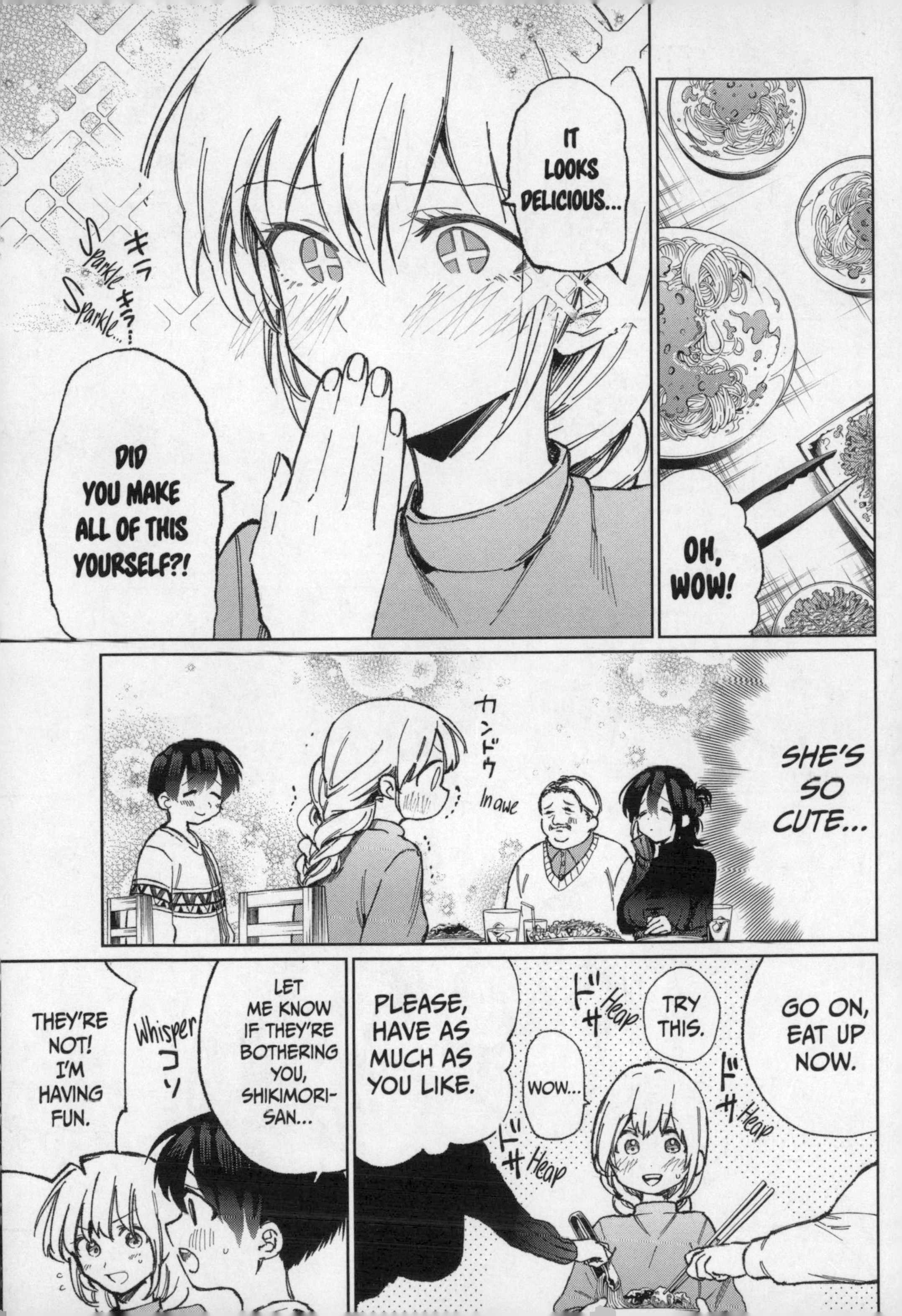

OH, WOW!
IT LOOKS DELICIOUS...
キラ Sparkle
キラ Sparkle...
DID YOU MAKE ALL OF THIS YOURSELF?!
SHE'S SO CUTE...
カンドウ In awe
GO ON, EAT UP NOW.
TRY THIS.
ドサ Heap
ドサ Heap
WOW...
ドサ Heap
PLEASE, HAVE AS MUCH AS YOU LIKE.
LET ME KNOW IF THEY'RE BOTHERING YOU, SHIKIMORI-SAN...
Whisper コソ
THEY'RE NOT! I'M HAVING FUN.

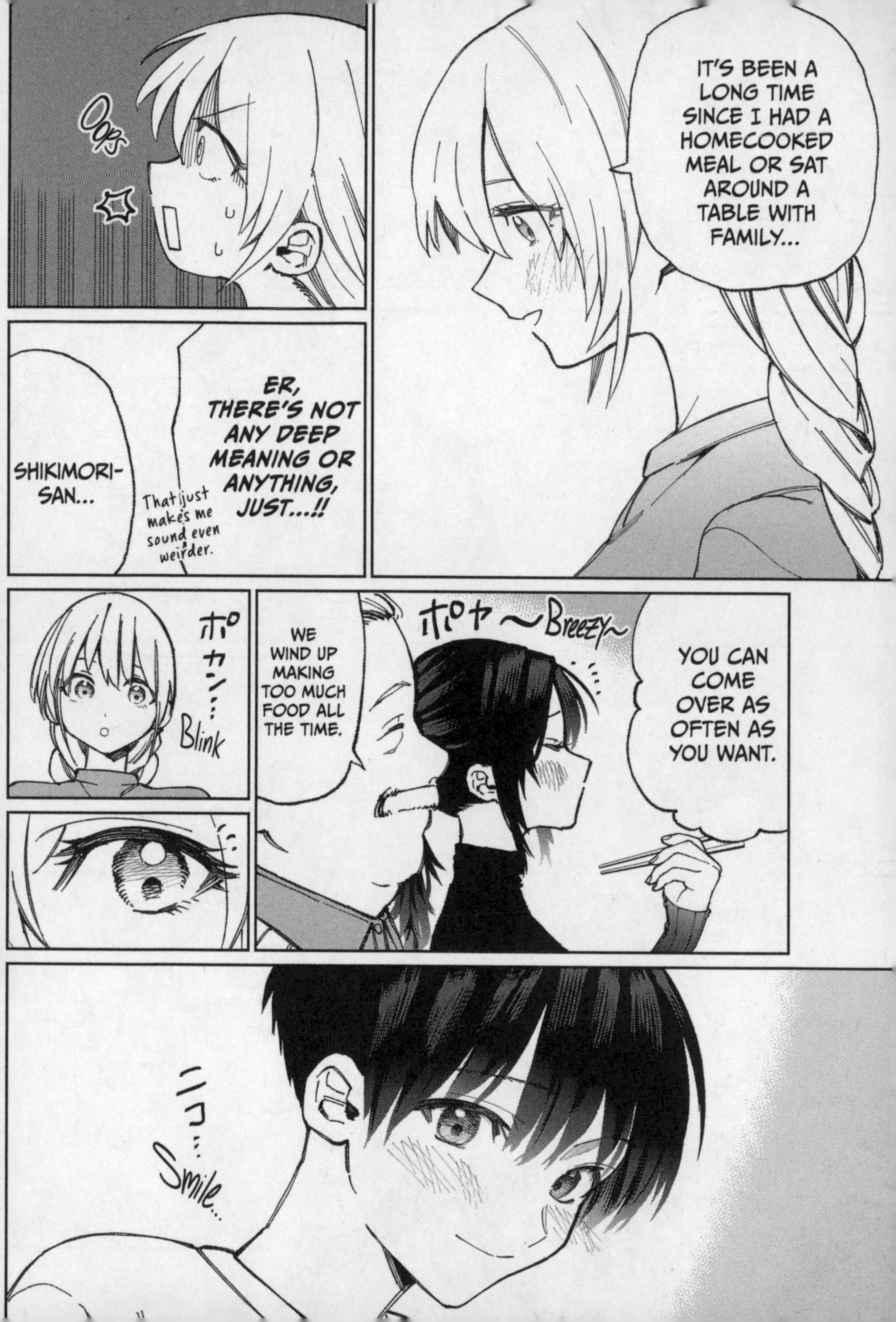
IT'S BEEN A LONG TIME SINCE I HAD A HOMECOOKED MEAL OR SAT AROUND A TABLE WITH FAMILY...
Oops
ER, THERE'S NOT ANY DEEP MEANING OR ANYTHING, JUST...!!
That just makes me sound even weirder.
SHIKIMORI-SAN...
Breezy~
YOU CAN COME OVER AS OFTEN AS YOU WANT.
WE WIND UP MAKING TOO MUCH FOOD ALL THE TIME.
ポカン... Blink
ニコ... Smile...

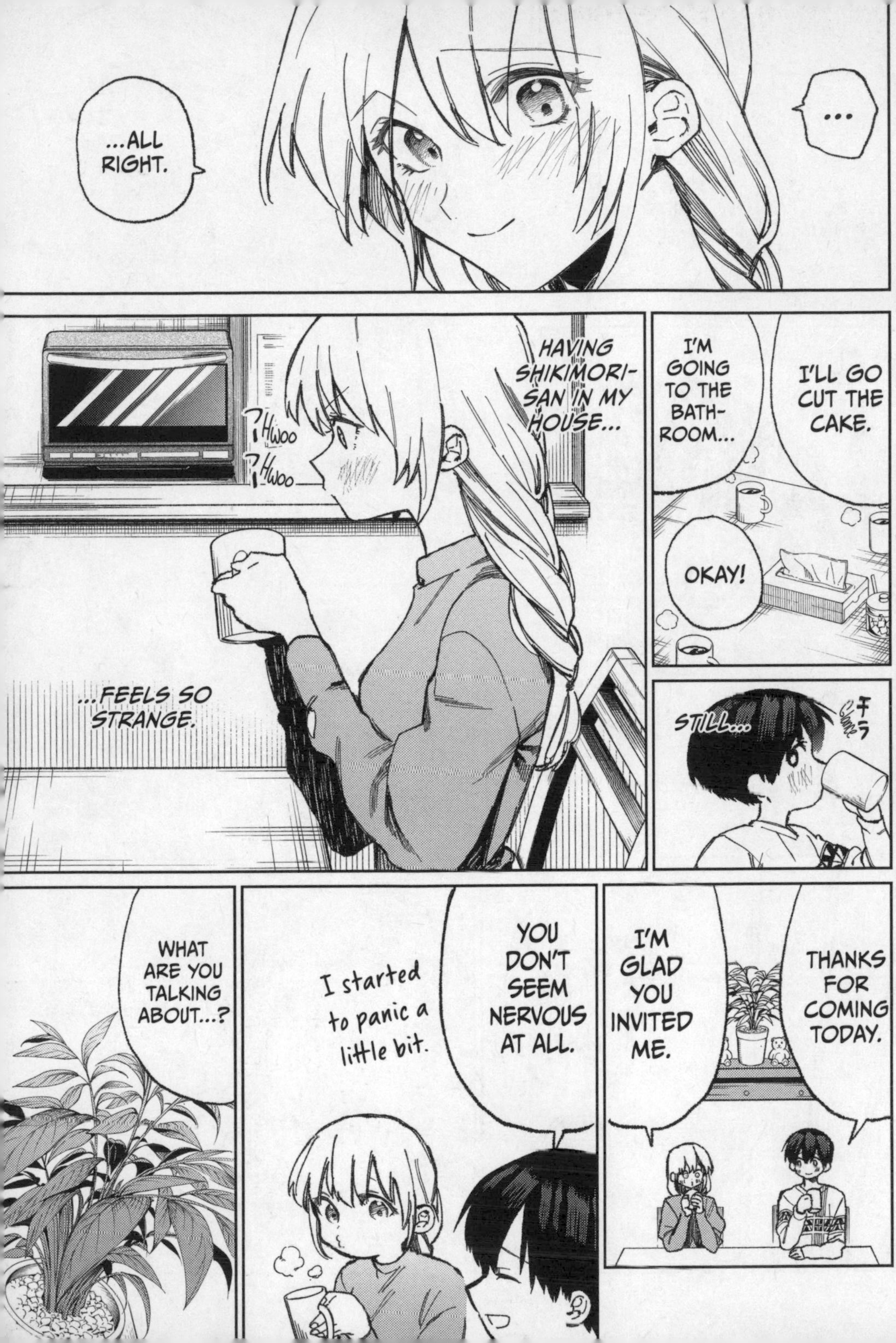
...
...ALL RIGHT.
I'LL GO CUT THE CAKE.
I'M GOING TO THE BATHROOM...
OKAY!
STILL...
Glance
HAVING SHIKIMORI-SAN IN MY HOUSE...
Hwoo
Hwoo
...FEELS SO STRANGE.
THANKS FOR COMING TODAY.
I'M GLAD YOU INVITED ME.
YOU DON'T SEEM NERVOUS AT ALL.
I started to panic a little bit.
WHAT ARE YOU TALKING ABOUT...?

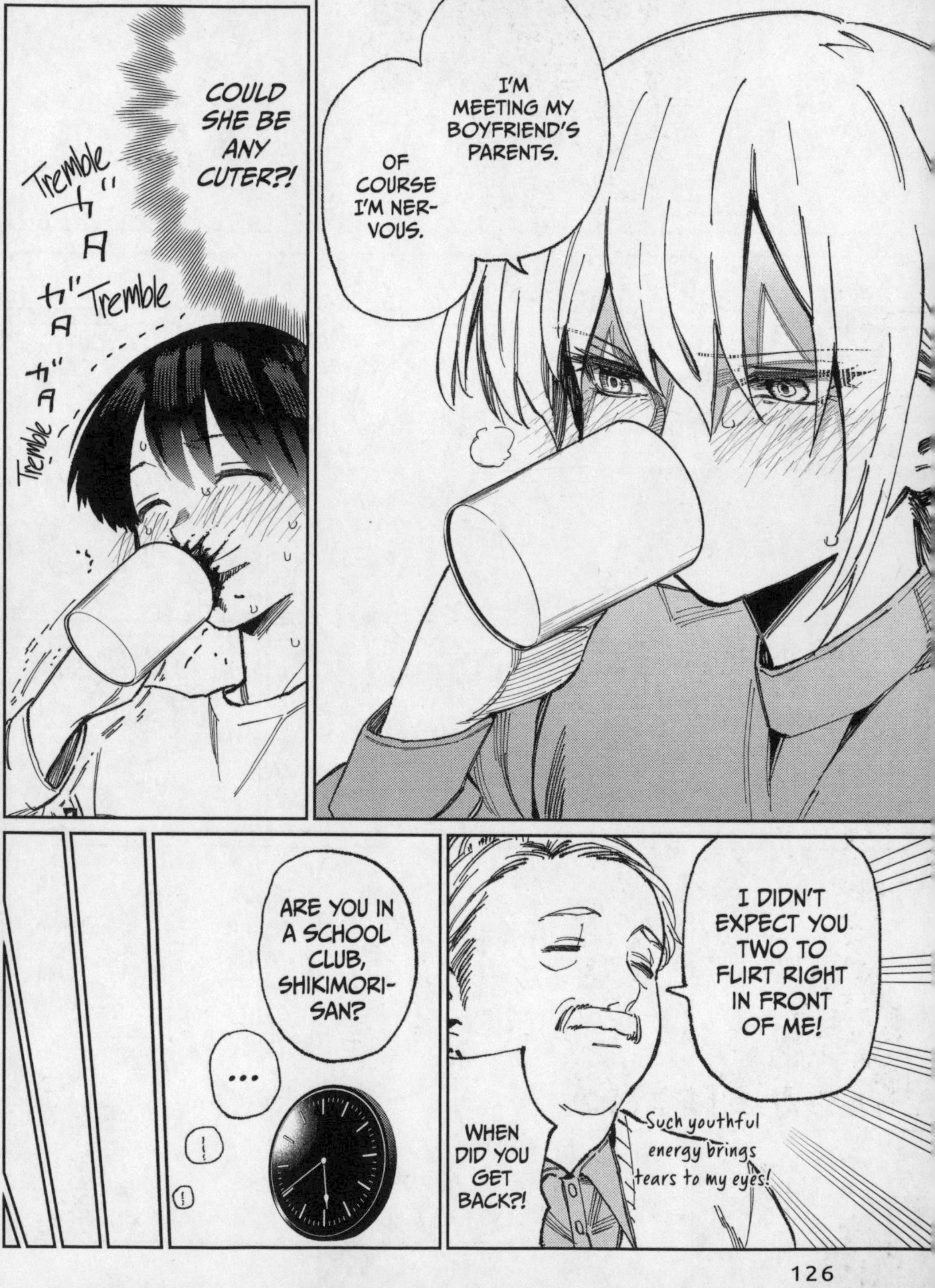
I'M MEETING MY BOYFRIEND'S PARENTS.
OF COURSE I'M NERVOUS.
COULD SHE BE ANY CUTER?!
Tremble
ガタ
Tremble
ガタ
Tremble
ガタ
I DIDN'T EXPECT YOU TWO TO FLIRT RIGHT IN FRONT OF ME!
Such youthful energy brings tears to my eyes!
WHEN DID YOU GET BACK?!
ARE YOU IN A SCHOOL CLUB, SHIKIMORI-SAN?
...
!
!

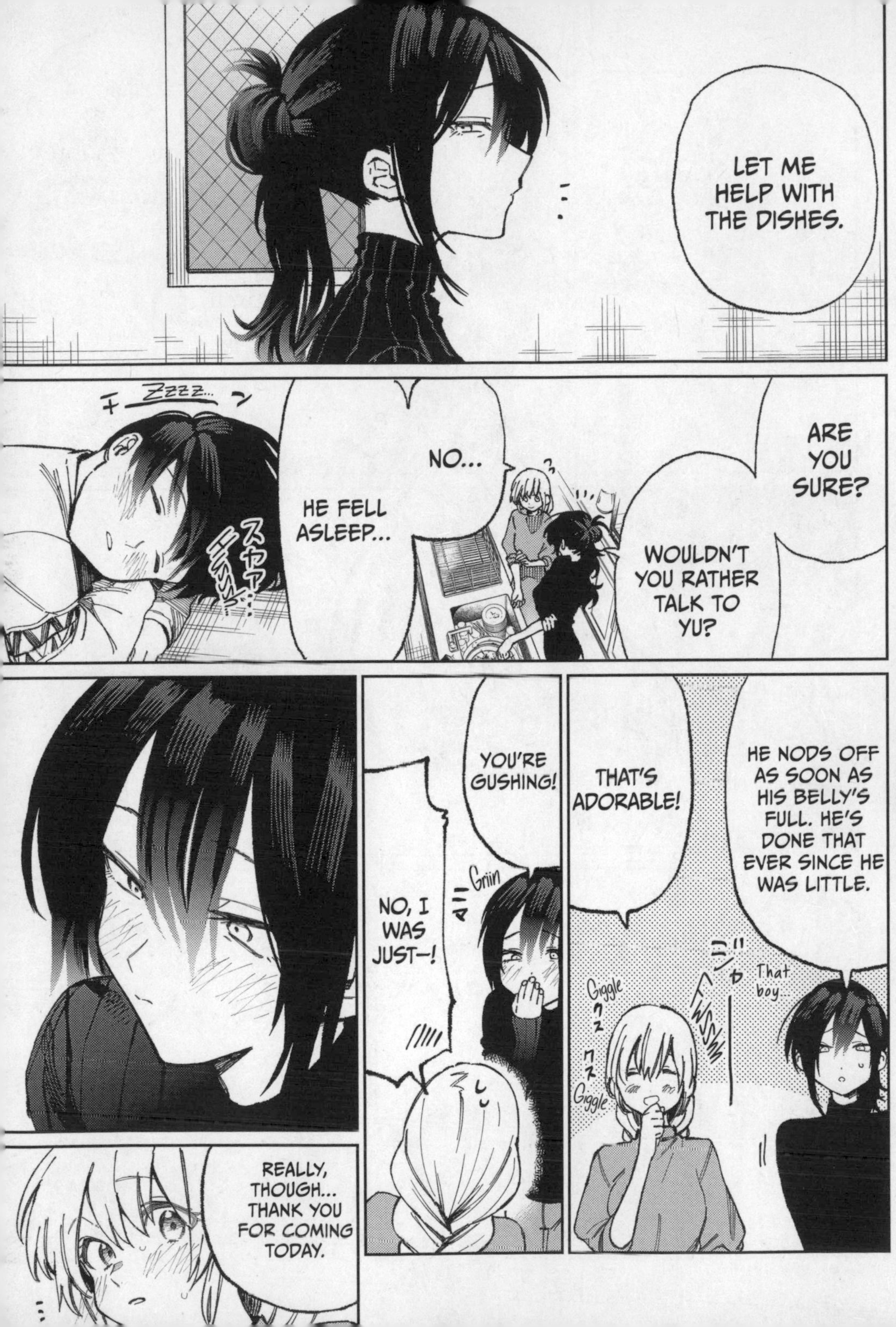
LET ME HELP WITH THE DISHES.
...
ARE YOU SURE?
WOULDN'T YOU RATHER TALK TO YU?
NO...
HE FELL ASLEEP...
Zzzz...
HE NODS OFF AS SOON AS HIS BELLY'S FULL. HE'S DONE THAT EVER SINCE HE WAS LITTLE.
That boy...
THAT'S ADORABLE!
Giggle
Giggle
FWSSH
YOU'RE GUSHING!
Griin
NO, I WAS JUST—!
REALLY, THOUGH... THANK YOU FOR COMING TODAY.
...

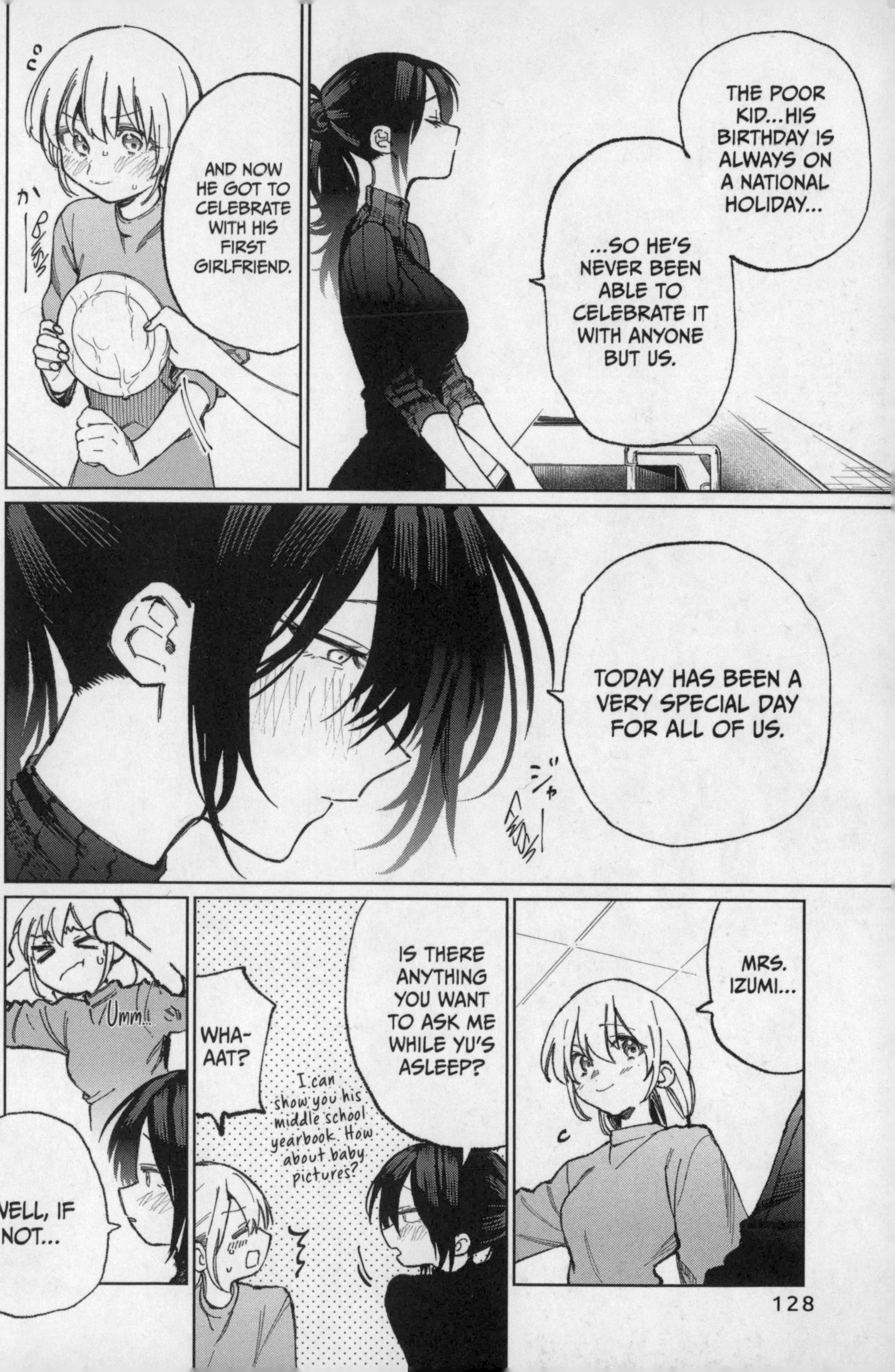
THE POOR KID...HIS BIRTHDAY IS ALWAYS ON A NATIONAL HOLIDAY...
...SO HE'S NEVER BEEN ABLE TO CELEBRATE IT WITH ANYONE BUT US.
AND NOW HE GOT TO CELEBRATE WITH HIS FIRST GIRLFRIEND.
Blush
TODAY HAS BEEN A VERY SPECIAL DAY FOR ALL OF US.
Fwsh
MRS. IZUMI...
IS THERE ANYTHING YOU WANT TO ASK ME WHILE YU'S ASLEEP?
WHA-AAT?
I can show you his middle school yearbook. How about baby pictures?
Umm..
WELL, IF NOT...

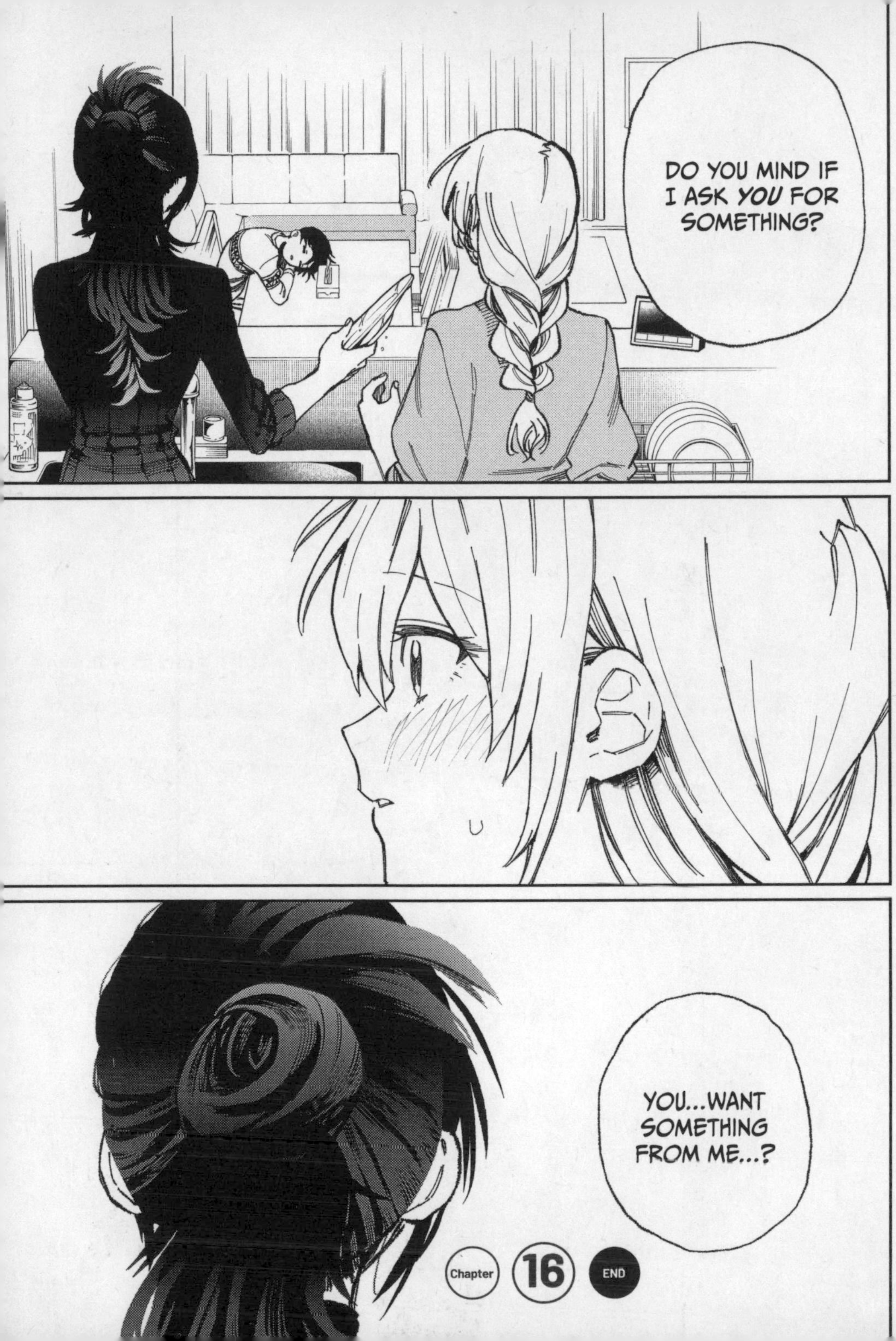
DO YOU MIND IF I ASK *YOU* FOR SOMETHING?
YOU...WANT SOMETHING FROM ME...?
Chapter 16 END

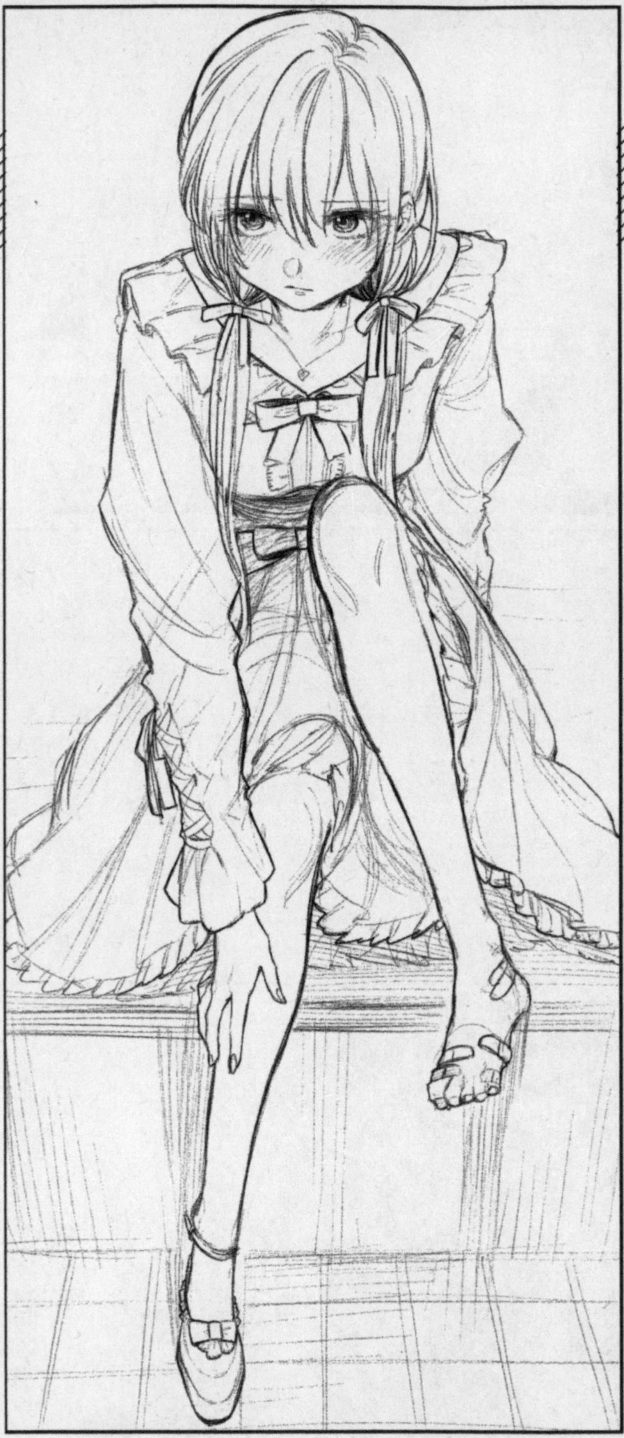

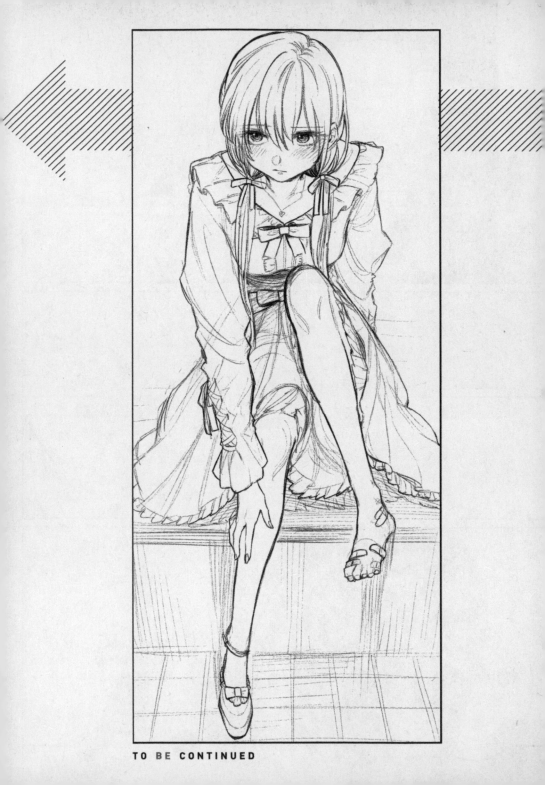

TO BE CONTINUED

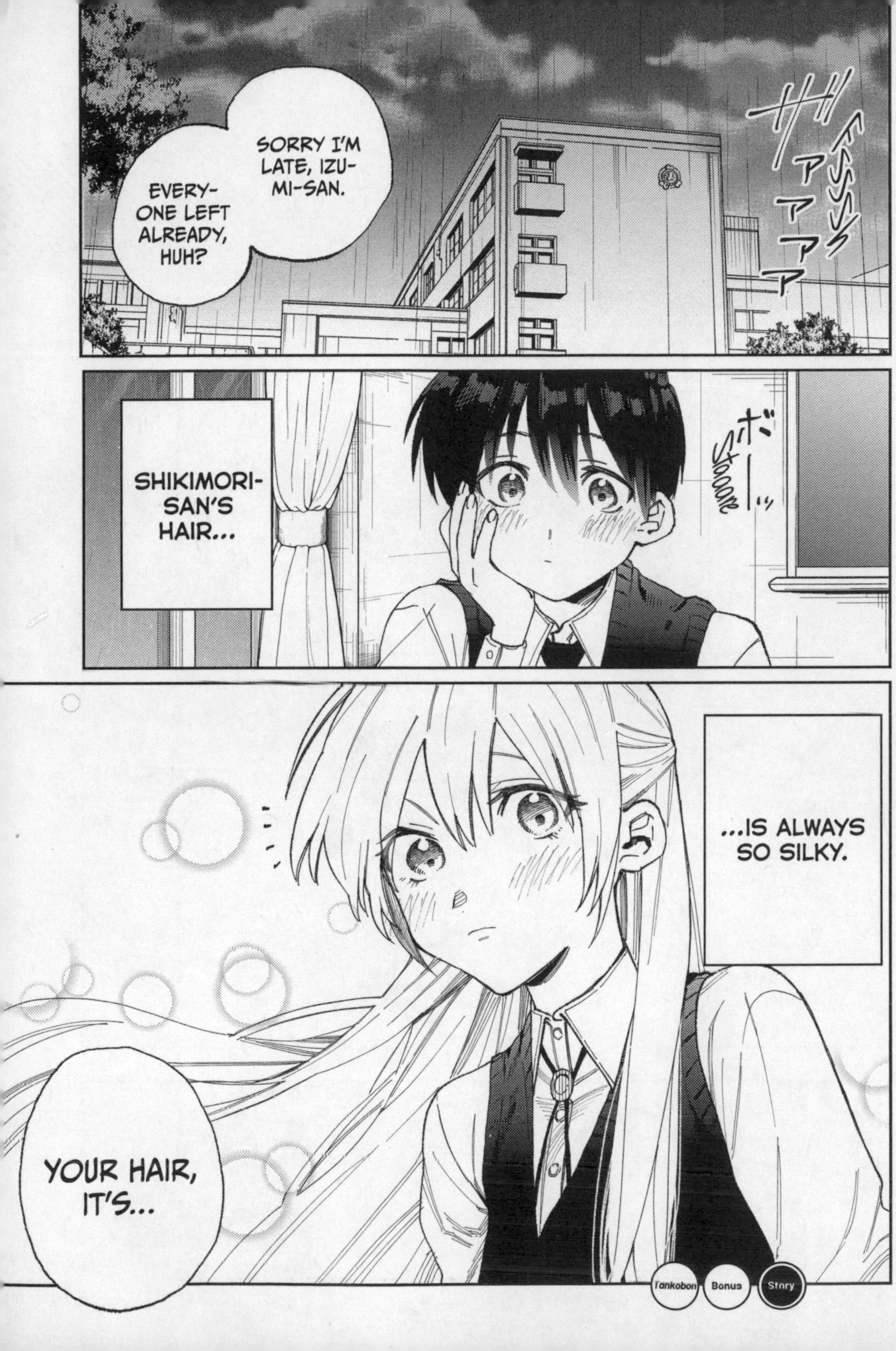
ザァァァァ
FSSSSH
SORRY I'M LATE, IZU-MI-SAN.
EVERY-ONE LEFT ALREADY, HUH?
ボーッ
Staaare
SHIKIMORI-SAN'S HAIR...
...IS ALWAYS SO SILKY.
YOUR HAIR, IT'S...
Tankobon
Bonus
Story

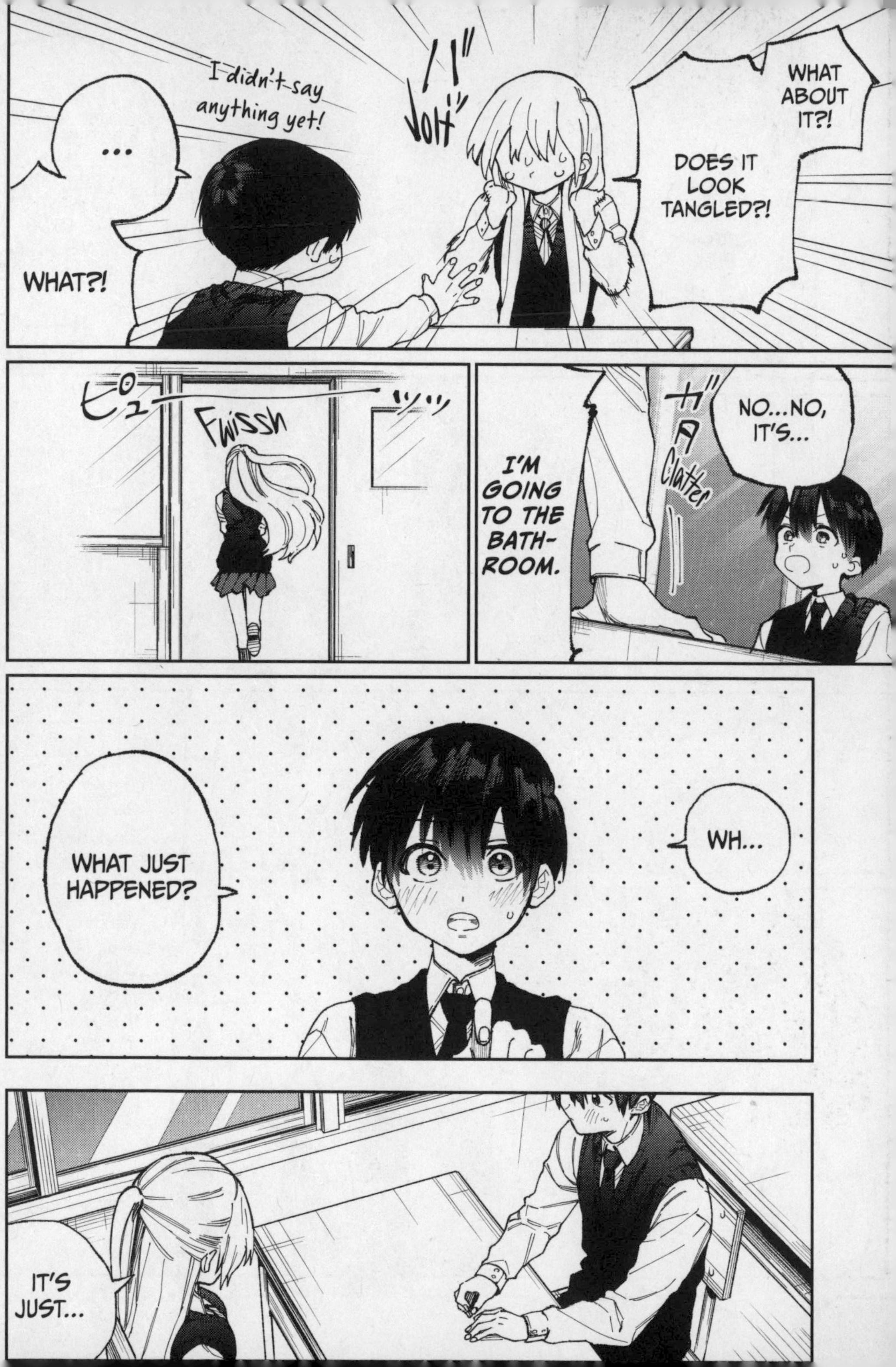
WHAT ABOUT IT?!
DOES IT LOOK TANGLED?!
Jolt
I didn't say anything yet!
...
WHAT?!
NO...NO, IT'S...
Clatter
I'M GOING TO THE BATH-ROOM.
Fwissh
WH...
WHAT JUST HAPPENED?
IT'S JUST...

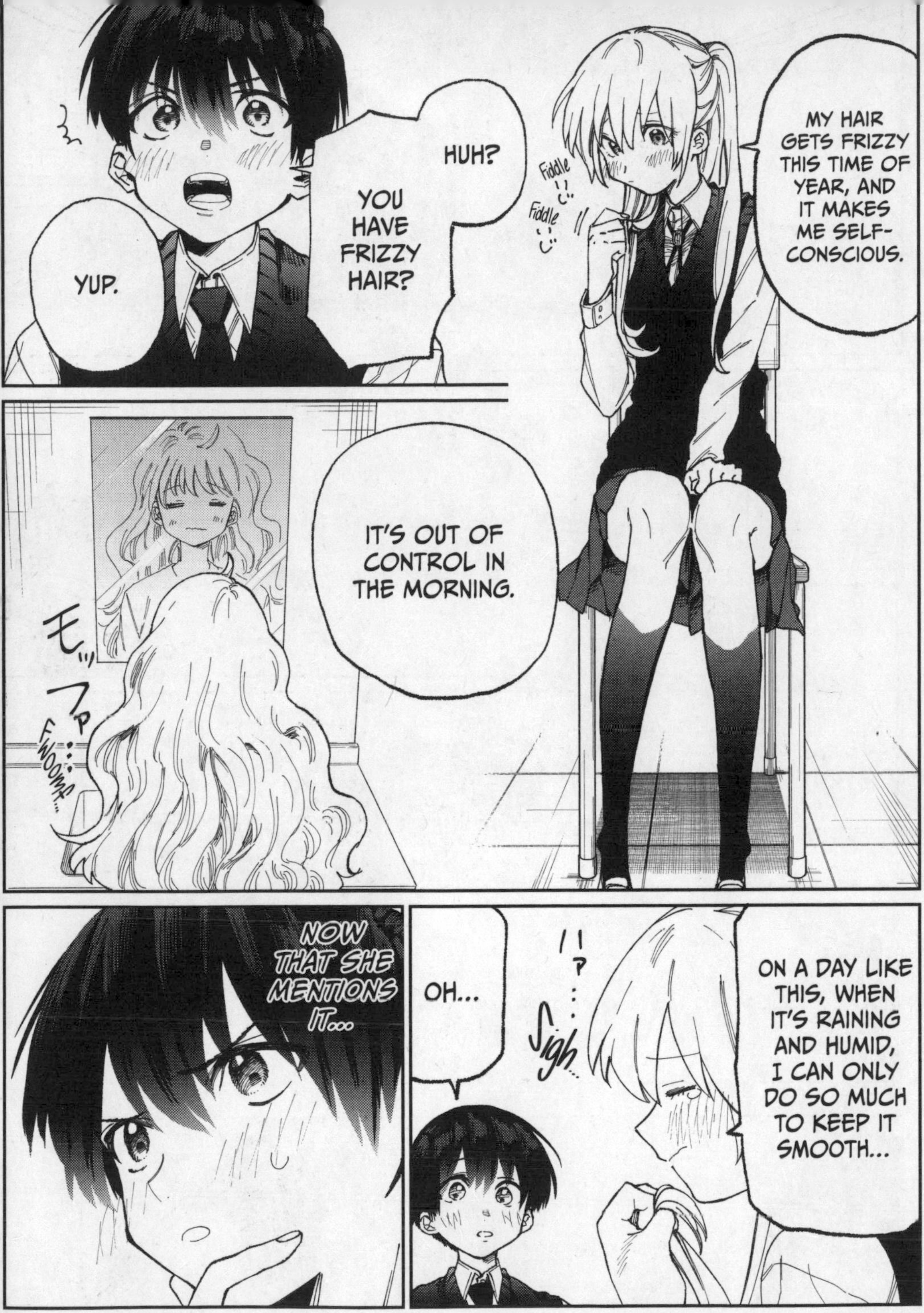
MY HAIR GETS FRIZZY THIS TIME OF YEAR, AND IT MAKES ME SELF-CONSCIOUS.
Fiddle
Fiddle
HUH?
YOU HAVE FRIZZY HAIR?
YUP.
IT'S OUT OF CONTROL IN THE MORNING.
FWOOMF...
ON A DAY LIKE THIS, WHEN IT'S RAINING AND HUMID, I CAN ONLY DO SO MUCH TO KEEP IT SMOOTH...
Sigh...
OH...
NOW THAT SHE MENTIONS IT...

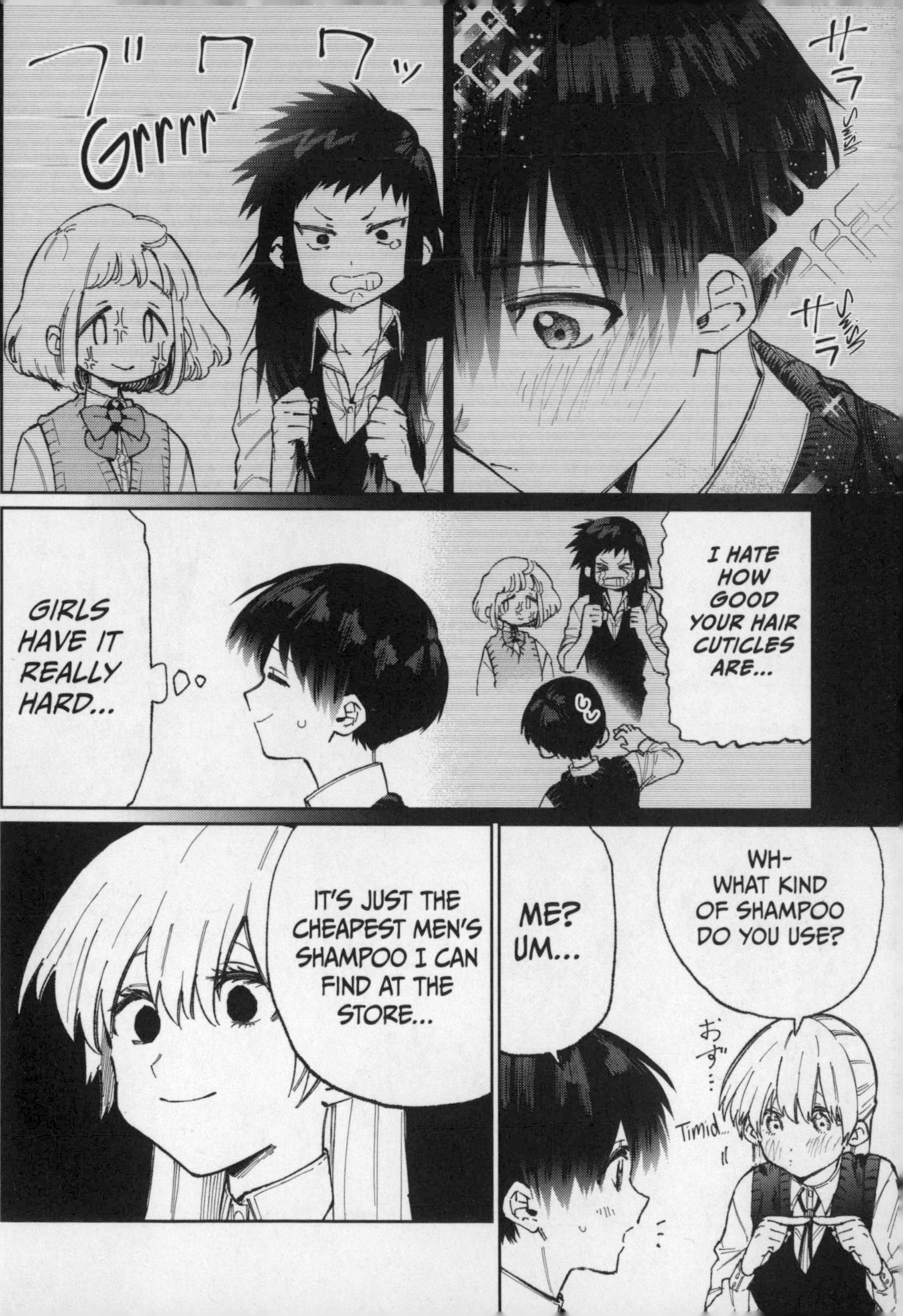
サラ
Swish
サラ
Swish
ブワワッ
Grrrr
I HATE HOW GOOD YOUR HAIR CUTICLES ARE...
GIRLS HAVE IT REALLY HARD...
WH- WHAT KIND OF SHAMPOO DO YOU USE?
ME? UM...
おず…
Timid...
IT'S JUST THE CHEAPEST MEN'S SHAMPOO I CAN FIND AT THE STORE...

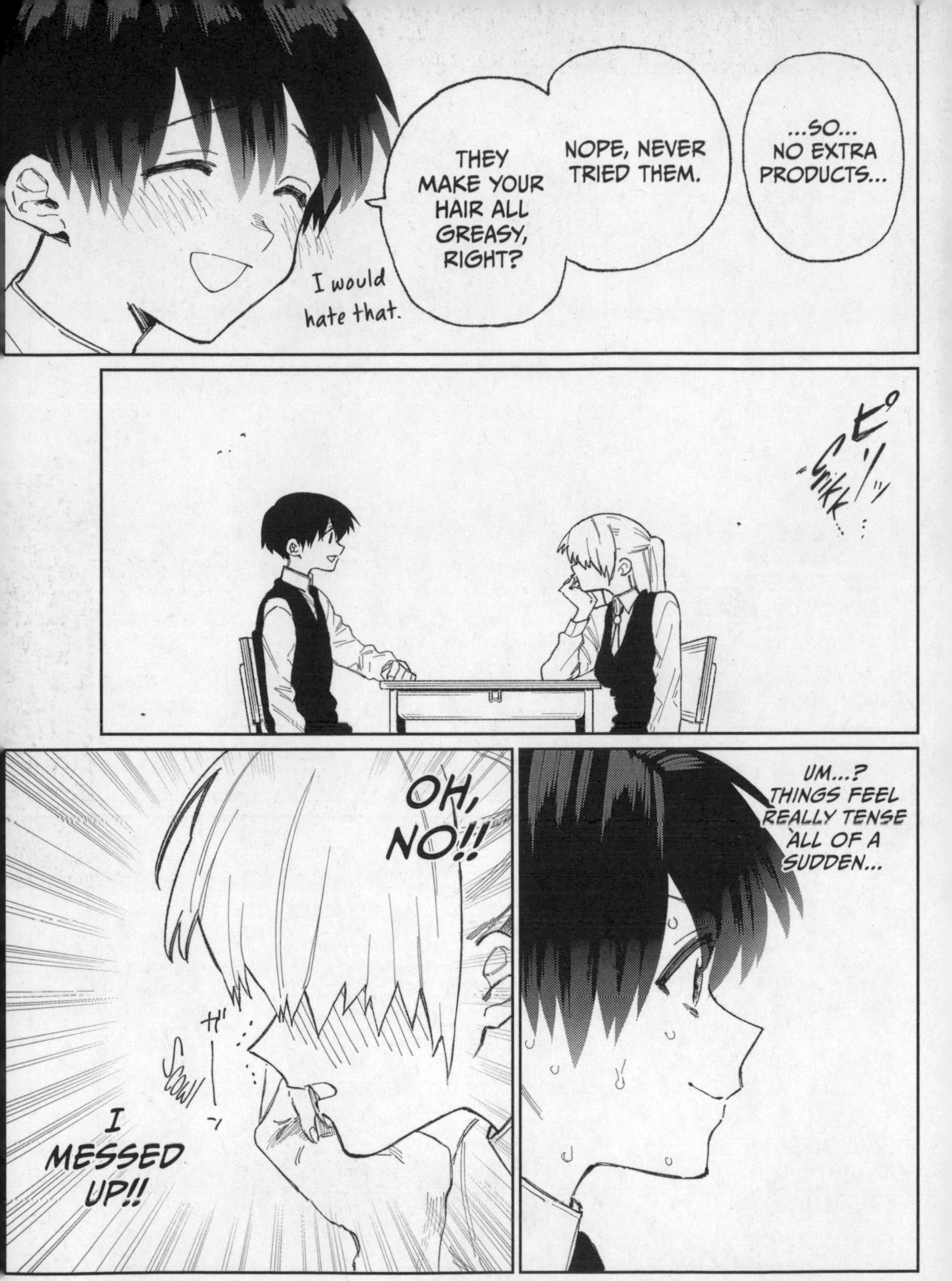
...SO... NO EXTRA PRODUCTS...
NOPE, NEVER TRIED THEM.
THEY MAKE YOUR HAIR ALL GREASY, RIGHT?
I would hate that.
Snikk
UM...? THINGS FEEL REALLY TENSE ALL OF A SUDDEN...
OH, NO!!
Scowl
I MESSED UP!!

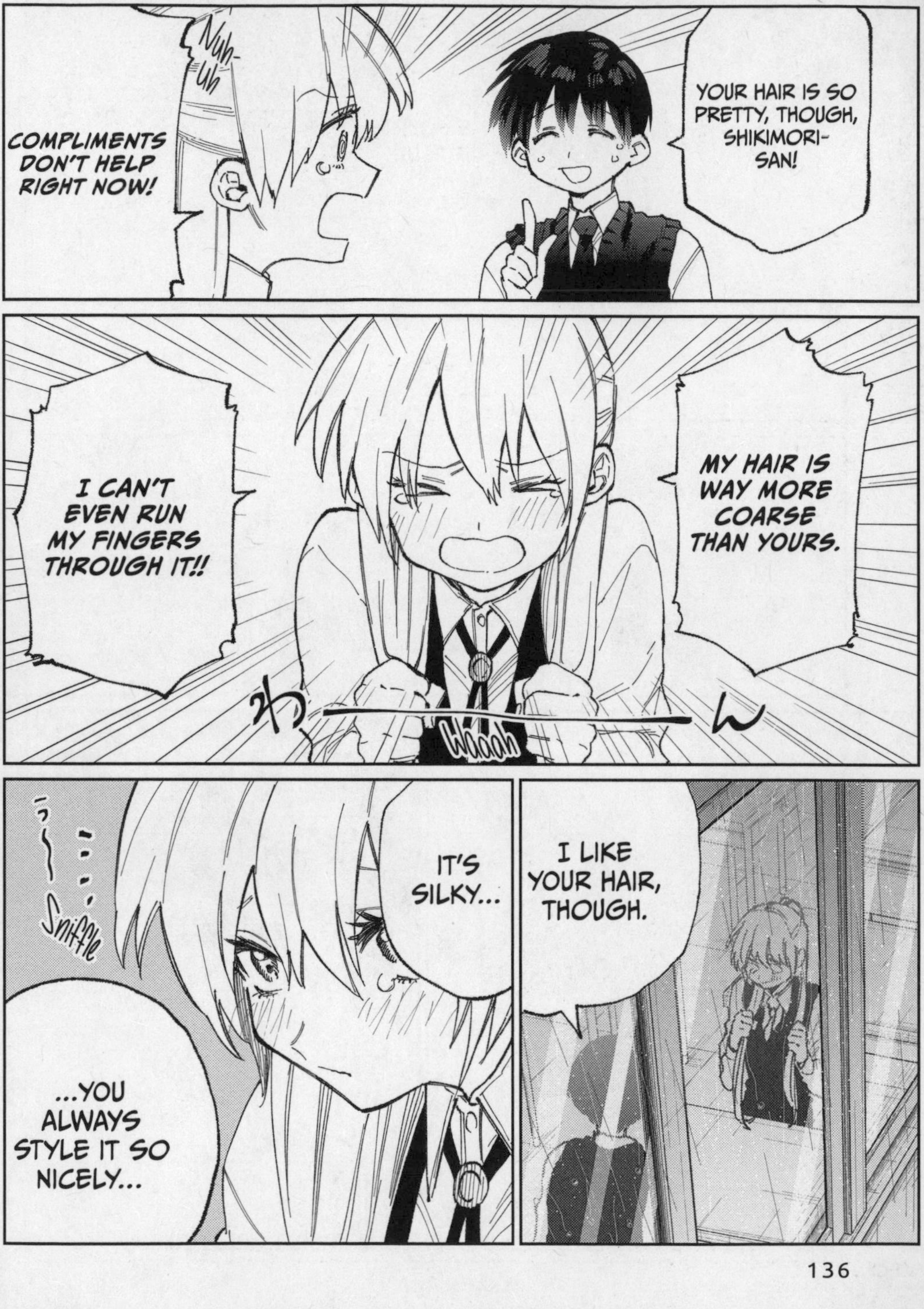
YOUR HAIR IS SO PRETTY, THOUGH, SHIKIMORI-SAN!
Nuh-uh
COMPLIMENTS DON'T HELP RIGHT NOW!
MY HAIR IS WAY MORE COARSE THAN YOURS.
I CAN'T EVEN RUN MY FINGERS THROUGH IT!!
Waaah
I LIKE YOUR HAIR, THOUGH.
IT'S SILKY...
Sniffle
...YOU ALWAYS STYLE IT SO NICELY...

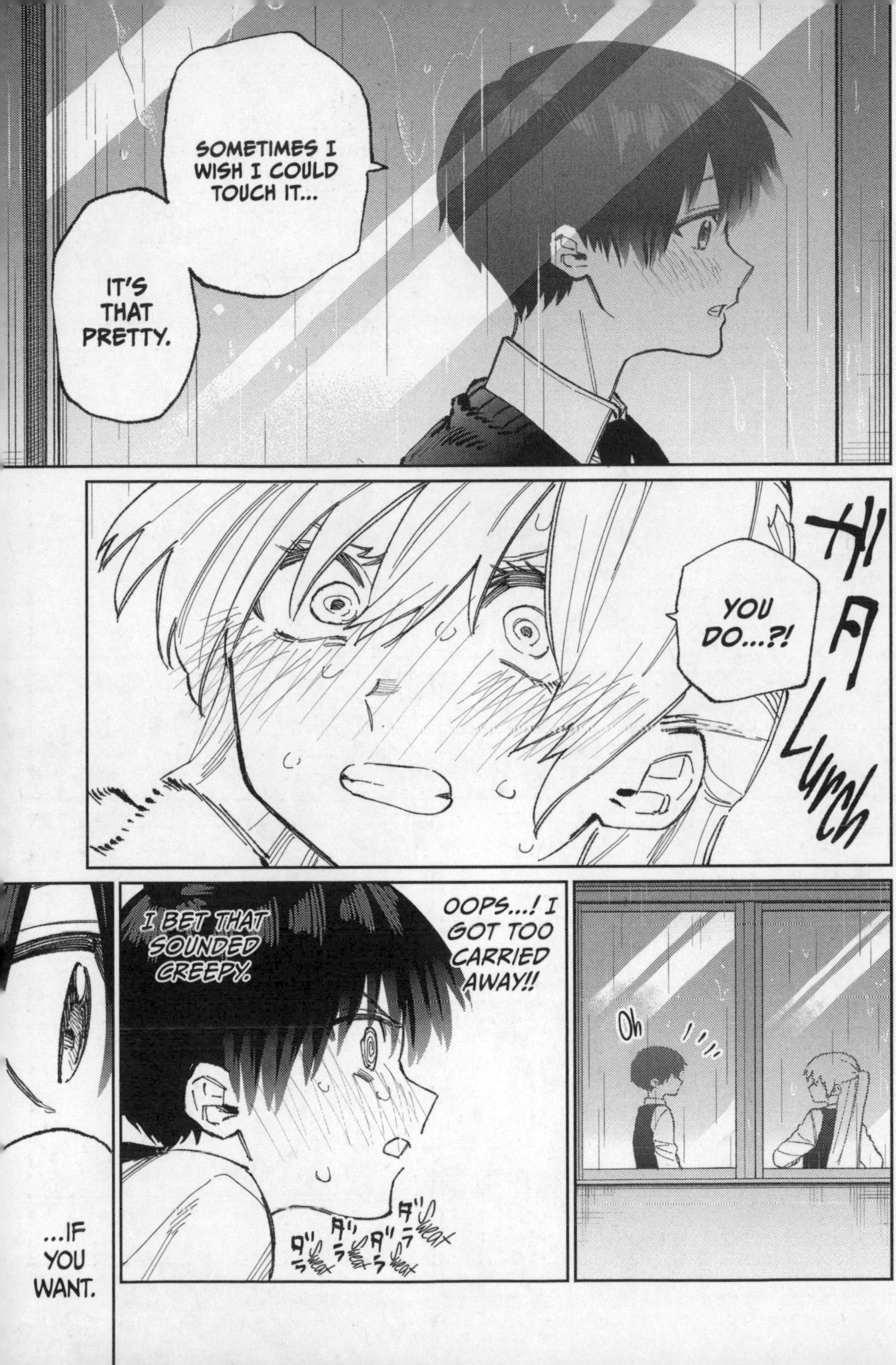
SOMETIMES I WISH I COULD TOUCH IT...
IT'S THAT PRETTY.
ガタ Lurch
YOU DO...?!
Oh
OOPS...! I GOT TOO CARRIED AWAY!!
I BET THAT SOUNDED CREEPY.
ダラ Sweat
ダラ Sweat
ダラ Sweat
ダラ Sweat
...IF YOU WANT.

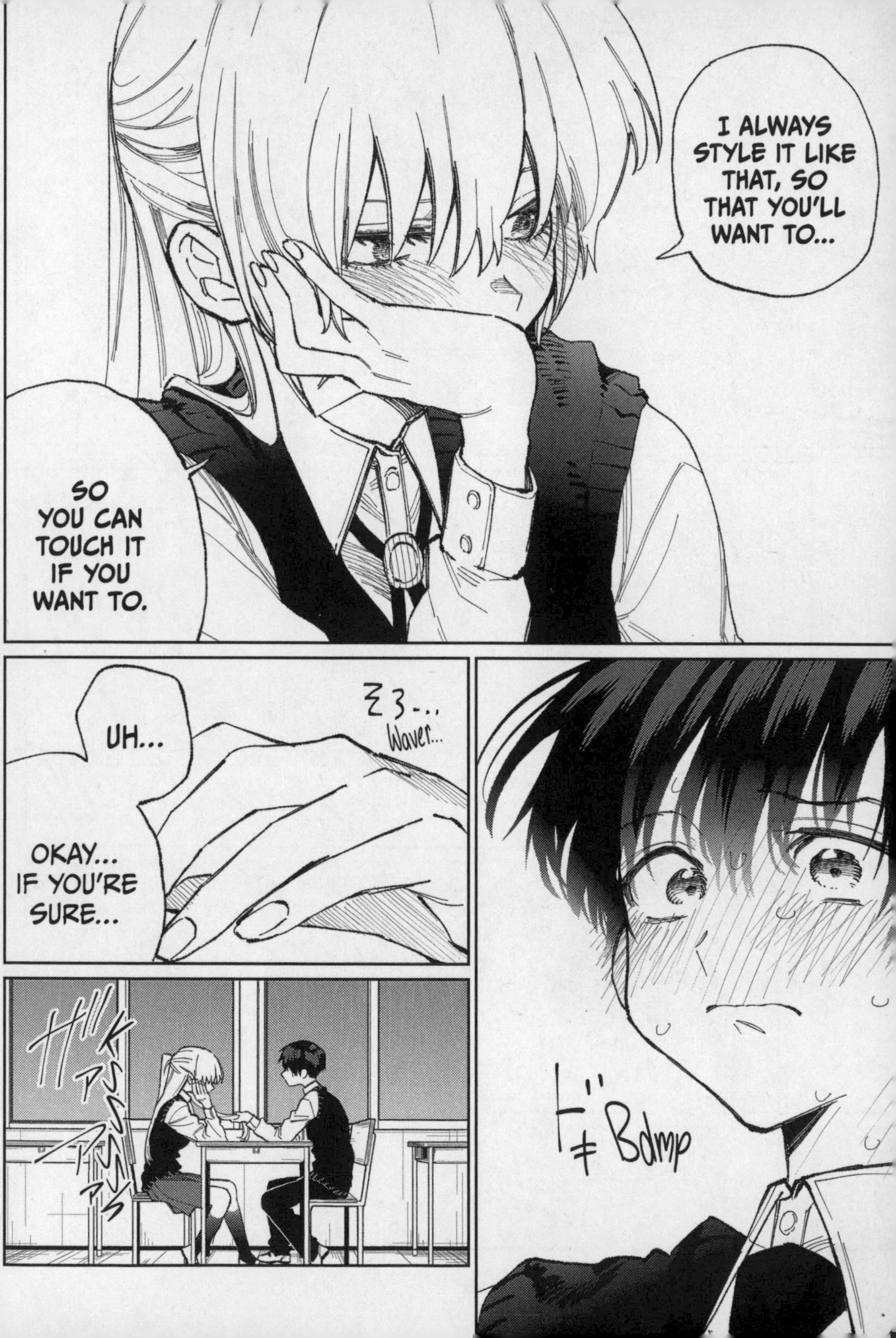
I ALWAYS STYLE IT LIKE THAT, SO THAT YOU'LL WANT TO...
SO YOU CAN TOUCH IT IF YOU WANT TO.
Bdmp
Waver...
UH...
OKAY... IF YOU'RE SURE...
KSSSSS

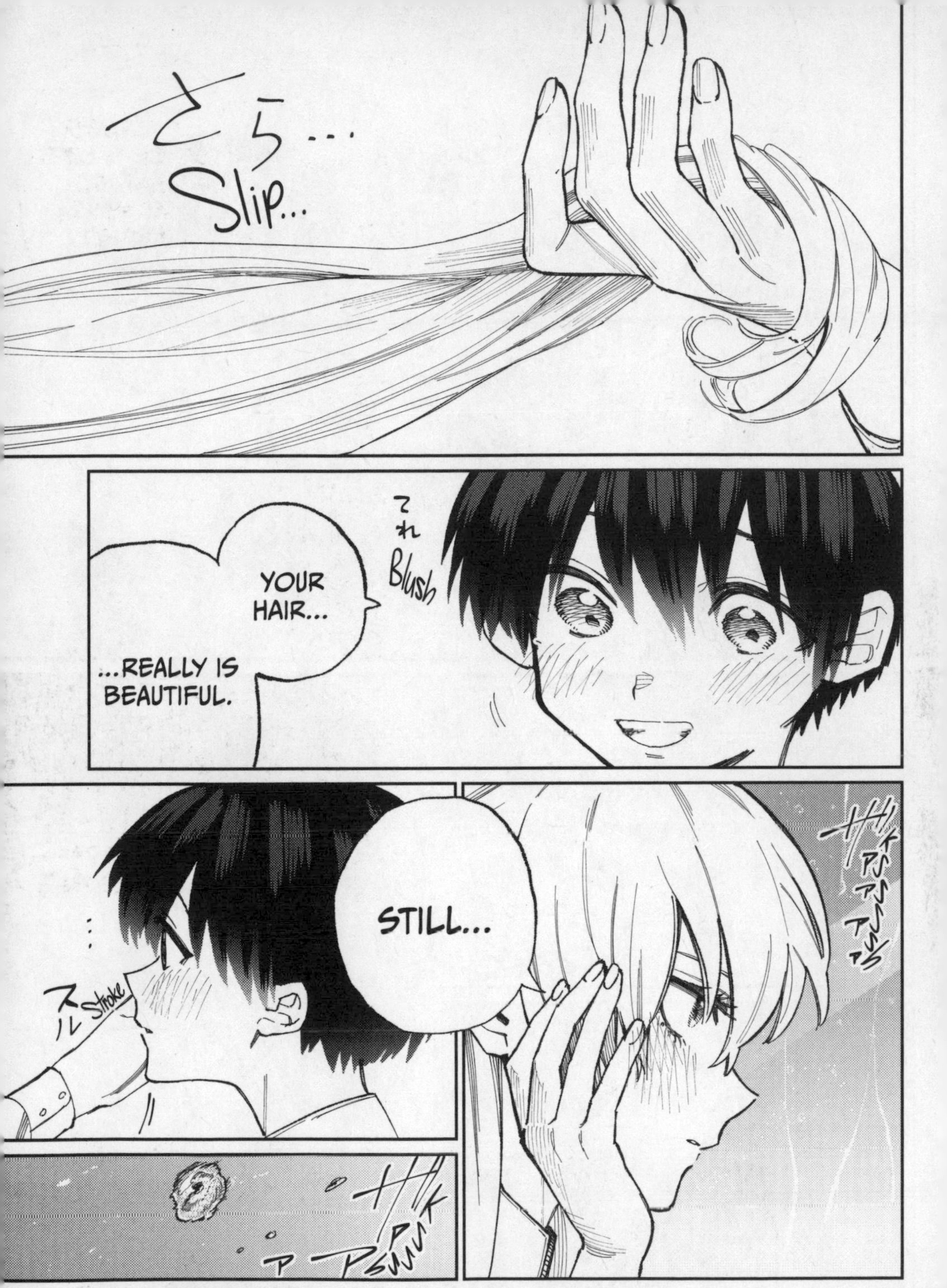
さら…
Slip...
てれ
Blush
YOUR HAIR...
...REALLY IS BEAUTIFUL.
STILL...
…
スル
Stroke

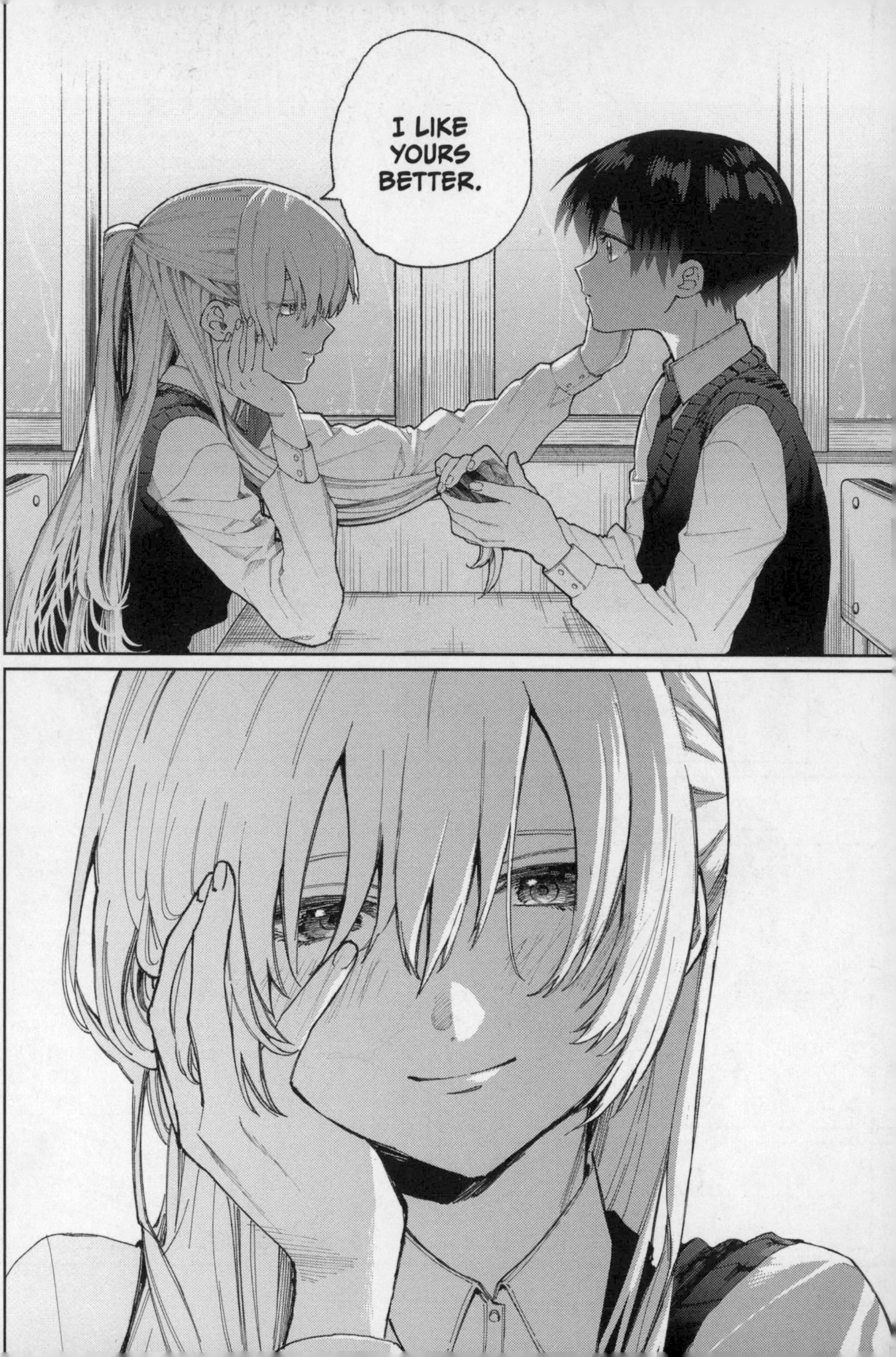
I LIKE YOURS BETTER.

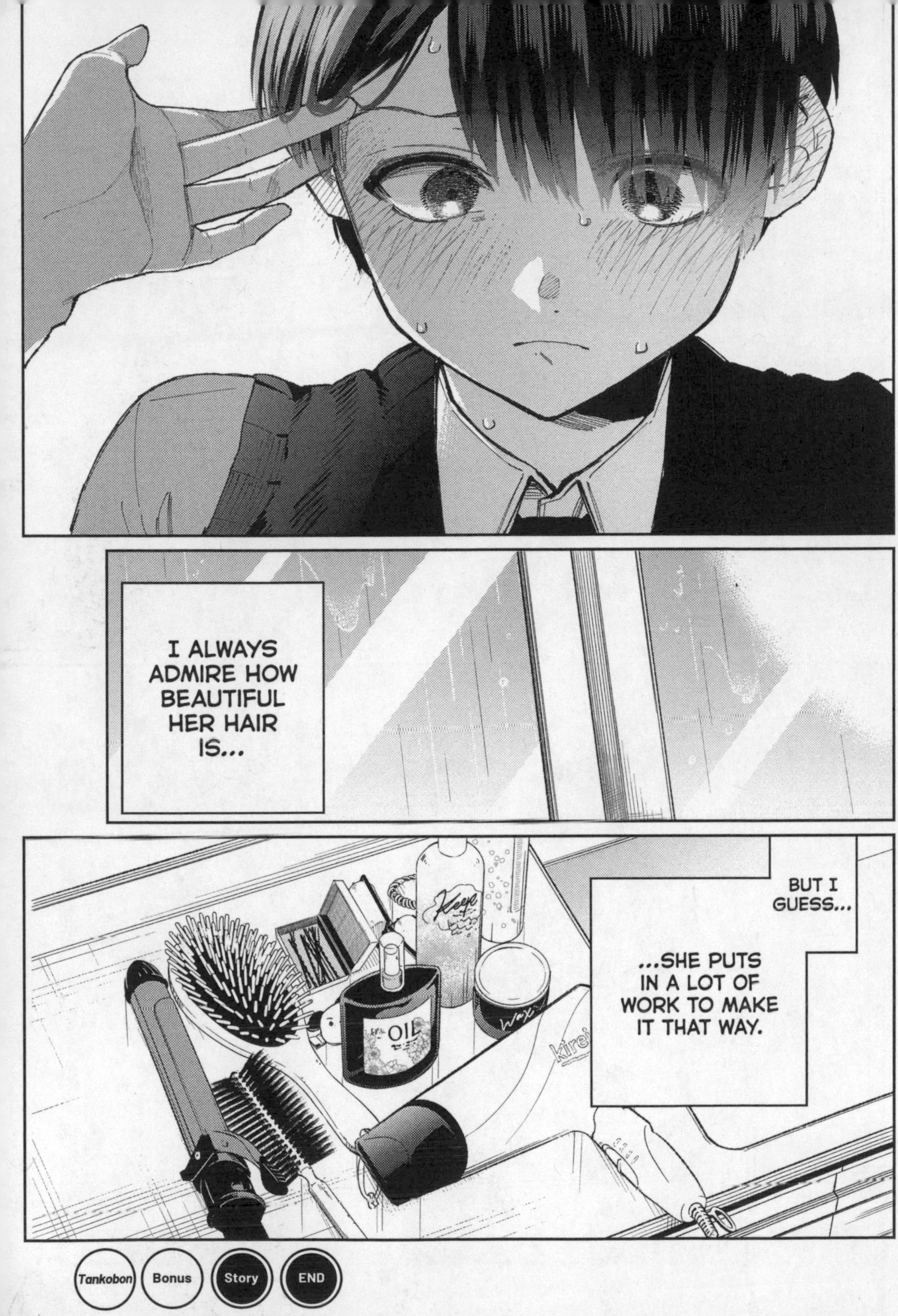
I ALWAYS ADMIRE HOW BEAUTIFUL HER HAIR IS...
BUT I GUESS...
...SHE PUTS IN A LOT OF WORK TO MAKE IT THAT WAY.
OIL
kirei

Tankobon Bonus Story END

IF Gallery 1

Shikimori-san, laser-focused on protecting her client

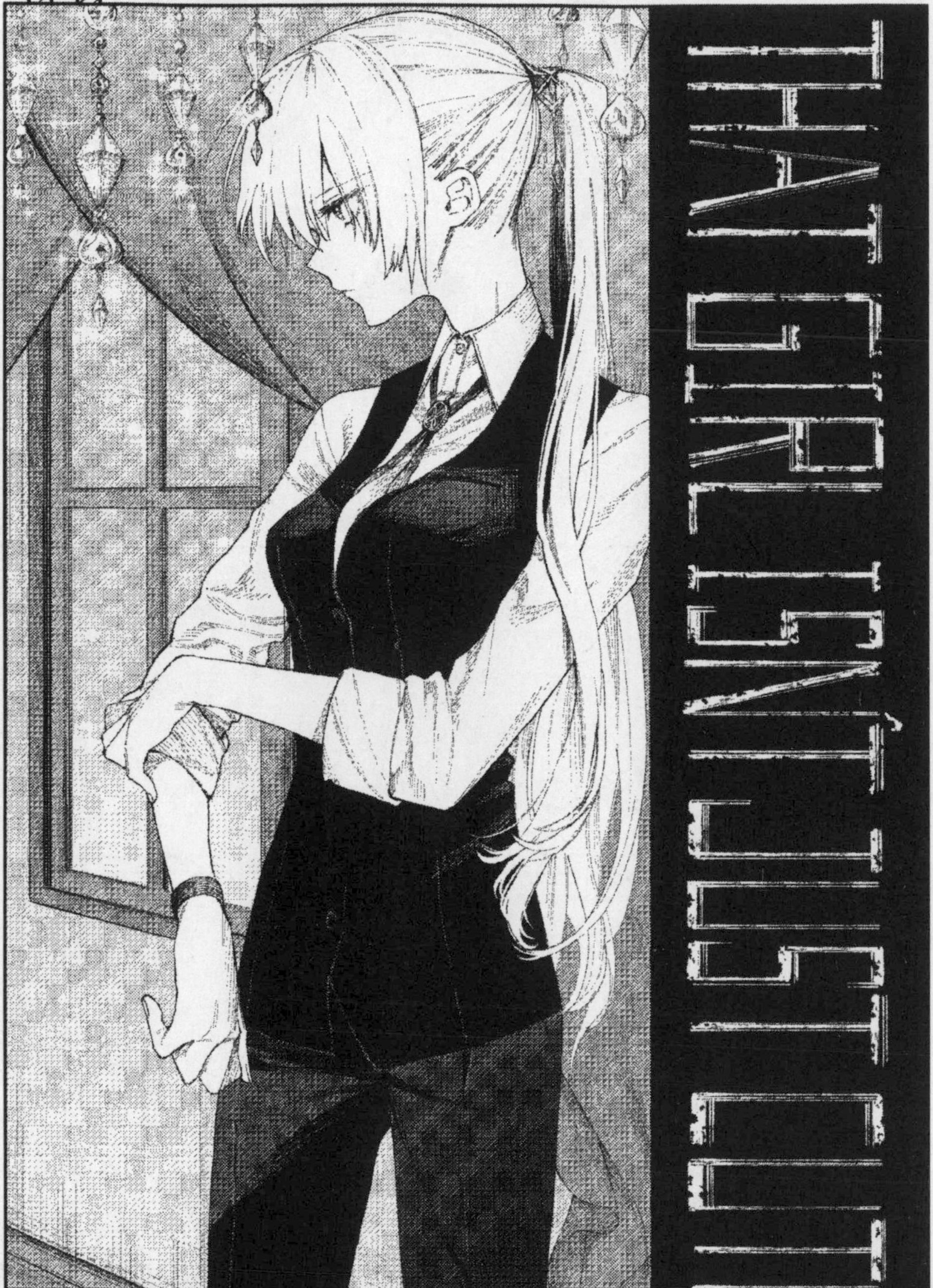

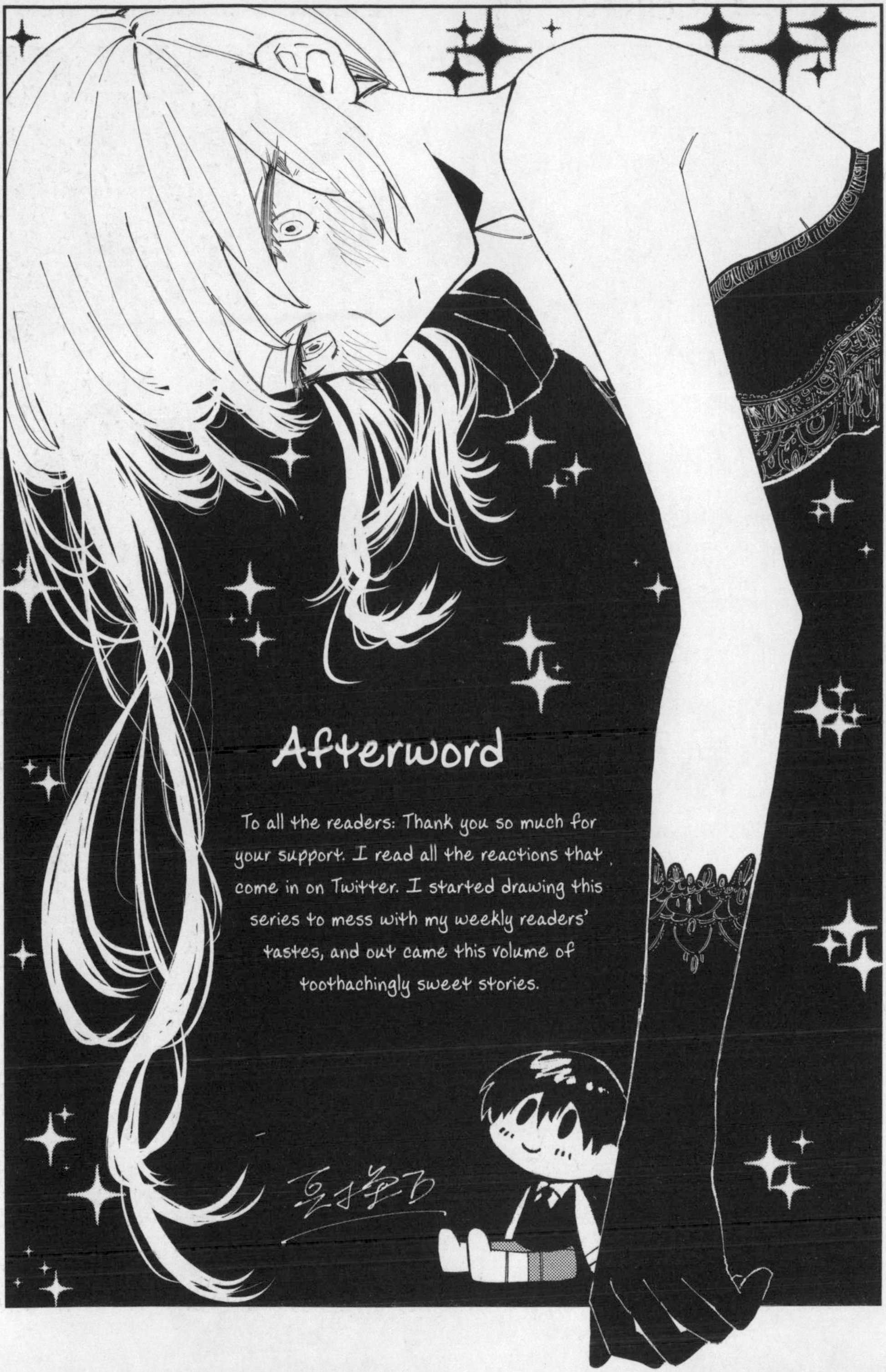
Afterword
To all the readers: Thank you so much for your support. I read all the reactions that come in on Twitter. I started drawing this series to mess with my weekly readers' tastes, and out came this volume of toothachingly sweet stories.

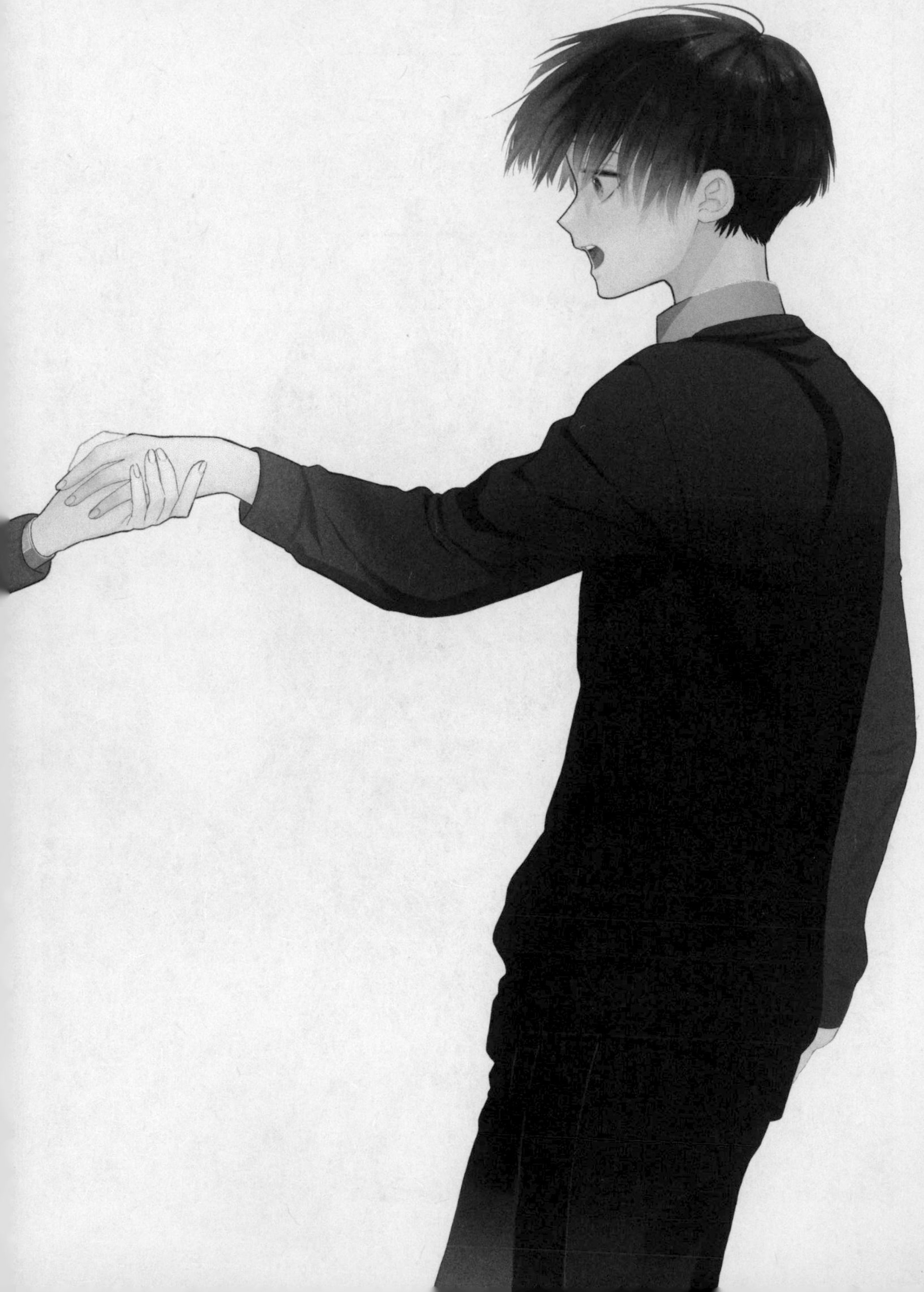

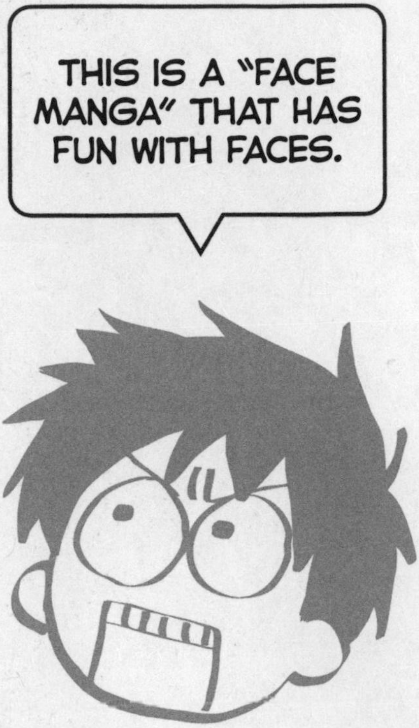
THIS IS A "FACE MANGA" THAT HAS FUN WITH FACES.

KEIGO MAKI

SHiKiMORi'S
not just a cutie

TRANSLATOR'S NOTES

Bean-tossing competition, page 89

The class is throwing beans and shouting "Demons begone!" as part of the traditional celebration of Setsubun. Celebrated on February 3, Setsubun occurs close to the Chinese New Year in the lunar calendar, so it has the spirit of "in with the new and out with the old." But bad luck might try to sneak into the new year, so to make sure things start out right, people throw beans at the demons who might bring bad luck in order to scare them away for the year.

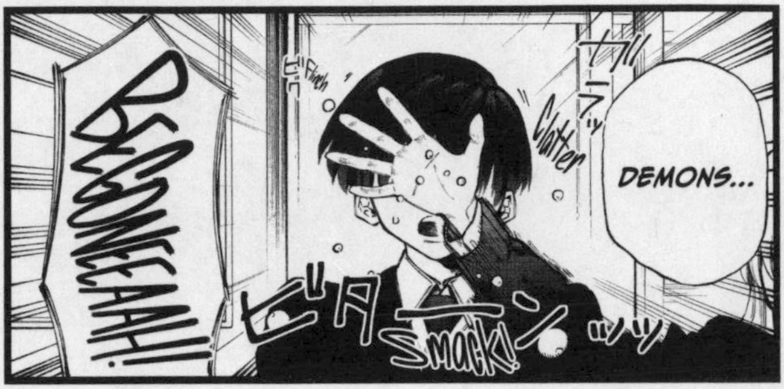

DEMONS...
Clatter
Flinch
BEGONEEAAH!
ビターンッッ
SMACK!

Hashimaki, page 103

Hashimaki is a kind of Japanese street food and is basically *okonomiyaki* (a thick, savory pancake) on a stick and drizzled with sauces.

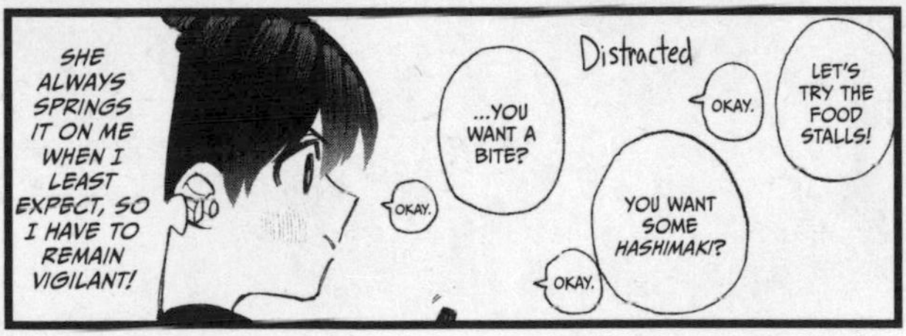

LET'S TRY THE FOOD STALLS!
OKAY.
Distracted
YOU WANT SOME HASHIMAKI?
OKAY.
...YOU WANT A BITE?
OKAY.
SHE ALWAYS SPRINGS IT ON ME WHEN I LEAST EXPECT, SO I HAVE TO REMAIN VIGILANT!

MAGIC KNIGHT RAYEARTH

25TH ANNIVERSARY EDITION

CLAMP

A BELOVED CLASSIC MAKES ITS STUNNING RETURN IN THIS GORGEOUS, LIMITED EDITION BOX SET!

This tale of three Tokyo teenagers who cross through a magical portal and become the champions of another world is a modern manga classic. The box set includes three volumes of manga covering the entire first series of *Magic Knight Rayearth*, plus the series's super-rare full-color art book companion, all printed at a larger size than ever before on premium paper, featuring a newly-revised translation and lettering, and exquisite foil-stamped covers.

A strictly limited edition, this will be gone in a flash!

THE SWEET SCENT OF LOVE IS IN THE AIR! FOR FANS OF OFFBEAT ROMANCES LIKE *WOTAKO!*

Sweat and Soap © Kintetsu Yamada / Kodansha Ltd.

In an office romance, there's a fine line between sexy and awkward... and that line is where Asako — a woman who sweats copiously — meets Koutarou — a perfume developer who can't get enough of Asako's, er, scent. Don't miss a romcom manga like no other!

1 PERFECT WORLD

Rie Aruga

A TOUCHING NEW SERIES ABOUT LOVE AND COPING WITH DISABILITY

An office party reunites Tsugumi with her high school crush Itsuki. He's realized his dream of becoming an architect, but along the way, he experienced a spinal injury that put him in a wheelchair. Now Tsugumi's rekindled feelings will butt up against prejudices she never considered — and Itsuki will have to decide if he's ready to let someone into his heart...

"Depicts with great delicacy and courage the difficulties some with disabilities experience getting involved in romantic relationships... Rie Aruga refuses to romanticize, pushing her heroine to face the reality of disability. She invites her readers to the same tasks of empathy, knowledge and recognition."
—Slate.fr

"An important entry [in manga romance]... The emotional core of both plot and characters indicates thoughtfulness... [Aruga's] research is readily apparent in the text and artwork, making this feel like a real story."
—Anime News Network

KC
KODANSHA
COMICS

A SMART, NEW ROMANTIC COMEDY FOR FANS OF *SHORTCAKE CAKE* AND *TERRACE HOUSE!*

A romance manga starring high school girl Meeko, who learns to live on her own in a boarding house whose living room is home to the odd (but handsome) Matsunaga-san. She begins to adjust to her new life away from her parents, but Meeko soon learns that no matter how far away from home she is, she's still a young girl at heart — especially when she finds herself falling for Matsunaga-san.

Young characters and steampunk setting, like *Howl's Moving Castle* and *Battle Angel Alita*

Beyond the Clouds © 2018 Nicke / Ki-oon

A boy with a talent for machines and a mysterious girl whose wings he's fixed will take you beyond the clouds! In the tradition of the high-flying, resonant adventure stories of Studio Ghibli comes a gorgeous tale about the longing of young hearts for adventure and friendship!

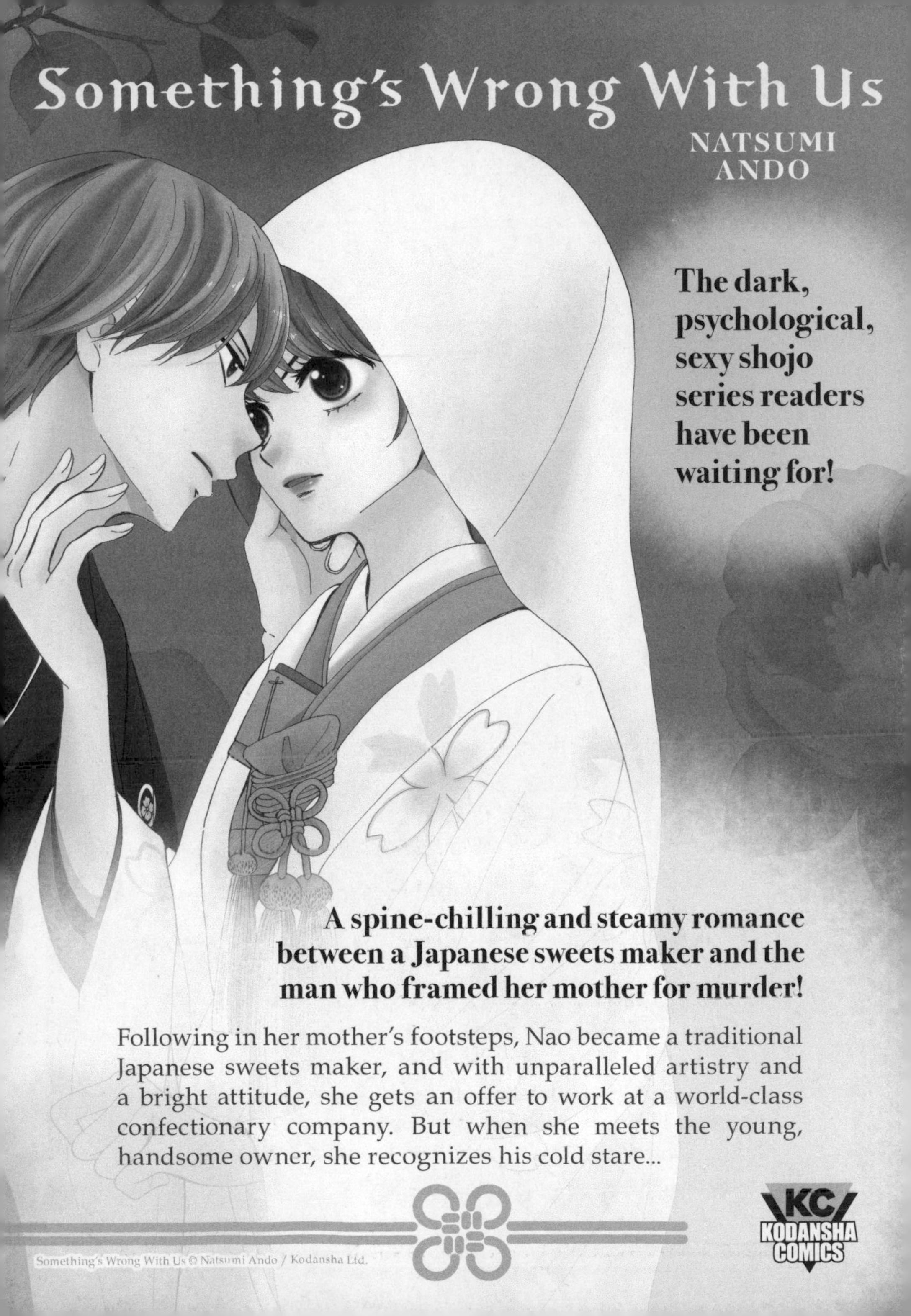
Something's Wrong With Us
NATSUMI ANDO
The dark, psychological, sexy shojo series readers have been waiting for!
A spine-chilling and steamy romance between a Japanese sweets maker and the man who framed her mother for murder!
Following in her mother's footsteps, Nao became a traditional Japanese sweets maker, and with unparalleled artistry and a bright attitude, she gets an offer to work at a world-class confectionary company. But when she meets the young, handsome owner, she recognizes his cold stare...
KC KODANSHA COMICS
Something's Wrong With Us © Natsumi Ando / Kodansha Ltd.

CUTE ANIMALS AND LIFE LESSONS, PERFECT FOR ASPIRING PET VETS OF ALL AGES!

YUZU THE PET VET

1

BY
MINGO ITO

In collaboration with
NIPPON COLUMBIA CO., LTD.

Yuzu the Pet Vet © Mingo Ito / NIPPON COLUMBIA CO., LTD / Kodansha Ltd

For an 11-year-old, Yuzu has a lot on her plate. When her mom gets sick and has to be hospitalized, Yuzu goes to live with her uncle who runs the local veterinary clinic. Yuzu's always been scared of animals, but she tries to help out. Through all the tough moments in her life, Yuzu realizes that she can help make things all right with a little help from her animal pals, peers, and kind grown-ups.

Every new patient is a furry friend in the making!

The adorable new odd-couple cat comedy manga from the creator of the beloved *Chi's Sweet Home*, in full color!

Sue & Tai-chan

Konami Kanata

Sue is an aging housecat who's looking forward to living out her life in peace... but her plans change when the mischievous black tomcat Tai-chan enters the picture! Hey! Sue never signed up to be a catsitter! *Sue & Tai-chan* is the latest from the reigning meow-narch of cute kitty comics, Konami Kanata.

KC
KODANSHA
COMICS

SAINT ☆ YOUNG MEN

A LONG AWAITED ARRIVAL IN PREMIUM 2-IN-1 HARDCOVER

After centuries of hard work, Jesus and Buddha take a break from their heavenly duties to relax among the people of Japan, and their adventures in this lighthearted buddy comedy are sure to bring mirth and merriment to all!

"Brilliant…the physical comedy and facial expressions will make you literally LOL."
—Sam Humphries
(host of *DC Daily*; writer, *Green Lanterns, Legendary Star-Lord*)

Saint Young Men © Hikaru Nakamura/Kodansha Ltd.

The boys are back, in 400-page hardcovers that are as pretty and badass as they are!

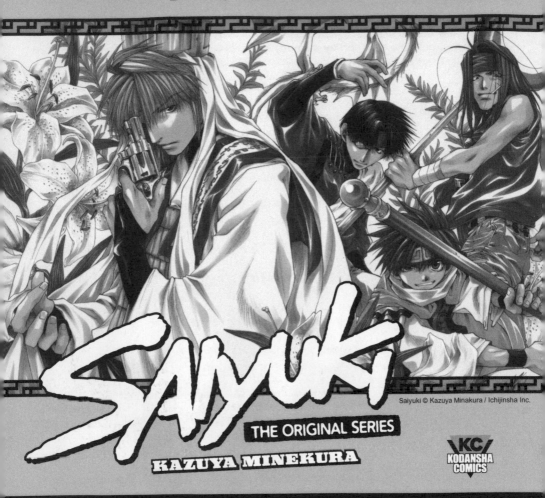

Saiyuki © Kazuya Minekura / Ichijinsha Inc.

SAIYUKI
THE ORIGINAL SERIES
KAZUYA MINEKURA

"AN EDGY COMIC LOOK AT AN ANCIENT CHINESE TALE." —YALSA

Genjo Sanzo is a Buddhist priest in the city of Togenkyo, which is being ravaged by yokai spirits that have fallen out of balance with the natural order. His superiors send him on a journey far to the west to discover why this is happening and how to stop it. His companions are three yokai with human souls. But this is no day trip — the four will encounter many discoveries and horrors on the way.

FEATURES NEW TRANSLATION, COLOR PAGES, AND BEAUTIFUL WRAPAROUND COVER ART!

A Kodansha Comics Trade Paperback Original
Shikimori's Not Just a Cutie 1 copyright © 2019 Keigo Maki
English translation copyright © 2020 Keigo Maki

Published in the United States by Kodansha Comics, an imprint of Kodansha USA Publishing, LLC, New York.

Publication rights for this English edition arranged through Kodansha Ltd., Tokyo.

First published in Japan in 2019 by Kodansha Ltd., Tokyo.

ISBN 978-1-64651-175-4

Printed in the United States of America.

www.kodanshacomics.com

9 8 7 6 5 4 3 2 1
Translation: Karen McGillicuddy
Lettering: Mercedes McGarry
Editing: Ben Applegate
Kodansha Comics edition cover design by My Truong

Publisher: Kiichiro Sugawara

Director of publishing services: Ben Applegate
Associate director of operations: Stephen Pakula
Publishing services managing editor: Noelle Webster
Assistant production manager: Emi Lotto, Angela Zurlo
Logo and character art ©Kodansha USA Publishing, LLC